GROUP 1 WINS: 104

PUMPER

PUMPER
Jim Cassidy
with Andrew Webster

MACMILLAN
Pan Macmillan Australia

For Mum and Dad

First published 2016 in Macmillan by Pan Macmillan Australia Pty Ltd
1 Market Street, Sydney, New South Wales, Australia, 2000

Cataloguing-in-Publication entry is available
from the National Library of Australia
http://catalogue.nla.gov.au

Typeset in Fairfield 12.5/17pt by Midland Typesetters, Australia
Printed by McPherson's Printing Group
Endpapers image: Shutterstock
Jacket, case, endpapers and picture sections designed by
Deborah Parry Graphics

MIX
Paper from
responsible sources
FSC
www.fsc.org
FSC® C001695

The paper in this book is FSC® certified.
FSC® promotes environmentally responsible,
socially beneficial and economically viable
management of the world's forests.

Contents

Prologue   VII

Chapter 1   Size Matters   1

Chapter 2   Kiwi   23

Chapter 3   'Bet Up, Boss'   43

Chapter 4   The Pumper   57

Chapter 5   Cruising   69

Chapter 6   Getting Off The Canvas   83

Chapter 7   The Boss   95

Chapter 8   Jockey Tapes   107

Chapter 9   Exiled   135

Chapter 10   Divine Intervention   149

Chapter 11   Longy   171

Chapter 12   The Day The Earth Rumbled   183

Chapter 13   Ring-A-Ding-Ding   201

Chapter 14   The Odd Couple   221

Chapter 15   Mokbel   239

Chapter 16   The King   255

Chapter 17   Pain   271

Chapter 18   The Hundred   283

Chapter 19   'Who's The Magic Man Now?'   299

Chapter 20   The Game   313

Epilogue   325

Acknowledgements   343

Index   345

Prologue

It's four o'clock in the morning, on the first Tuesday in November, and there are only two people at Flemington. Just two people and the horses.

We're not supposed to be here. Not at this time of the day. It's so early we've had to slip 50 bucks to the security guard to let us in, but it's money well spent because later in the day it will return more than anyone could ever imagine.

It's not quite dawn and here, in the sauna and steam room near the jockeys' room, it is dead quiet. They'll open the gates at 7.30 am, and all walks of life will start spilling into the course. There will be about 94,000 people packed in as the main race nears. Some come for the drink and the fashion and a good time, but many of them come to bet and most of the money will be on Might And Power to win the 1997 Melbourne Cup.

PUMPER

He is the 4 to 1 favourite. He is expected to lead from start to finish – just as he did in the Caulfield Cup a fortnight earlier – and they are all expecting him to win.

But I know differently.

I know it won't be that easy. I know he's carrying more weight and must cover more distance than Caulfield. Different track, different atmosphere. There was no pressure leading into the Caulfield Cup, but there's been a shitload coming out of it.

I know about all of this expectation because I will be the one riding Might And Power today.

Luckily, I also know I've got the horse to get the job done.

I knew it the moment I won a nothing race at Canterbury on him earlier that year. This big monster of a horse just towed me around, like he does every person who's ever been on his back.

I knew it after he went past the line in the Caulfield Cup. Everyone was talking about the 8 lengths he put on the rest of the field. I was more worried about the way he kept charging beyond the winning post. How I couldn't hold him as he kept going and going and going . . .

I knew I could win the Melbourne Cup but I could only do it if I had someone in my corner.

I know that much.

There's been many bosses in my life. Trainers. Owners. I've mostly done what they've told me. Sometimes I haven't. I call all of them 'Boss'.

But there's one boss at the top of the heap and his name is Malcolm Ayoub.

A week out from the race, Malcolm is lying in a hospital bed in Perth, struggling to breathe because of emphysema.

PROLOGUE

I call him.

'Boss, I think this horse is the real deal,' I tell him. 'Do you feel up to it?'

'Yes, I do,' he says.

'Boss, you get me right, the horse will win the Melbourne Cup.'

And that's why we are here, as the sun starts to poke its head above the city skyline in the distance. The silence of Flemington is only broken by the tap of boxing gloves on boxing pads.

I'm wearing the gloves. Boss is holding the pads. As always.

Boss is wearing a white singlet with holes in it. I'm sweating bullets, but I won't stop punching. I won't give up.

'You remember what happened two years ago, don't you?' Boss asks, not missing a beat.

'Yeah, Boss,' I reply, still punching, trying to breathe.

'What?' he asks.

'Yeah, Boss.'

'What happened?'

'I got cucumbered.'

Then he starts pounding the shit out of me with the pads. I am fending them off, ducking and dodging the punches, trying to keep away from the onslaught.

That's Boss for you. He never, ever lets me drop my head. If I'm ever down, he gives it to me. As fat as he is, and how slow he seems, his hands are always too quick for me.

'You ready?' he has asked me countless times over the years.

And then *slap!* He whacks me in the head with the pads.

'No, you're not ready.'

PUMPER

Fact is, I'd been belted everywhere I turned in the past two years. 'Jockey Tapes' had ruined my life. Nobody has seen the cost of that more than Boss. *You're a crook! You're a dog!* Boss has seen all of that.

I will never, ever say I've been squeaky-clean because I am no different to anyone else: where there's an edge, you take it.

And if people in racing can't admit to that, they're full of shit. They can't lie straight in bed. Racing has always been bent. Well, some of it. It's been like that since I've been involved. It all depends on who you are, who you do or don't know. There's never been a pencil sharpened that rules a straight line.

After 'Jockey Tapes', everyone abandoned me except those who now matter the most.

I was cucumbered. In other words, fucked over. Time to pay it back.

'You go out there and do that today,' Boss says. 'You give it all back to them today. Every bit of it.'

Then he hugs me and kisses me on the forehead.

I've been broke plenty of times. I've been ripped off by some of the biggest owners, done over by the biggest trainers. But I've never had a poor day since I've been with Boss. He's seen me get money, then throw it away. He's seen me get ripped off, not get paid, promises not followed through. Some days we've drunk champagne, some days we've drunk water. Some days we've had lobster, some days we've had bread.

But I've never had a poor day with Boss.

With his hands, and his secret ways, he put the blood in my veins, more than any other person in almost three decades of my life as a jockey.

PROLOGUE

'Go out and win the Melbourne Cup,' he says. 'Show them how good you are.'

Then Boss leaves Flemington to get on a plane as the rest of the world arrives.

And I go out and win the Melbourne Cup.

1

Size Matters

WHEN I WAS KID, I HAD TWO AMBITIONS IN LIFE: TO BE a jockey or to play for the All Blacks.

I stopped growing when I was fifteen years old. I was 5 feet tall. The idea of leading New Zealand to Bledisloe Cup glory against the Wallabies was over before it really started.

My size has never been my weakness. My size is my strength. My size allowed me to achieve the first of those childhood ambitions, for the next 30 years.

Some men were born to play for the All Blacks. I was born to be a jockey.

You mightn't have known as much when I crashed through the barriers on 21 January 1963, in Wellington on New Zealand's North Island. It was Wellington Cup Day and I was in a hurry. My mum, Francis, tells the story about how I was born in the hospital lift. I've been going up and down in life ever since.

I was a big baby; just under 8 pounds (3.6 kilograms), according to Mum.

Mum and my dad, Arthur (although everyone knew him as 'Blue' because he had red hair), worked as hard as any people I have known. They had seven children living in a three-bedroom house in the small North Island city of Lower Hutt: Mandy, Ricky, Fiona, Jimmy, Pamela, Larry and Colin. Life was a struggle, but we were happy.

Dad was an upholsterer by trade. He'd work on everything from hot rods to dining suites and lounge chairs. Sometimes, he'd find money in sofas while taking them apart and that would help make ends meet. He'd work all through the night, and sometimes Ricky and I would help. Mum and Dad would scratch and scrounge and would go without. But us kids, we never seemed to miss out on anything.

We lived for the weekends. And for me it was about two things: footy and the races.

We'd finish playing footy on a Saturday morning and if the races were at Wellington or Foxton or Palmerston, it was nothing for us to get in the car and head to the track for the afternoon.

If we weren't playing footy on the Saturday, we would all pile into the van and drive to Tauherenikau, which was over the hill from Lower Hutt. We'd go there on the Friday night and camp out, put on a barbecue, and then go the races the next day. I'd pick up discarded TAB tickets strewn all over the course, then go home, get the paper and sort through them, hoping some drunken punter might've accidentally thrown away a winning ticket. I once found one worth $70. Dad cashed it in and we used it to buy food.

SIZE MATTERS

My brothers and I played footy for Hutt Old Boys in the Wellington competition. I started playing when I was about six years old. The first position I played was hooker, but I was getting poleaxed too much so I got out of there and switched to halfback. This might surprise a few people but I had a bit of front, even at that age. I had to. I was little and I'd get pushed around, so I had to stick up for myself.

When I was at intermediate school (years seven and eight), I played in the firsts and seconds sides, starting at halfback for one and five-eighth for the other. Then, in 1974, the opportunity came up for an under-11s team from Hutt Old Boys to tour Australia. We did sponsored walks and held raffles to raise money to fly over.

We were the youngest team representing New Zealand to tour Australia, playing at Manly and being billeted out to strangers' houses all over Sydney's Northern Beaches. I was smaller than bantamweight then – about 34 kilograms – and about 4 feet 3 inches. I was front and centre of the haka, poking my tongue out and trying to spook the opposition players.

I remember we played four games and we were paid 50 cents per match. We never won a game – but we never lost a fight.

Growing up, that was often the way. I had to learn how to look after myself.

'You'll be good for nothing,' I was often told because of my lack of height.

'Yeah, you watch,' I'd shoot back. 'Good things come in little packages.'

It's not about being the biggest present, but what's inside it that matters.

In my final year at Hastings Boys High, when I was fourteen, there were three of us who were all the same size but the others were soft cocks. They tried to stand up to me and I just belted them.

But there were some kids who were just too big to belt, and they bullied me like you wouldn't believe. I would take the lunch order for the class – pies, apple turnovers, whatever – and then take the order down to the canteen at 11 am each day. A couple of Maori boys once grabbed me, belted me and took all the lunch money. I had to go back and tell the teacher that I had been robbed. By the time I left the class-room at the end of the day, the same boys had discovered I'd dobbed them in. All that was left of my pushbike was the frame. I carried my bike home instead of riding it.

At school, I was never good at any subject. I was a dunce. The best mark I ever got in English was one – because I'd spelt my name right. I could add in fives and tens but I could never subtract. I was put in the class for disadvantaged kids. Some couldn't read or write at all because they had learning difficulties. But they were my type of people. I'd take them bacon and eggs and banana cake from home to eat. Or I would just read with them.

Or I'd take the form guide to school and study that. The teacher would ask me to engage in class. And I always had the same answer: 'I'm going to be a jockey.'

The signs had been there all along. I often climbed onto the arm of Dad's lounge chair and start whipping away with a tree branch listening to the races on the radio. If not the armchair, it would be one of Dad's old sawhorses. I'd get some leather and make some stirrups, then put a set of reins on the sawhorse and ride the shit out of it. I was Gary

4

Willetts on Battle Heights, or Noel Harris on Grey Way, or Bob Skelton on Van der Hum. The sport was in my blood.

More than once, I was given detention and sent home from school but on the first Tuesday in November each year, it didn't matter. I walked out the door early no matter what.

'I'm going home to watch the Melbourne Cup,' I'd tell the teacher.

'You can't go,' the teacher would say.

'Watch me.'

I'd be glued to the black-and-white television, soaking up everything that was happening at this magical place called Flemington. It was gold: the people, the atmosphere, the parading of the horses. It was a magnet to me. It always has been. I was obsessed, and I just sat there, not budging for the whole afternoon.

'I'm going to win one of them,' I said to Dad one year.

Most fathers would've laughed and dismissed it. But my dad didn't. He was always supportive.

'If you work hard enough, you'll give it a good shot,' he said. 'But it's never going to come to you. When you want something bad enough, you take it.'

*

When I came back from our rugby tour of Sydney, I told Mum and Dad that whenever I wasn't at school I wanted to be near horses. I wanted to work at any stables, wherever I could. So Mum phoned the Racing Conference – the sport's controlling body in New Zealand – and told them her son wanted to be a jockey.

I was directed to two trainers. The first was Alan Kay, who was a good horseman but for the first two weeks I barely saw a horse. I was milking cows the whole time. Stuff that.

Then I got sent to a bloke called Peter McLean, who was a pig-farmer-turned-horse-trainer. I worked seven days a week, getting up before dawn to work a couple of hours before school, then come home and work a bit more. I was getting paid $5 a week. If I missed the bus coming home at the end of the day, I would have to walk for four hours to get home.

And I was given a lot of responsibilities. I was 44 kilograms wringing wet by then, but I would ride a 500-kilo racehorse down the road and lead two others at the same time. If some chooks came out at us, they would all spook and take off. Then, once a week, we'd take the horses to the races and that meant washing, grooming and all the work that comes with strapping them.

Around this time, Dad became very ill. He came down with pneumonia and it was so bad we were worried he might die. To ease the burden on Mum at home, I went and lived with another family for a while.

They were butchers – and they weren't too generous. They'd have a leg of lamb for dinner and give me baked beans on toast because I was only paying $15 a week for rent and board. When I came home from work, I'd always have sawdust on my boots and they got sick of it. In the end, they got the shits and asked if I wanted to make the old shed out the back into a room for myself.

The old shed was a chook pen. So I ended up killing the chooks with a shovel, and turning it into a room for myself. The family would lock me out so I couldn't get inside the house in the morning to brush my teeth or have a wash. Then I would have to run 4 miles to work in my gumboots. I would jump the fence into people's gardens and eat asparagus because I was that hungry.

SIZE MATTERS

They were tough days but I didn't care. I was riding horses. I had an affinity with them straightaway. I wasn't intimated by them. I probably should've been because I was so little. But I never got scared. I simply loved them.

The first horse I rode was actually a pony. I still remember her name: Daphne. I'd be bobbing up and down, going as fast as I could.

'He'll be able to ride, this kid,' Peter said to Mum one day.

Ride? Fuck that. I wanted to race them.

Then I graduated to full-grown racehorses, tearing around the paddock with no helmet and bare feet. I don't know how many times I had my feet and toes broken from horses standing on them. I should've been killed twenty times after getting thrown off racehorses I should not have been on.

My brother Ricky wanted to be a jockey, too, and he started his apprenticeship with Peter. He was four years older than me, and a big inspiration. And he could ride. He had no fear at all, smashing himself up badly on a few occasions with broken arms and teeth. He rode a few good winners, too, but keeping his weight down was a struggle.

When I turned fourteen, I left Peter and went to the stable of Patrick Campbell. He was better known as 'Felix'. His father's name was actually Felix, but I reckoned Patrick looked like the cartoon character Felix the Cat because he had eyes as big as dinner plates. It was a great nickname – and he was a great bloke.

Patrick was flamboyant: a fancy dresser, always immaculate. And he was a bachelor, a shagger, and he was always outstanding fun to be around. He lived in a shack off the side of the chief steward's place near his stables at Hastings, in the Hawkes Bay region.

He was also a great boss who wasn't afraid to get his hands dirty and ride trackwork with us if necessary. He wanted to see me flourish. He knew I was keen, so he bought all of my riding gear for me.

In the first few months of my apprenticeship, he made me sit in the grandstand on race day, with a pad and pen, making notes on what the leading jockeys had done in certain races.

'I want you to watch Maurice Campbell today,' he would tell me. Maurice was one of the country's leading jockeys at the time.

After the race, I'd report back what I had noticed.

'He came out of barrier four, he was fourth or fifth in the run. He was third at the 800 metres. He pulled to the outside and whipped it eight times.'

At the end of 1977, at the age of fourteen, I was just old enough to get a licence to ride.

I still remember my first ride in a race, like it was yesterday. It was at a meeting at Wairoa. We'd go every year in February, racing over three days: Saturday, Wednesday and Saturday. It was a great course, with a great crowd it had an amphitheatre feel. When we walked in on the first day of the 1978 meeting, I didn't expect to get a ride because there were no horses that were suitable.

So there I am, sitting in the jockeys' room, chest puffed out like Lester Piggott – even though I don't have a ride, even though I've never had a ride – and a trainer walks in. I can't remember his name, but I remember how the conversation went.

'You got a ride in the fifth, mate?' he asks.

'No, no, no,' I reply. 'I'll ride it for you.'

The bloke throws me the colours and I bolt out of the jockeys' room, into the carpark where punters are necking beers and eating sandwiches. I'm trying to find my boss.

'Boss! Boss!' I say when I find Patrick. 'I've got a ride! Can I ride him?'

'I better come up and see what it is,' he says.

I get back to the jockeys' room and the trainer asks me how many rides I've had today.

'None today,' I told him.

'How many have you had? Ever?' he asks.

'None at all.'

'Well, you can't ride this one.'

He took me off it. I was gutted.

There were eight races that day, but the last race was a trial; a non-tote race. Alan Pringle had a runner and his regular jockey had been injured earlier in the day. He saw I had a long face. And the long face said this: 'I will never have a ride.' So he put me on his horse. I didn't care that they weren't betting on it. It was a ride!

The horse was a filly called Rauhine Lass. I weighed 38 kilograms wringing wet, and I was given this massive saddle to throw on her back. We finished fourth, and it meant that much to me we snapped a photo afterwards. It's still in a scrapbook at home: a fifteen-year-old Jimmy Cassidy, with a bowl haircut, standing like a statue holding the silks.

After that ride, Alan gave me a chance on his horse Irish Moss in the Wairoa Cup. I was built like a matchstick, and the horse just took me everywhere in the race. Irish Moss came second but for me it was like winning the Melbourne Cup. In reality, it was the equivalent of a picnic race. But I didn't care.

Soon after, Patrick asked me to ride a few of his horses in some barrier trials. Seven of them.

'If you can't win on all of these today, you can't ride,' he said.

Sure enough, I came out and won on all seven. I'd taken my first steps as jockey. But success took a long time to come when it mattered most.

New racing rules meant apprentices could claim a four-and-a-half kilogram reduction in the weight that had to be carried.

Don Sellwood had stables next door to Patrick's. He had seen me grow up, and started to use me on his sprinter, El Donte. He'd throw me on him and I'd claim four-and-a-half kilos on account of my apprenticeship. I had six rides on that horse, and had four seconds and two thirds. I got beaten twice by the width of a spider's dick. I was the ultimate bridesmaid.

That's how it went for me for a long time. I was beaten by a nose in photo finishes in about fifteen races. Every time. *Every time.* I'd ridden in 87 races without a win. All I could think was, 'Is this ever going to happen for me?'

John Jenkins is a New Zealand racing journalist who wrote for the *Hawke's Bay Herald-Tribune*. He was with me at the start. He recalls those early years:

Jimmy and I go back a long way. I started out as a racing journalist in Hastings in 1974 and he came along about three years later. I used to drive him around to the different race meetings before he got a driver's licence.

Often we would be driving home from a meeting somewhere and he would be on a downer because he had managed to pick up a couple of placings but was still winless.

SIZE MATTERS

I used to say to him: 'Don't worry mate, once you ride your first winner you are going to take off and make it right to the top.'

I was never going to give up riding in races because I just loved it. Not once did I think about tossing it all in. To me, second was better than third, and third was better than fourth. I was like that throughout my entire career. Going without that breakthrough win kept me striving. I knew one day it would come. I knew that, for sure.

Other jockeys were supportive, too. Noel Harris was the man. So was Chris McNab. Maurice Campbell, Bill Skelton, all the local boys.

'Don't worry son, it will come,' they'd say. 'Once you ride your first winner, they won't stop.'

The problem was pretty evident: I was little, I was light, I was weak. But that improved with time. To be a successful jockey, you need strength but you also need some maturity and common sense. Safety has to come into it somewhere: you can't go out there and take risks. When you're riding a motorbike, it has brakes. Riding horses, we don't have brakes – we have our judgement. One wrong decision and it can be catastrophic.

Bad falls? I had a heap of them early on. One afternoon, at Whanganui, I had a bad smash. Three or four of us fell and I was coming second last. I went over the top of them and fell amongst the horses. I broke both wrists and all the bones in my hands. But I recovered, then kept pushing on.

I never got a lot of rides for Patrick when I was starting off because his horses weren't suitable. They were either mongrels or hard pullers.

But then a horse came along called Tarlton. He was a Northern Hemisphere–bred horse, and he was owned by Patrick's father. Tarlton was one of the first imports to come into New Zealand. He was an open handicap horse at this stage. Patrick put me on him for a race at Wairoa.

'We'll claim today,' Patrick said. 'You can ride the big horse.'

And then I went out and won on the big horse. My first winner. Beautiful. I still recall the day: 26 August 1978. It was a big relief to finally get a win, but it was also special because my boss trained the horse.

I was away. After that win, the floodgates opened. I rode 82 winners for the 1979–80 season and became New Zealand's leading apprentice.

Patrick says of that breakthrough season:

During his time with me, he learnt a lot from Chris McNab, who was another outstanding New Zealand jockey. I know it's easy to say this now, but even after his modest start everybody around the track knew he would make the grade. He just couldn't find a winner but it was only a matter of time before it happened. He was totally dedicated. If he was a foot taller, he would've been an All Black.

*

When I turned eighteen, I really started to notice the difference. I was stronger. I had more control. I won the apprentice jockey's premiership for the 1979–80 season, just three years after being indentured to Patrick.

After winning the 1981 Hawke's Bay Cup on Four Crowns – a time-honoured race at the Hastings racecourse – I was headed to Australia for the first time. We were after the Brisbane Cup, a 3200-metre handicap at Eagle Farm. I look back now and there is only one word to describe those ten days of my life.

Wild.

The horse was prepared by Dave Enright, and he was on a shoestring budget. We arrived about ten days before the race, and booked into the iconic Breakfast Creek Hotel but only stayed there for one night because the rate was too expensive. We moved out and into another place around the corner. It had a double bed.

'Why don't I sleep in the bed with you?' I pleaded with Dave. 'I have to ride tomorrow.'

Nope. So I slept in a lounge chair with the horse's rugs over me while he slept in the bed on his own. I woke up in the morning and couldn't move because I was so stiff.

We sent Four Crowns around in the P.J. O'Shea Stakes at Eagle Farm – one of the key lead-up races to the Brisbane Cup. It was a weight-for-age race, over 3200 metres, and it was my first ride in Australia.

This was the big time. I looked around the jockeys' room. There was Peter Cook, Mick Dittman and Gavin Duffy. These were superstars in their prime. I was an eighteen-year-old apprentice from Lower Hutt, New Zealand.

In the mounting yard, Four Crowns looked anything but a winner. The horse had been given his name because of four distinctive hair crowns on his forehead – but there was nothing regal about him. He'd come out of our winter and into 28 degrees of warm Queensland weather. He was a chestnut and his coat had been clipped all over except for his head. There were bits of hair coming off his legs too. He looked awful.

The bookies put him up at 30 to 1 . . . but he won in a canter. I couldn't believe it. My first ride in Australia and it's a winner!

I didn't have any more rides that day, so after I got showered and changed I went up into the grandstand and looked around. I knocked back two vodkas, soaking up the moment.

Then came an announcement over the loudspeakers.

'Jockey Jim Cassidy wanted in the weighing room,' said the announcer. 'Jockey Jim Cassidy.'

'Shit!' I thought. 'I must be in trouble.'

I figured I mustn't be allowed in the grandstands or something like that.

Instead, I'd picked up a ride. I didn't tell a soul that I'd had two vodkas. The horse was a 100 to 1 shot. I came out and won on it.

The next morning, I went home to New Zealand but then returned the day before the Brisbane Cup. Once again, Dave made me sleep in a lounge chair. I could barely move by the time we arrived at Eagle Farm for the race the next morning.

Four Crowns had dropped 6 kilos from the O'Shea Stakes to the Brisbane Cup. He went from a 33 to 1 outsider to the 5 to 1 favourite.

This really was the big stage. Over there in the corner of the jockeys' room was Malcolm Johnston. He rode for Tommy Smith, the best trainer in the country. 'Miracle' was the best jockey in the country. It was like being in the same room as Tom Cruise. He was riding a horse called Granite King.

But if there's one thing I know it's that superstars are there to be beaten. They're all the same on the track. I was about twelfth in the run, and by the 1000-metre mark I snuck up a few more spots. By the time we were 200 metres from home, there were two horses, and two jockeys, fighting it out. Tom Cruise on Granite King, and me on Four Crowns.

The racecaller, Wayne Wilson, described it like this:

Here's Granite King with a big run on the outside. Granite King settling down to fight it out with Four Crowns. Four Crowns on the outside. Four Crowns and Granite King. Granite King and Four Crowns. They go towards the line and it's a photo. By golly it's close! Almost a dead heat . . .

As I loomed outside of him, Malcolm's horse was drifting me off the track. I only beat him by a nose. If I had been beaten, I would've protested and won the race anyway, I reckon.

When the result was announced, I couldn't believe it: I had outridden Malcolm Johnston, who was riding a horse prepared by the great T.J. Smith, to win the 1981 Brisbane Cup. I was on cloud nine.

We celebrated long and hard that night, although I was kicked out of the pub because the barman didn't believe I was eighteen and I didn't have any identification on me. So I went around to the bottle shop, got half a dozen beers, slipped the bloke behind the counter twenty bucks, and then went back to the hotel room and got on it. I flew home the next day.

I recall a mate of mine had backed Four Crowns in doubles betting – that was the way to bet back then – in the O'Shea Stakes and Brisbane Cup. A massive collect. He then went and knocked it off at the casino.

*

PUMPER

My first Group 1 winner in New Zealand came on 9 December 1981, on a horse called Alice in the Avondale Cup over 2400 metres at Ellerslie in Auckland.

Johnny Jenkins remembers it well:

That day he and I flew up from Napier to Auckland for the meeting and on the way he said he thought he could win three races on the card. They were Della Rand in a minor race, Alice in the Cup, and Tudor Sky in the feature 1200-metre open sprint, the Concorde Handicap.

Neither of us had too much money in those days but we decided to put in $10 each and take an all-up bet on the three. They duly won and we had a nice pool to divvy up at the end of the day.

Just to emphasise Jimmy's tremendous will to win, he drew the extreme outside barrier on Tudor Sky that day and carved up a couple of runners inside him to get across and lead soon after the start. It cost him a $250 fine so one of the guys that he had arranged to pick us up from the airport and take us to the races dipped into his pocket and gave Jimmy the $250, saying he and his mates had cleaned up big time on the three winners.

I knew then that he had it in him to become one of the best jockeys New Zealand has produced. He not only had a perfect seat and balance on a horse but he also had a tremendous will to win and, most importantly, that killer instinct that every top sportsman has to have.

I should also add that the guys who cleaned up on Jimmy's three wins at Avondale that day took us out on the town in Auckland that night. I was supposed to be Jimmy's minder and we were in a bar somewhere when he suddenly

went missing. I shot outside to try and find him and, after
searching down a couple of side streets, here he was standing
at a mobile takeaway munching on a big hamburger. The
poor bugger had to ride Tudor Sky at 48.5 kilograms in the
Concorde and had hardly eaten a thing all day.

I started getting a lot of support from a few key New
Zealand trainers. Without them, I would not be where I am
today.

Eric Ropiha was renowned for being a trainer who could
set horses for races to the minute and then pull off a big
plunge. He got me to ride for him one day.

'I'll put you on this horse,' he said.

'Will you be there, Mr Ropiha?' I asked.

'No, I'll be on the shithouse at home counting the
money, son.'

Then I went out and won.

Eric was an amazing horseman. One day at Whanganui,
the horse I was riding for him ran off the track. He asked me
to ride it again for him on the Monday.

'It won't run off again, son,' he promised.

'Why's that?'

'When I got the horse off the float, I tied its tongue to
its tail.'

He'd literally tied a piece of string from the tongue of
the horse to its tail, so for the whole weekend it was turning
inwards, going around in a circle. At the next start, when it
jumped out, it went to the rail like a greyhound and absolutely shitted in.

One day, I really saw the command Eric had with horses.
He made a horse lie down on some straw like a dog. When

he told it to get up, it wouldn't get up. So he got a match and flicked it on the straw and set it on fire.

'It'll get up now,' he said.

From then on, the horse did exactly what Eric told it to do.

Colin Jillings, a Hall of Fame trainer, put me on a horse called McGinty, who was a bit of a wonder horse of the early 1980s in New Zealand. He ran a world-record time over a mile as a three-year-old and he was one of the great horses I rode early in my career. I was also given a lot of opportunities by people such as Bruce Marsh, who is now based in Singapore.

But the more chances I got, the more headlines I created – although not all of them for winning races.

There was one meeting at Wairoa. The track had been like concrete the day before, and then it rained on race day. The first horse I rode nearly slipped over.

'The track's dangerous, Boss,' I told Patrick. 'There's going to be an accident.'

'Just ride,' he said.

No way.

'I'm not riding,' I told the stewards. 'The track's not safe. My horse almost fell over. I'm not scared but I don't want to come off.'

One of my biggest supporters in those early years was Graeme Rogerson, 'Rogey' to anyone who knew him. He was the New Zealand training equivalent of T.J. Smith, and he had horses running from one end of the North Island to the other.

But he wasn't pleased that I was standing my ground on this day.

'If you don't ride today,' Rogey said, 'I'll ban you from my horses for six months.'

'Good as gold,' I said to Rogey.

The stewards weren't happy, either. They stood me down after a lengthy inquiry and I was fined $300 for being rude and arrogant. Who was I to say the track was unsafe?

Sure enough, the jockey who replaced me in the next race came down. Fuck. And then they called the meeting off.

I've always spoken up. But I would like to think I could back it up with actions. As the 1981–82 season came to a close, in my fourth and final year of my apprenticeship, I was chasing history and the overall jockey's premiership.

Rogey might've banned me for six months after Wairoa, but he was one of my biggest supporters. He still is.

I rode for him one day at Auckland, and I was hauled before the stewards after shortening one up. I was charged with careless riding for allegedly causing interference and ruining the winning chances of other horses around me.

Rogey came into the inquiry to represent me. As the stewards grilled me, he looked to be writing down notes on his cigarette packet.

'I just want to ask some questions,' Rogey said, before disputing a few things he had seen on the video. 'As far as I'm concerned, he shouldn't be charged. He hasn't done anything wrong.'

As we waited outside the stewards' room for their decision, he said to me: 'You'll be right. I'll get you out of this.'

When we went back in, I was handed a warning and nothing more.

'Rogey,' I said as we left the room, 'give us a look at what you wrote on your cigarette packet.'

'I didn't write anything down,' he said.

That's the type of person he is: a happy-go-lucky bloke but the shrewdest of operators. You know where you stand with him. If he likes you, he likes you. If he doesn't, he won't have anything to do with you.

Rogey was one of the most solid, genuine trainers I've ever had anything to do with, and when it came to possibly winning the jockey's premiership that year, he flew me all over the place to ride his horses. He was desperate to see me win. I needed the support because it was going to be tight.

I'd already notched up a record during that 1981–82 season. Brent Thomson had been the country's most successful apprentice, having won 250 races during his time – a record. In late December, I got Peace Pipe home at Awapuni from a long way back in the field to break the record. I then went on to notch up 257 wins as an apprentice. I was eighteen years old.

'It's the biggest thrill of my career so far,' I told Tony Hilton from *The Dominion*. 'Now, I've got this, I'm all out to get Bill's record.'

That was Bill Skelton's record of 124 winners for the season, set in the 1960s. I was already on 54 wins with seven months remaining to get there.

On the last day of the season, I was sitting on 119 wins. I was five ahead of David Peake. He was riding in Auckland, I was riding at Whanganui, and as the day went on he was reeling me in. *Peake's won another one! Peake's won another one!* The radio was running hot, and it told the story of how close it was going to be.

David rode five winners, making us equal at the top the premiership ladder. I had eight rides that day and coming into the final race not one of mine had so much as placed.

'Shit!' I thought. 'I'm going to get done here on the last day.'

SIZE MATTERS

In the final event of the day, I was on a horse called Lord Raywood for Evan Rayner. It was a 2000-metre race and I drew barrier 13. So I'm sitting in the jockeys' room, working out a plan.

'Fuck this,' I thought. 'I'm going to take this into my own hands.'

So I got straight out to the lead, dictated the race, and won. In Auckland, David failed to place. I went into the last race of the premiership needing to win.

And win I did.

2

Kiwi

Have you ever been rolling in money?

Days after the 1983 Melbourne Cup, I was supposed to be back in New Zealand riding trackwork but I didn't turn up. Instead, I was still in Australia. Two days of wild partying had finally come to an end, and I found myself at the foot of the bed in my hotel room holding a little green Air New Zealand bag.

There was $22,000 cash inside; a fortune in those days. The money had been given to me in 'grey nurses' – hundred-dollar bills – but I had them cashed into twenties and fifties.

I ripped back the sheets, emptied the money onto the bed, and then stripped off all of my clothes. My two mates from New Zealand, Rod Croome and Dave Johnson, were there alongside me.

'Watch this boys,' I told them.

Then I dived on the bed. I was literally rolling in cash.

I was twenty years old, a young punk jockey from the other side of the Tasman, and I had just won the Melbourne Cup on a horse called Kiwi – a six-year-old New Zealand farm horse bought for $1000 to round up sheep.

I knew I would win it, too.

'I'm going to win the Cup for you, Dad,' I said before I flew out for Melbourne. 'I'm going to win the Cup.'

He just gave me a big kiss and a cuddle and told me to do my best.

They still talk about Kiwi's last-to-first victory that year as one of the most thrilling in the history of the 2-mile race. Of the tens of thousands of races I've ridden in over the years, it remains the standout. A Kiwi jockey in Australia's greatest race, that stops the nation, that stops all of New Zealand as well, on a horse called Kiwi. Incredible.

It was the win that started everything for me. And I still haven't seen a Melbourne Cup winner – not even Saintly, not even Might And Power – be as bold as Kiwi that year. Kiwi would've kicked Might And Power's arse at 2 miles. I don't say that lightly. That's just how highly I rate him.

I was a seventeen-year-old apprentice when I first noticed him. Dianne Moseley, the leading female jockey of the day, rode him in his first few starts, but I knew straightaway that I wanted to be the next jockey on Kiwi's back.

'Saw a good horse today, Boss,' I told Patrick. 'I want to see if I can get on him.'

He told me to ring Kiwi's trainer, Ewen 'Snowy' Lupton.

That's where the real story of Kiwi starts. Snow and his wife, Anne, lived in Waverley on the North Island on a big sheep and cattle station, and they trained racehorses in their spare time.

KIWI

They had previously owned a horse by the American sire Blarney Kiss, and Anne wanted another one from the same stallion. She insisted that it had to be a chestnut. So they went to the Karaka yearling sales and out came this scrawny, undernourished looking thing . . .

'I like that one!' said Anne. 'I want to buy it.'

Snow put in a bid, the bidding went to a thousand dollars, which is as cheap as it gets for a racehorse, and they bought him. They took him home and named him Kiwi – not because of national pride, but because Anne liked kiwi birds.

So after I saw the horse run I phoned Snowy and said, 'I want to get on Kiwi next start, if that's possible.'

'Yeah,' said Snow, with his slow, husky voice. 'You can come and ride him.'

What I didn't know was that his next start was at New Plymouth, in the Taranaki region on the west coast of the North Island. I lived in Hastings, on the east coast. To get there I would have to drive. It was a seven-hour trip.

The only problem was I didn't have a car. But my boss had one. A big V8 Charger.

'Boss, I have no way of getting there but I want to go and ride him,' I told Patrick.

He threw me the keys to the Charger. Can you imagine me in a V8 Charger? No, neither can I.

I took the cushions off my couch, put them on the driver's seat, perched myself up and away I went, driving all the way to New Plymouth. Kiwi was in the last race, a 1200-metre sprint. It was the only ride I had on the day. He was back last the whole trip, flashed home and got beaten by a nose, finishing second. I was paid $30 for the ride. It didn't cover the petrol money.

But it didn't matter because I loved the horse. You couldn't get me off him from then on.

The legend goes that friends convinced Snow and Anne to race Kiwi after they had initially bought him as a farm horse. But even after the horse started racing, Snow, along with his old cattle dog, would round up sheep and cows on Kiwi. Over there, they jump anything, including big sheep fences. I was always praying the horse wouldn't break a leg getting caught up in the wire fences.

Sometimes, I'd ring up Snow at the farm and have a chat.

'Where are you going to run the horse next, Snow?' I'd ask. 'Are you going to run him in the Pahiatua Cup?'

'No,' Snow would say. 'I'm going to take him hunting next week.'

'You're gonna what?'

'I'm taking him hunting.'

In between rounding up livestock and hunting, Kiwi was also racing with me all over the North Island, and often winning.

One day, I called my mate Dave Johnson. He was the publican at The Carlton Hotel in Palmerston North where many of the All Blacks drank.

'I've found a good horse – we should try to buy him,' I told Dave.

We offered Snowy $40,000 to buy the horse midway through 1981.

'I'd never sell him,' replied Snow. 'But I'll make you a promise: if I ever decide to sell him, I'll give you first bite.'

'Beautiful,' I said. 'But if you're not going to let me buy him, can you let me keep riding him?'

'He's yours.'

Then Kiwi went out and won the Waverley Cup (2175 metres) carrying 54 kilograms. That was his first open handicap. He should've had 47 or 48 kilos on his back that day – the handicapper was harsh – but he won anyway. He carried more weight then than he did in the Melbourne Cup. That's how tough he was.

The first Tuesday in November wasn't in anybody's plans until he won the Wellington Cup in late January.

The Wellington Cup at Trentham is one of New Zealand's long standing races. It was first run in 1874. In recent years it became a 2400-metre race, but when Kiwi went to the barriers for the race in 1983, it was over 3200 metres (2 miles). He'd never raced over that distance before.

'It would be a great thrill to win the race because I was born in Wellington and first got interested in the game by going to the Trentham track,' I said to the press before the race.

A day before my twentieth birthday, the dream came true. John Jenkins wrote in the *Herald-Tribune*:

Kiwi had to produce a Herculean effort to win. He was a lonely last until the home turn and powered past horse after horse in the last 300 metres to get up in the last stride.

The northerner, Maurita, looked to have the cup won when she dashed to the front close to the finish. But Kiwi, bulldogging his way through on the inside, got up to snatch victory by a nose.

Commentator Peter Kelly was not game to say which of the two horses had won as they flashed over the line locked together. But both Jim Cassidy and Maurita's rider Greg Childs were sure of the outcome.

Luckily, I was right. That's when the plan came into our heads to take Kiwi to Australia for the Melbourne Cup.

About a month before the race in Australia, he raced at Hawera in the Egmont Cup over 2100 metres, winning by two-and-a-half lengths with 57 kilograms on his back. He came from last to first again. He was always coming from last. Now he'd be carrying 5 kilos less for the Melbourne Cup.

For me, this was going to be something magical. I'd grown up watching New Zealand horses, trainers and jockeys go over and win one of the world's biggest races. I remember Bruce Marsh winning on Silver Knight in 1971. And Bob Skelton's win on Van der Hum in 1976, on a bog track.

I also remember an Australian jockey, the great Harry White, winning in 1979 on Hyperno. He was riding for Bart Cummings, and he was so patient in the race. Waiting, waiting, waiting . . . I would have to do the same on Kiwi.

I felt so confident. I'd ridden in the Cup for the first time the previous year for George Hanlon on a horse called Amarant. That was the year Gurner's Lane knocked off the famous Kingston Town. I'd finished tenth. It was a wonderful experience but Amarant was a 50 to 1 outsider in that race. Now I was on a horse that I knew could win. On a horse called Kiwi.

And that had me pumped.

*

I'm standing in the mounting yard at Flemington.

The cream of the crop is here. I see Bart Cummings. I see Tommy Smith. I see Colin Hayes. And then I see Snowy, a tall, thin man with a roll-your-own cigarette in the corner of his mouth, the ash about 2 inches long and ready to fall onto his suit at any moment.

'What are we doin'?' I ask him.

'I don't know,' Snow replies. 'I'll leave it to you. You know what you're doin' on him. Just don't annoy him. Let him do what he wants.'

That was the thing with Kiwi: he was just like Snowy. You couldn't make Snow go any quicker, you couldn't make him go any slower. The closest thing I ever saw to a horse being human was Kiwi. You had to see them together. Kiwi was more like Snow's son than his racehorse. Wherever Snow went, the horse would follow. Even if Snow let him off the lead, he'd just hang around. He was a pet.

Kiwi was never a big, robust horse. He was fairly tall, just under 17 hands, but he wasn't as big and strong as Phar Lap. He was this rangy thing and he never carried a lot of weight on his bones, although towards the end of his career he developed.

But he had a nature I've never seen in another horse. Very laidback. Like Snow. I reckon it was because of how he was prepared around the farm.

Now, here we were at Flemington on Melbourne Cup Day.

I can't recall another time during my entire career when I was so relaxed going into a race. It was like I was at the beach and about to slip into the water for a nice swim.

I'd been relaxed since arriving in Melbourne the Sunday before the Cup. Snow and Anne booked me into the Park Royal in St Kilda. Shortly after arriving, Snow phoned my room.

'Why don't we walk the track?' he said.

'What's the use of that?' I replied half-joking. 'I'm going to see enough of it from where I'm going to be on Tuesday.' But there's no slacking with Snow so begrudgingly I joined him at Flemington.

We walked into the racecourse, past the mounting yard, past the clocktower, and the members' stand, heading to the little side gate where you walk out onto the course proper. The first event on Cup Day back then was a jumps race, and the hurdles were already up.

Jockeys are a superstitious bunch. Bill Skelton, God bless his heart, would never swear. He wouldn't even say the word 'bloody'. So he said 'blummy' instead. He's in a wheelchair now, but when I was an apprentice I would look up to Bill and watch him ride. He used to say to me, 'Son, you always need that blummy bird on your shoulder in this game. That little birdie will always help you.' I would often think, 'Yeah. I'd like a little birdie helping me. A two-legged one.'

As Snowy and I walked the course that Sunday – blow me down – I saw this little bird in the middle of the track at Flemington. It was on the ground, flapping around with an injured wing.

'I have to catch this bird, Snow!' I bellowed and dashed off towards it.

'What are you doing?' Snow asked when he reached me.

'See this bird? This is the omen I need to win the Cup.'

I picked up the bird, carried it over to the winning post and set it down in a shady spot near the post. 'So what?' you might think. But for me, that blummy bird was a sign.

On the Monday afternoon, I went to the sauna at St Kilda baths, had a swim, and then returned to the Park Royal about 6.50 pm. The back bar was chock-a-block, as you would expect the night before the Melbourne Cup.

I walked up to the corner of the bar and elbowed my way to the front.

'Excuse me, mate,' I said to the barman. 'I need two Crown Lagers.'

'Who is the other one for?' a bloke standing next to me asked.

'Me,' I said, throwing down the first.

'What are you doing, mate?' he said, bewildered. 'Aren't you riding in the Melbourne Cup tomorrow?'

'Who gives a fuck?' I laughed and threw down the second beer. 'I'm going to win it anyway.'

And besides that, my mouth was as dry as a birdcage. I'd been at the sauna for a few hours and I needed a drink. I told the stranger the story about the little bird, and went back to my room. I knew I wasn't riding until mid-afternoon the next day, so I slept like a baby.

*

In those days, before the main race they would have a parade of successful jockeys and horses from the 1200 metres, up the famous Flemington straight, to the winning post.

Bob Skelton couldn't make it this year to sit in a carriage behind Van der Hum, so they asked me to fill in. 'How beautiful,' I thought, as it would be a good chance to get some clues on how to win the Cup.

I knew there was at least one man in the parade who could help me – Roy Higgins, the legendary jockey who had twice won the race for Bart Cummings with Light Fingers (1965) and Red Handed (1967). Roy had retired earlier that year.

This was a chance to pick the brains of one of the best riders the world had ever seen.

'Mr Higgins, I'm Jim Cassidy,' I said shyly. 'I'm riding Kiwi in the Melbourne Cup.'

'How you feeling, son?' he asked.

'Good, actually. I feel relaxed. Any pointers for riding in the Cup?'

Roy was happy to oblige. 'From the time you jump, you have to get your position,' he advised. 'By the time you get to the finishing post the first time, you want to be as close to the fence as you can so you're not covering extra ground.'

'I'll be right, Mr Higgins,' I said. 'I'll probably be back near last.'

'Oh yeah?' he said with a puzzled look on his face. 'Well, when you get to the 2000 metres,' he continued, 'you have to make sure you're close to the fence. Once you get up that side, if you haven't got your position then you're in all sorts of trouble.'

'I'll be last by then.'

'That's all right . . . As the race goes on, and you're at the 1000 metres, you're near the turn at Chiquita Lodge, and then you have that run up to the half mile, you really have to be aware that horses that can't run two miles start to get the stitch . . .'

'That won't worry me, Mr Higgins. I'll be last.'

Roy gave me that puzzled look again. I looked straight back. He kept going.

'From the half mile to the 600 metres, the race is on,' he said. 'The tired horses are starting to come back, some are getting a stitch, and when they get a stitch, they start to wobble . . .'

'I'll be able to see everything. I'll be last.'

'Well, when you turn for home and you're back last, what are you going to do?'

'I'll weave my way through. I'll win this race at the clocktower.'

Roy looked at me with disbelief. I looked at him full of belief.

'Good luck, son,' he said smiling as he walked off. 'All the best.'

If I didn't know I could win then, I knew I could as soon as I saw Kiwi when he came into the mounting yard before the race. He was the only horse that didn't have a sweat mark on him. Look at the horses before the Melbourne Cup now: very few horses don't have sweat on them. Kiwi was so relaxed he was almost asleep.

I climbed on board and we made our way out onto the course proper . . .

I have watched replay after replay of what happened in the next few minutes. I get goosebumps looking it now. There were several racecallers describing what happened that day, but the voice in my mind will always be the late Clem Dimsey, who called the Cup for the Channel 10 network for many years.

I am coming out of barrier 2, and I am the first one dropping back on the fence, coming back through the field. Combat goes out at a hundred miles an hour. I'd told Roy I would be last at the clocktower the first time around, last at the winning post, last at the 2000 metres, and I was.

And last of all is Kiwi . . .

Then Amarant, the horse I rode the previous year, drops back behind me. He has bled and is pulled up.

At the 1600 metres, I am 25 lengths off the leaders. Now we are coming to the home turn. The pace is quickening. They all fan out across the track, but I stick to the inside, ready to come through the middle. There I am in the blue cap, ready to make my move.

And last of all is Kiwi . . .

I haven't spent any petrol going around a horse. Because I am last, and doing absolutely nothing, all I have to do – which I always tried to do in the big ones – is make sure I have an uninterrupted run. Your navigation has to be clear. I'm already looking at the other horse in front of me. I have to know whether I am going in or out. I have to make that decision and I have to make it quick, because it comes like *that*. I don't want to stop my run because then I have to get going again. Once I stop, I'm gone.

I don't know the horses in front of me, or what they are going to do. I know that Bart Cummings, Colin Hayes and Tommy Smith are the best trainers and I know they have the best stayers. I don't know anyone else. I just know Kiwi.

At the 400 metres, Chiamare (trained by Smith) has nosed ahead but is about to be tackled by Noble Comment (George Hanlon) and Mr Jazz (Cummings).

I am weaving through the pack, getting to the outside of the field. Then I see the clocktower.

Let me tell you why the clocktower is so important in my mind.

After Kiwi won the Egmont Cup, trainer Eric Temperton pulled me aside. Eric had won the 1971 Melbourne Cup with Silver Knight.

'Whatever you do,' Eric said that day, 'have him wound up at the clocktower.'

That stuck in my head for a month. *Have him wound up at the clocktower.* And there it is. Time to go.

I pull the stick and go as hard as I can. For a twenty-year-old from New Zealand with nothing to lose and everything to gain, I can't be more confident.

On any horse, it's all about momentum. On horses like Kiwi, you could drop your weight and use your balance to change the horse's stride and find another gear. It's like David Campese doing a goosestep. He could be running flat out then step and go the other way. That's the same on a horse. You can't be taught that – you learn it. It's all feel.

So now I angle out, and Kiwi changes stride. When he changes stride, he lengthens. He makes Noble Comment and Mr Jazz look like they're tied to the rail. He smokes them, because he has spent nothing early in the race.

Mr Jazz on the outside, Noble Comment and Chiamare settle down to a ding-dong struggle . . .

Clem still hasn't noticed me. Not many have. But in the last few strides the rest of Flemington will know what I knew back at the clocktower before I hit the straight.

Noble Comment about a neck in front of Mr Jazz on the outside – and Kiwi's flying. He might beat them all. Kiwi's come from last with a phenomenal performance to win the Cup!

Kiwi's last 100 metres was so quick he'd have outrun a fighter jet. I told Roy Higgins I would win coming from last, and I did.

After the race, in the madness of the mounting yard, a newspaperman came up to me. I didn't know him but I recognised the face from somewhere.

'I want to do an interview with you,' he said. 'My name's Tommy Brassel.'

Tommy was the racing editor for *The Daily Mirror*, an afternoon newspaper in Sydney, and – as it turned out – the bloke I'd chatted to yesterday in the bar while I knocked back my two beers. I'd told him about the little bird, and he wrote about it in the paper the next day.

The New Zealand press went mad, as you can expect. The headline in *The Dominion* read: 'Oh boy! This Kiwi can fly. Mystery horse stuns Melbourne.'

In the interviews I explained how I had thought about sneaking up on the inside, instead of weaving through the field and coming down the outside like I had. On the turn, three or four horses went wide so I just sat and waited. I saw Fountaincourt flat in front of me. I knew he wouldn't win. Once Kiwi straightened, I knew I had it won. I thought, *This horse can do anything.* In front, I could see Noble Comment going up and down in the one spot. I knew then that the race was mine. My blood was boiling. I don't know what I said or called at the line, but I knew I had won the Melbourne Cup. It was a marvellous feeling, quite out of the ordinary, and I'll never forget it.

Elsewhere in the mounting yard after the race, Roy Higgins was being interviewed on television about what he had just seen.

'I met that little Jimmy Cassidy at the parade before the Cup,' he said. 'He said he was going to be last at the 2000 metres, the 1000 metres, the 800 metres . . . Then he made the most outlandish statement: he was going to be last on the turn in the Melbourne Cup and he said he could win.'

I saw Roy later and I told him I had to look up the dictionary to see what 'outlandish' meant.

Snow, typically, was calm when I saw him. Anne was more ecstatic. She was proud of Kiwi. She never dreamt of having a horse run in the Melbourne Cup. It just happened.

I was proud of Snow and Anne for sticking with me. They could've put Noel Harris, who had ridden in a couple of Melbourne Cups, on the horse. They could've gone for any one of New Zealand's top jockeys. That was my concern after the Wellington Cup, but Snow never hesitated.

'No, you ride him in the Melbourne Cup,' Snow had said. He stuck to his word.

Without sounding rude or arrogant, I was also proud of myself. Proud of my self-belief that I would win. Proud that I was right. If I had flashed home and finished third or fourth, the media would've buried me. That didn't worry me. Who were the media to me? I was young. I didn't give a fuck.

Later in the afternoon someone from the Victoria Racing Club approached me and said I had to attend the Melbourne Cup dinner.

'No, no,' I said. 'I can't do that. I'm here with my two mates. We're going out on the town. We just won the Melbourne Cup!'

The VRC hassled me to attend, but there was no way I was going without my mates, Dave Johnson and Rod Croome. They'd backed Kiwi, of course, and were ready to hit the town with me.

'Unless you get the other two into the function, I won't be coming,' I said.

Before that, I had to appear on *Hey! Hey! It's Saturday* with Daryl Somers. They did the show on Cup night in those days. They picked me up in a stretch limo, and there was a bottle of champagne waiting for us in the back. I thought, 'How good is this?'

'You're a little bloke,' Somers said when we were on air. 'What makes the Kiwi horses so good?'

'It's all the green grass,' I told him. 'The way they're brought up.'

'Grass?!' he joked, referring to another type of grass.

Then the three of us went to the Melbourne Cup dinner. I can't recall much of the night, but I can remember leaving the event.

There was a sculpture in the hotel foyer: a big frozen statue of a horse made out of margarine and chocolate.

'I wouldn't mind taking that horse,' I told the boys.

I didn't know it was this buttery, chocolate thing. I went to pick it up, and it collapsed on me. I was covered in margarine. It was all over my suit. Then we ended up at a nightclub. It was wild.

It went on like that for two more days in Melbourne until I found myself at the end of the bed, holding the little green Air New Zealand bag.

I'd come to Melbourne with $2000 in cash. That was my life savings. It was basically everything I had.

The day before the Cup, I wanted to make sure I knew how long and how much a taxi would cost to get from the Park Royal to Flemington and back. I wasn't leaving anything to chance. The trip cost me $1.98. I remember that, because I handed a green two-dollar note to the cabbie.

That left me with $1998. I gave it to Dave and asked him to put a bet on Kiwi.

You need to remember that I wasn't allowed to bet. It's against the rules of racing for jockeys to punt. But Dave got on at 11 to 1 with a bookmaker.

The bet wasn't for me. It was for my dad. I'd told him that I would win the Melbourne Cup for him. I didn't tell him I would be winning $22,000 for him. Now I had.

But before I gave it to him, I had one last thing to do with it. I wanted to roll in the cash.

*

You will never, ever again see a Melbourne Cup run and won like that. The European stayers won't do it, because they race close together. The Aussie stayers, well, there won't be any left before too long. There will never be another Kiwi.

But there were other horses for me to ride back in New Zealand. If I look back on my career, there were two that really put me on the map, alongside Kiwi.

The first was Burletta, a tiny grey filly trained by Patrick Campbell. We had her set to win an 800-metre race first-up for two-year-olds at Hawke's Bay. She missed the start by 7 lengths and in an 800-metre race, when you don't have enough time to fart, that's a big setback.

But she picked them up by the time she got to the straight, and then won by 6 lengths. *Six lengths*. She had a wing on every foot, despite being so small. People were flabbergasted and wondering, 'What's this little thing?'

She was a flying machine. She went on to have four wins as a two-year-old from eight starts. Then, the next season, she was unstoppable, winning the Thousand Guineas a few days after I arrived home following the Melbourne Cup. In the end, I had seventeen rides on Burletta for ten wins.

Burletta ended up being named New Zealand Filly of the Year as a three-year-old – and I was crowned New Zealand

Racing Personality of the Year. I was the first person from Hastings to receive the award.

Then there was Commissionaire, who was trained by Noel Eales. I shifted from Hastings to Woodville to ride for Noel, and while I wasn't really his number-one rider we had enormous success, no matter where we went.

Noel was just as good as any of the legendary trainers in Australia. He was very patient with his horses, and knew how to time their preparation to the minute. In 1993, we combined to win the Group 1 Mackinnon Stakes with The Phantom. Held on Derby Day, the Mackinnon is the key lead-up race to the Melbourne Cup. We were favourites for the Cup the following Tuesday, but the heavens opened up the night before the race and on the wet track we went no good.

Noel wasn't a great traveller, though, so he never took Commissionaire across the Tasman for any of the big races, but I believe he was the only horse at the time that could've come to Australia and given the mighty Kingston Town a run for his money over 2000 metres. That's how highly I rate the horse.

I won a maiden on him at Foxton by 2 lengths over 1400 metres. The total prizemoney for the race was $1300. I could barely buy a beer out of my percentage. From there he took off, winning at Group 2 and 3 level before going into the more difficult weight-for-age races. The problem was finding him strong enough races to compete in. If he was around now, he would've had a string of Group 1 races to his name. Back then, they were only Group 2.

I compare him to Might And Power because I would ride him up on the speed, or lead on him, and I would always ride him to run at 10 furlongs in two minutes. Once, he broke two minutes. He just had an enormous will to win. He didn't know how to give in. I had 32 rides on him and won eighteen times.

They were great horses. But there was only one Kiwi.

The cruel part of the Kiwi story is that he was robbed of winning the Melbourne Cup the following year when he could've joined the likes of Archer, Rain Lover, Think Big and Makybe Diva as one of the horses to win back-to-back.

I reckon Kiwi would've pissed in because he was going even better than the year before.

VRC chief vet John Bourke decided to scratch Kiwi on the eve of the race. The official verdict was a pastern injury, the bone above the hoof, which Bourke diagnosed in one of the horse's front legs.

As far as I'm concerned, it was up there with the Trevor Chappell underarm incident from the one-day cricket match between Australia and New Zealand in 1981. Disgraceful. I'm not really sure of the reasons, but there were plenty who thought there was no way you could have a Kiwi horse, trainer and jockey winning Australia's biggest race for the second year in a row.

It was bullshit because the horse was not injured and he was fit to run. He was more sound than the winner, Black Knight, who had been galloped on three times in the Geelong Cup and had cuts and scars all over his legs when he lined up in the Melbourne Cup.

Snow was gutted. It was humiliating for him because he knew his horse better than anyone and he knew the horse was not sore. He galloped him, he did figure-eights on him, he did all the tests they asked for, and they still said the horse wasn't fit to race. I was standing right there when they vetted Kiwi. They were twisting his joints and banging his leg. It was appalling. If they had vetted every horse in the race like they did Kiwi, they would've only had four runners. What a joke.

I also know this: three weeks later, I rode Kiwi in the Japan Cup over 2400 metres and he came an admirable fifth. Pretty good for a horse that was vetted out of the Melbourne Cup.

It was hugely difficult for Snow because it embarrassed him. As far as I was concerned, the VRC officials responsible had only embarrassed themselves.

Snowy passed away in 2004, aged 84. Kiwi had died in 1995, aged eighteen. He was buried on Snow and Anne's farm. The headstone reads: 'Kiwi, 1983 Melbourne Cup'. Straightforward, just like Snow.

3

'Bet Up, Boss'

THE PHONE CALL THAT TURNED MY CAREER ON ITS HEAD came at 8.30 pm on a Thursday in March, 1984. I was lying in bed, back home in New Zealand.

'Hello, this is Bob Lapointe,' said the voice with a Canadian accent.

I thought, 'Who the fuck is Bob Lapointe calling me at this time of the night?'

'Hello, Bob,' I said.

'I'm calling from Sydney. I race this good mare called Emancipation. I want to talk to you about a job in Sydney.'

Bob's name didn't ring an immediate bell but I knew about Emancipation. She was the champion grey filly who in 1983 had won the George Ryder Stakes at Rosehill, beating the champion Manikato, then the Doncaster Handicap at Randwick, and the George Main Stakes at Warwick Farm. Ron Quinton – a jockey I admired a great deal – had been in charge for most of her starts.

Naturally, I thought the phone call was a mate taking the piss. So I hung up.

Ten minutes later, the phone rang again.

'I don't know if you know who I am,' said Bob. 'I race a lot of horses. We want to send you some air tickets and fly you over to discuss a stable we're setting up.'

I was still the stable rider for Noel Eales at Palmerston. So I asked Noel if I should fly over and check this out. It was a no-brainer, he said.

Before I knew it, I was on a plane bound for Sydney. As we flew in, all I could see were rooftops. Orange-tiled rooftops. It was a concrete jungle. I was from Lower Hutt, with twenty houses along our road. Sydney was mind-boggling.

When I came through customs at Sydney airport, there was a driver holding a sign with my name on it. He led me to a brand-new black Merc and we weaved through the heavy traffic to Point Piper, the harbourside suburb in Sydney's east that is famous for its mansions.

The waterfront mansion we pulled up in front of was pink. The door swung open and I was greeted by a butler wearing white gloves and a top hat.

'Come in, Mr Cassidy,' he said. 'Come through to the conservatory, Mr Sangster will be there in a minute.'

I waited in the conservatory for ten minutes before another man, immaculately dressed in a suit, entered the room.

'I'm Robert Sangster,' he said.

I had some idea who he was – but only later did I realise how *big* he actually was.

Robert Sangster was a British multi-millionaire who, in the 1970s, turned thoroughbred racing around the world on its head. He spent millions of pounds with John Magnier's Coolmore Stud in Ireland, breeding superstar horses that won the world's biggest races. He owned The Minstrel, which won the Epsom Derby, Britain's richest race. He owned Alleged, twice the winner of the Prix de l'Arc de Triomphe in Paris. And he owned Beldale Ball, which was trained in Australia by Colin Hayes and won the 1980 Melbourne Cup with Johnny Letts in the saddle.

Sangster moved to Australia in the late 1970s, and was also known for his flamboyant lifestyle. He married the socialite Susan Rossiter – the wife of former Liberal Party leader Andrew Peacock and later to become Lady Susan Renouf – in 1978, but by the time I came into his life he was seeing a woman called Susan Lilley. The English racing correspondent Julian Wilson once said of Sangster: 'His pleasures were boxing, champagne, golf, racing and beautiful women, in no particular order, and often more than one at the same time.'

No wonder we got on so well.

'Can I get you a Coke?' Robert asked.

'Nah. Can I have one of those blue labels up there on the shelf?' I said, waving to the expensive bottles of scotch I'd spotted as soon as I'd walked in. 'If we're here to talk business, we may as well drink the good stuff.'

He just laughed. The racetrack is full of all different types of people, from the top to the bottom. From sheiks and princes and property tycoons, to people just like me, who came from very little. You treat people as they treat you. People like Robert Sangster didn't intimidate me. They never have.

He looked at my hands.

'Just what I want,' he said. 'For a little bloke, you've got awfully big hands.'

In terms of riding, big hands are good. Your upper-body strength must be good. You need good, strong biceps. You need them to control the horse.

'You can fit a lot of money in them,' I said.

When Sangster put his offer on the table, I realised that this was serious stuff. He was going into business with Lapointe – who had come to Australia as a 26-year-old and brought the KFC, Pizza Hut and eventually Sizzler franchises with him. Also involved was Millie Fox. She had been married to the late Stan Fox, who had established 120 boxes at Nebo Lodge at Rosehill. This was where the legendary Jack Denham trained in the 1970s.

The operation was due to start on 15 May. Queensland's Brian Mayfield-Smith was to be the trainer, and I was being considered as the stable's number-one jockey. Their plan was straightforward: to end Tommy Smith's long reign as Sydney's leading trainer.

I was given a guided tour of Nebo Lodge, and then we went out to Lapointe's pre-training property at Wisemans Ferry, on the Hawkesbury River, about an hour's drive away.

My trip to Sydney was not a secret. Bert Lillye interviewed me for *The Sydney Morning Herald*:

> Winning the Melbourne Cup on Kiwi was my biggest thrill, especially the way it was received by Australian race-goers . . . It was a dream come true, but the challenge of the Melbourne Cup does not compare with being appointed the number one stable jockey for Brian Mayfield-Smith. It will be the start of a new life for me.

Lapointe was also quoted in the same article, and he said it wasn't the victory on Kiwi that sparked their interest in me but the Brisbane Cup win two years earlier on Four Crowns.

'He more than held his own in a titanic struggle over the last 200 [metres] with Malcolm Johnston, who was on the runner-up Granite King,' he said. 'The margin was only a nose, but Four Crowns carried three kilograms more than Johnston's mount. We have also interviewed Wayne Harris for the appointment and are now in the process of making a firm decision.'

Bert also wrote that a decision would be made in the coming week and 'it will surprise me if Cassidy does not get the job'. He was right. I was given the nod, and moved to Australia soon after.

*

When I started with Nebo Lodge, I was based in Brisbane. I would ride there on a Saturday, then be flown to Sydney for the Wednesday meeting, have three or four rides, and then fly back. Within a few months they were sending me down for a Saturday in Sydney, before flying me back to Brisbane again.

I started winning more and more and by the time I moved into a big four-bedroom house in Sydney's west, not far from Rosehill racecourse, I was ready to rip for the start of the season on 1 August.

Sangster and Lapointe were prepared to be patient, which is rare in racing. Nebo Lodge had a pool of 150 horses: 85 of them were two-year-olds and about 60 of them were in full training. 'We plan to take things quietly at first,' Lapointe told *The Herald*. 'We will have a lot of young, untried horses, fresh from schooling, in the early months. But by the end of this year we will have a hundred horses in training year-round at Rosehill.'

But, in my mind, the pressure was on. One of the richest men in the country, and one of the best known figures in global racing, had thrown this lifeline to me. Now, I had to prove myself.

I was daunted enough by the traffic. I recall the first time I drove from Parramatta to Randwick. I took a wrong turn and ended up on the wrong side of the Sydney Harbour Bridge. I had to ditch my car and pay for a taxi to get me to Randwick racecourse.

Then there was the pressure in the jockeys' room. I had to prove myself there, too. I was in the same room as the likes of Ronnie Quinton, Mick Dittman, Peter Cook, Kevin Langby and Bruce Compton. Wayne Harris was the leading apprentice at the time. Darren Beadman was just starting out. I was the two-foot-nothing Kiwi who'd jagged the Melbourne Cup the year before. And now I had landed the big job at Nebo. There was enormous pressure on me to stand up and be counted.

There was also pressure to make sure there was money in the back pocket. Les Young, who was a spokesman for Nebo Lodge, explained to *The Sun-Herald* what my deal was. 'Our guarantee isn't a huge amount and, with normal luck, I have no doubt Jim will be able to earn more from rides and percentages,' he said. 'However, we will be supplying a car and house.'

Brian Mayfield-Smith was hard to work for because he was a perfectionist. He was a stockman, raised in Cairns in Far North Queensland, and he'd been the main trainer for Stan and Millie Fox for many years. As a Queenslander, he enjoyed getting on the rum – but apart from that he was a straighty-one-eighty. All he wanted to do was train winners. He didn't want to bet. Didn't tip. Nothing.

We had a few blues, but then we would sort things out. I would usually have a full book of rides for the day, no matter where we raced, and I never rode for other stables unless Nebo didn't have a horse in a particular race. Tommy Smith started using me. I'd win a couple for him and Brian would want to kill me.

I won for Nebo Lodge with my first ride for them, on Glen Vista, and the last race of the season, on Fix The Date, on protest.

That twelve-month period had many highs and lows.

I won the 1985 Levin Bayer Classic on the great Bonecrusher, who went on to win the Cox Plate in that amazing finish with Our Waverley Star the following year. Bonecrusher was unknown when I won on him. I started him on his winning way.

The only other time I rode him was three years later in the Queen Elizabeth Stakes in Canberra. He finished second by a snotball to Bart Cummings' Beau Zam.

Before that race, I was in the mounting yard when Bob Hawke, then prime minister, approached me.

'Um, er, I'd like you to meet the Queen,' he said.

I turned around. And there was the Queen. I didn't know what to do. So I just stuck out my hand. She was wearing white gloves.

'How you goin'?' I said.

'Very well, thank you,' she replied as she shook my hand.

I was primed to win the 1985 AJC Derby on Sir Zephyr, but a setback in his preparation cost him that win for sure.

A month later, he won the South Australian Derby but I missed the ride because I had badly hurt my back while riding him in the Adelaide Cup the week before. Sir Zephyr clipped the heels of the horse in front of him, and he catapulted high in the air and I landed on my back. It should've killed me but it didn't. I was given the green light to ride again, but then I fell down the stairs at home while rushing to answer the phone and I sprained my ankle.

It wasn't until late June that I finally made it back into the saddle, and come the end of the season I finished fourth in the jockeys' premiership with 52 wins, behind Mick Dittman (83), Bruce Compton (76) and Ron Quinton (72). I'd done so despite missing about four months of the season.

But I was still to win a major race for Nebo Lodge.

That all changed as Handy Proverb came down the Flemington straight, hitting the lead in the 1985 VRC Derby to win by a length from Acumen.

That win set the ball rolling for me. Sangster and Lapointe put a deal to me that included a house, a car and a good retainer of about $4000. It was big money back then. Throw in the 5 per cent of prizemoney that is awarded to jockeys per race win, and the fact that I didn't have any real expenses, and things were going good. Brian Mayfield-Smith didn't know about the deal. I never told him a thing.

That following autumn, there was a lot of pressure to win the Sydney Cup, the Group 1 over 3200 metres at Randwick, on a lightly raced five-year-old called Marooned. Sangster had brought him out from England. Brian put the screws on me that the horse had to win at all costs in his first start. The race was at Canterbury, over 1500 metres. He missed the start and we were last the whole way. We kept chasing, chasing, chasing . . . and came second.

I feared Brian would sack me from the horse and give Johnny Duggan the ride on him. Even though I was doing most of the riding for Nebo Lodge, Johnny was being used for many of the bigger races. He'd won the 1977 Melbourne Cup for Bart Cummings on Gold and Black. He was a great jockey but he was getting towards the end of his career.

And I was getting the shits because I wasn't getting the pick of the rides.

'Fuck this,' I said one day. 'I want first pick.'

So I got in Bob Lapointe's ear.

'Listen, if you're not going to ship me up, ship me out,' I said. 'I'm here, I want first crack.'

They got rid of Johnny, but then they started using Ron Quinton for some big races. I was in and out, in and out.

Meanwhile, Marooned and I kept on winning. As the Sydney Cup drew near, I thought he was the standout to win the race. The only problem was he was looking at being slugged only 48.5 kilograms. That weight was too light for me.

I could ride comfortably at about 50 kilograms back then, but anything less was a real stretch. In reality, due to the weight of the gear, I had to get down to 47 kilos to ride that weight. To get it off and keep it off and be strong was almost impossible.

'Fuck it,' I thought. 'He's unbeatable. I'm going to ride him.'

So for the next month I lived on water, lettuce leaves, carrots and beetroot.

Before the meeting, I told Brian I didn't want too many other rides that day because I wanted to make sure I could win the Cup on Marooned. I rode two others, including a horse called Dance Hall Girl. I told Sangster to back her and he did. He won about $150,000.

I will never forget the conversation in the mounting yard before the 1986 Sydney Cup later that day.

'What are we doing?' Sangster asked me.

'Bet up, Boss,' I advised. 'Bet up. Put the whole lot on him to win.'

It was a lot of money, but $150,000 to Sangster was like $200 for me. His wife, Susan, was there as well. She was wearing a white see-through dress that day. She didn't agree with the bet and tried to talk him out of it.

'I'll tell you what we'll do,' Sangster said. 'You toss the coin, Susan. If it's heads, we bet. If it's tails, we won't.'

I knew what I wanted. *Heads. Heads. Heads. Heads . . .* He tossed the coin.

It was heads. Fuck yes!

'That's $150,000 to win, Boss,' I said.

Then I went out and won the Sydney Cup on Marooned by 4 lengths.

Whenever you tipped Sangster like that, he always wanted to pay you in women. I said, 'I'll get my own.' I just wanted the money.

*

Success brought unwanted publicity. The word on the street, or at least in racing circles, was that a gang of thieves was going to knock off a prominent jockey or trainer. When I felt the sawn-off shotgun at the back of my head, I figured it was me.

I can laugh about it now but it scared the shit out of me at the time. I thought they were going to kill me.

It happened late on the Friday night before a meeting at Rosehill. I was married to Helen then. We had met in New Zealand and Patrick Campbell had married her sister.

We were lying in bed in our place at North Parramatta when I heard a loud bang in the kitchen. I got up and looked around but I couldn't see anything so I went back to bed. About ten minutes later there were three blokes in my bedroom, each of them holding a sawn-off shotgun.

I was half asleep but I woke up very quickly when they punched me in the face. *Wooshka!* Then they tied up Helen and me with pantyhose and tape, gagged us and turned us over on the bed and shoved the shotguns in the back of our heads.

That's when I thought we were going to die. I'd heard about the rumours but thought nothing of it. Just racetrack scuttlebutt. But suddenly it was very real.

'Where's the money?!' they yelled. 'Where's the money?!'

There was a perception around that time – and this is the case for many jockeys – that I was swimming in money. I was asked in an interview with *Turf Monthly* if I was a 'millionaire'.

'People think you go home and stack the money in a drawer,' I said in the article. 'That's not the case. I have bills to pay, like everyone else.'

I definitely didn't have tens of thousands in cash in the house at this time. I had three thousand Kiwi dollars in a briefcase, because I'd just come back from New Zealand and I'd been at the sales.

The robbers went through the house and left – but not without taking my red convertible Mercedes-Benz with them. Helen managed to get her hands untied, and then mine. I looked at my face in the mirror. It wasn't pretty. They'd picked me up and dropped me face-first on the floor, breaking my nose and smashing it across my face.

I went to phone the police, but discovered the phone lines and electricity had been cut by the robbers. So I threw on some clothes and banged on the neighbour's door. They wouldn't let us in. Can you believe it? I ran down the street and managed to find a mate who drove us to the cop shop.

While we were sitting there, a phone call came through to the station. It was a reporter from *The Sydney Morning Herald*.

'We need to speak to somebody in charge,' the reporter asked. 'We believe a jockey at Parramatta has been robbed and bashed and held up.'

They'd heard all about it on the radio scanner.

'It's all right,' they were told. 'He's here with us.'

We were sitting there with the panty hose and tape still around our wrists. I had no eyebrows left because the robbers had wrapped tape over my eyes, and when it came off it ripped my eyebrows clean away.

Then the questioning from the police started to go down a weird line. It sounded like they thought it was an inside job. For what reason, I don't know.

'Mate, don't worry about it,' I said to the officer interviewing us. 'I'm going home. I have to ride tomorrow.'

It was now approaching dawn. Maxie Lees, the great Newcastle trainer, and his wife Vicki were driving down the F3 freeway on their way to the races. They had planned to drop in to our place first, but then they heard on the radio that a jockey had been held up and bashed. The word spread fast, as it does in racing, that I was the jockey.

Maxie was trying to ring my home phone but the line was cut. He pulled his car into the driveway. The unfortunate coincidence was that he also drove a red Merc. Unbeknown to anyone, two coppers had been staking out my place in case the thieves returned to the scene of the crime.

'On the ground! On the ground!' they screamed with guns drawn at all of us.

Maxie had his hands up. They had me spread eagled on the front lawn, wanting to cuff me.

'I live here! I live here!' I insisted.

They wanted Maxie on the ground, too.

'No, that's my horse trainer!' I yelled.

We sorted it out and went into the lounge room. The phone rang. It was John Schreck, the chief steward of the Australian Jockey Club.

'I don't think you should ride today,' he said.

'Really? Why's that?'

'You're on favourites today and carrying a lot of money for the punters.'

'I haven't got a broken arm. I'll be fine.'

I walked into Rosehill wearing sunglasses to cover up my two black eyes. The sunnies couldn't hide the broken nose, though. It was sideways across my face.

I'm glad I did ride. I rode four winners at Rosehill that afternoon, taking me to 67 wins for the 1985–86 season. It was an unassailable lead in the jockeys' premiership.

The headline in *The Herald* read: 'Cassidy goes gunning for a premiership'. There's a photo of me holding up four fingers. And the story underneath it explained how I had ridden Maxie's three-year-old Cenchire to victory over 1500 metres. The story read:

> Showing no signs of Friday night's ordeal, the jockey looked down at Broadmeadow trainer Max Lees and quipped, 'It was easy, mate'.

*

In the end, Sangster, Lapointe and Mayfield-Smith all got what they had wanted. That season, they won the Sydney trainers' premiership, ending the 33-year reign of T.J. Smith. I got something I had wanted, too: I won the jockeys' premiership with 82 wins. Mick Dittman was second with 73.5 winners.

I'm sure Sangster didn't need the money – he just loved horses and racing and everything about it. Later that year, during the Melbourne Cup Carnival, I won the VRC Oaks on Diamond Shower for him.

After the last race, he wanted me to come and see him in the Flemington carpark. I found him with a bunch of people drinking champagne out of these hand-painted glasses and eating lobster and caviar.

That's not my scene. It never has been. All I wanted was a beer. Some of that blue-label scotch would've done, too.

4

The Pumper

ONE MORNING IN 1987, DURING TRACKWORK AT ROSEHILL, Glenn Robbins approached me. Robbo wrote for *The Sun* back then.

'I want to ask you a favour,' he said.

'What's that?'

'I want to call you "The Pumper".'

'Why's that?'

'Because of the way you ride: up and down, up and down.'

The Pumper. I've been called many things over the years – not all of them nice – but that is the one that most people know me by. I used to say that it's because my first girlfriend was six-foot-two, but it's because of Robbo that the name first came about.

It also became a brand. I started using it more and more, carrying on and putting my neck on the line. Racing was different in the 1980s. Trainers and jockeys weren't afraid to back themselves. They'd have strong opinions and stir things up.

T.J. Smith knew the value of publicity before anyone else. He told me when I first arrived in Sydney in 1984 to never be afraid of it, because it kept you front and centre in everyone's minds.

'If you have to pay for publicity, and you're in the public eye, you're a mug,' he said. 'Watch me.'

As a result, Tommy was in the newspaper every day.

So I played up to the whole Pumper thing, but in fact my riding style is not so much about going up and down – it's about going with the horse.

Riding a racehorse is about poetry in motion. It's about being a part of something else. When you are weak, a horse can take you anywhere it wants. When you are stronger, you go with them. But you have to be a part of them. Perched on a small saddle, standing up on your toes and bending down low and close to the horse's neck, you can feel which way its 500-kilogram body will go.

Watch racehorses and watch them stretch. You can see which way their muscles are going. If you are going against them, and you are out of sync, you are a passenger. You are a dead weight. You are working against them. You are not poetry in motion.

The way I was taught to ride was to go with them. Use your upper body and your own strength to go forward, making them extend, squeezing every last bit of effort out of them. You mould yourself to the horse. The two of you are one.

Nowadays, jockeys fall over the top of the horse to try to get them going. Everyone has their own style. But I found mine worked – and I think my record shows it.

THE PUMPER

The best I ever saw at it was Lester Piggott, the English legend who many believe was the best of all time. He was tall for a jockey – about six-foot – but he'd go with the horse. He'd sit low, or sit back and up and whop them. He'd get them to lengthen. He had the feel to get them to lengthen.

He was amazing. I learnt watching Lester what it meant to 'lift a horse'. His balance, his whip action, his strength. He had it all. He was riding quality stock for the best owners in the world, from the Aga Khan to the Queen, but that also brings pressure. If any of today's kids coming through had brains, they'd get videos of Lester and just sit and watch.

My claim to fame is that I beat him in an 'international jockeys race' in Japan. After the race, I asked if I could have his silks. He said he'd be honoured.

A lot of jockeys over the years have been taller or skinnier than me. I look around the jockeys' room now and I see kids who are much bigger, because kids these days just are. But I've always been compact and small. I think the only jockey smaller than me is Chris Munce.

As I told *Turf Monthly* around that time: 'I don't ride horses to look pretty. I ride to get the best out of them. I ride to win.'

Unless I'm not allowed to ride at all.

Racing is all about getting on the right horse at the right moment, and it could be injury that changes the course of history. Or, in my case, suspension. In 1987, the curse of the Golden Slipper really set in.

The Slipper, for those who don't know, is the lucra-tive 1200-metre race for two-year-olds held every autumn at Rosehill Gardens. It's a mad scramble of lightly raced, juvenile horses but it's one of the races every jockey wants to win. It's part of the 'grand slam' along with the Melbourne and Caulfield Cups and the Cox Plate.

In the 1986 Golden Slipper, I was on Imperial Baron, and I thought I could win until he was flattened 200 metres after the start. I almost fell, but he still flashed home for third.

The following year, I was primed to win it with Brian Mayfield-Smith's promising colt Marauding. Unfortunately, my ride in the George Ryder Stakes a week earlier meant I would take no part in Slipper Day at all.

The horse I was riding was Magic Flute, which was trained by Brian and owned by a syndicate that included television reporter Mike Willesee. I was coming across from a wide gate, hoping to find the fence and lead.

But a Kiwi jockey, David Walsh, on Courier Bay decided to kick up on the inside. I was nearly ahead of him, trying to find the fence, and he kicked up again. His horse was stuck to the fence and took out 3 metres of running rail. I was just about to park in there. I thought, 'What is this guy doing?' He kept kicking up, kicking up . . . His horse was on the rail, it couldn't get off.

Magic Flute – the second favourite at 5 to 1 – finished third, while Courier Bay came dead last. I was charged with careless riding.

'Why would I put her into the rail?' I said to chief steward John Schreck.

Because it was a Group 1, he gave me a six-week holiday.

Then what happened? Marauding wins the Slipper (with Ron Quinton in the saddle) and Magic Flute wins the Doncaster Handicap (with Shane Dye riding).

THE PUMPER

According to the 'Racing New South Wales Disciplinary Report of James Cassidy', I had 23 charges levelled at me up until that point of my career. For each of those charges, I had been reprimanded, fined or suspended. I had been in Sydney for less than three years.

There are many critics on a racetrack but the loudest is the punter. I respect the punter, because the punter kept me in a job for 38 years. But don't be critical of the jockey who couldn't get through a gap, it doesn't work like that.

And I'm a gambler. I love gambling. I love taking a risk. My life was a risk, doing what I did every day.

But my philosophy for the punter is if you can't afford to lose, don't bet. If I can't afford to go to the casino, I don't go. If I can't afford to play Keno, I don't play.

What most punters don't appreciate is how dangerous the game is. I think of the deaths on the track over the years, from Simone Montgomerie in that terrible fall at Fannie Bay racecourse in Darwin a few years back, to Noel Barker who fell at the trials at Randwick one day when a seagull spooked the horse he was riding. All the young jockeys who have died doing what they love . . . For the number of race meetings we have each year, the amount of barrier trials, the amount of trackwork that's done, it's pretty good. The stewards police that side of it well.

I've had so many falls that I can't remember them all. I fell at Brisbane one day. The horse put its foot in a hole. I hurt both my knees, broke my ankle and seven ribs. I don't know how I didn't break my neck. There's a photo of the incident. You can't see my head because it's stuck in the ground.

I've ridden a horse that has broken both fetlocks in the race, so it's just running on two stumps. It was a two-year-old in

New Zealand, and I kept it up. If the horse snaps a leg on an even surface, you can get them to run on three legs until they stop. But if the horse puts a foot in the hole, they just go *bang!* The horse falls – and you have no choice but to fall with it.

What people need to realise – from the punter to the stewards, too – is that riding a horse is not like driving a car. When you drive a car down Parramatta Road, you are in something that has brakes, indicators, lights, a rear-vision mirror, and no mind of its own.

There are four things jockeys can do in a race, with the exception of falling off. We can go forward, go back, go left, go right. There's the barrier, canter around, go into them and then we jump out . . . Go forward. If you can't go forward, you go back. Or you can go in or out. So what else is there you can do in a race?

Nothing. I've been riding for more than 30 years. I don't know another way to go.

You make those decisions – forward or back, in or out – and each time it's either the right decision or the wrong one. There are four mistakes you can make, at one time. People don't understand that. They say, 'He's in behind the leader, why doesn't he get out?' If you're trying to get out, but there's a horse there, well, that's why.

It's about reading the play. *That favourite's going to take me to the corner. Fuck, it's not going that good. I better get out of here. Is this one going to come back? And now I'm getting caught on the inside. The track's playing out, not in. Why am I in here? Fuck . . .*

It's lightning quick. Have a look at the overhead camera angle on the big race days and you'll see it's not like driving a car down Parramatta Road. The horses are so close they bump into each other. If the punter is in a car, and I'm in a semitrailer, and they're inside me, do I just run them into the next lane?

Racing is much safer nowadays than it was in the 1980s. For some of the jockeys back then, money came first and life was secondary.

No matter what happens, you can always buy another racehorse. You can buy another cat. You can buy another dog. But you can't buy another kid, or another father. You can't buy another life. The jockeys who don't have respect for life on a racetrack should not be out there – and there's been a few of them.

I've blown up in the jockeys' room a few times: *If you want to put me on the deck, I'll bury you first. If you don't want to show respect for me, I'll show you none either. I'll be saving my neck first.*

The blokes who put money first can rot in hell.

*

The first time I saw him was on TV in 1979. He had the perfect suit, and wavy, well-combed hair. His horse Hyperno had just won the Melbourne Cup, with Harry White aboard. I wasn't in the mounting yard at Flemington. Instead, I was a wide-eyed apprentice trying to make his mark in New Zealand. The first time I remember seeing Mr Cummings was on TV.

So when I was walking around the same mounting yard eight years later, about to ride his three-year-old Omnicorp in the Victoria Derby, I had to pinch myself.

From the moment I met Bart Cummings – I always called him Mr Cummings from the start – he had that indefinable aura about him. We'd go out for dinner on a Saturday night after the races. His wife Val was always there alongside him. I'd sit there with my eyes wide open, just looking at him. Just listening to his stories. Whenever he talked, he knew exactly what he was talking about. People gibber on and on. Not Bart.

I'd noticed Omnicorp's win in the San Domenico Stakes over 1000 metres at Warwick Farm in early August. He was at 26 to 1. A young John Marshall rode him that day. I'd ridden Boasting, which finished near the tail of the field.

I approached Bart after the race.

'He's got Victoria Derby written all over him, Boss,' I told him.

It was obvious that I wanted to get on him in the spring.

'I'll see what I can do,' Bart said.

I'm glad he did. The 1987 Spring Carnival in Melbourne launched me onto centre stage.

On Cox Plate Day at Moonee Valley, I won the Crown Lager Handicap on Sandy's Pleasure for trainer Neville Begg. Rubiton won the main race, but the filly's win caught the eye of several trainers and owners, and the calls started flooding in, even though I was contracted to Nebo Lodge.

A week later, on Derby Day at Flemington, I got things started by riding Bart's Top Innings to victory in the Carbine Club Stakes. Then, in the $600,000 Victoria Derby, I had a dream run on Omnicorp, who was at 10 to 1 odds, to upset Beau Zam who was the 7 to 4 favourite. I completed a winning treble for the day when I got the Perth sprinter Sky Filou home at 16 to 1 in the Gadsden Stakes.

Later in the carnival, I rode Sandy's Pleasure in the VRC Oaks, the race I had won the previous year for

Robert Sangster with Diamond Shower. In the Wakefield Stakes on Derby Day, Sandy's Pleasure had been run down in the straight, but she had fought back well in the last 200 metres for a minor placing.

This time, in the Oaks, I hooked her back to the rear of the field. At the 600 metres, I bolted away, grabbing the lead. She held on to win.

'She's the gutsiest filly I have ridden,' I said as I climbed off her after the race. 'She's all heart.'

The wins kept coming for me. A week later, I won the Sandown Cup on Colour Page and the Sandown Guineas on Ascot Lane. A week after that, I was ready to pounce in the Queensland Cup with Our Jug, a stayer I part-owned with my good mate George Costi.

I first met George soon after moving to Sydney in August 1984. I'd ridden in Sydney on a permanent basis for only two weeks, and landed a couple of winners. Out of nowhere, there was a knock on the door. A cabbie stood there with two big eskies.

'I've got some boxes here for you,' the cabbie said. 'And this bloke's number. You have to give him a ring.'

George owned the iconic De Costi Seafoods business, which was based at the Sydney Fish Market. He'd sent me lobster, prawns, fish, scallops. I had no idea who the bloke was.

I phoned him up.

'I just wanted to say welcome to Sydney,' George said. 'I've backed some of your horses. Call me whenever you want some seafood.'

We've been great mates ever since.

We'd taken Our Jug to Melbourne for the last race on Caulfield Cup Day, a 2000-metre welter. He was 25 to 1.

'You should be having $25,000 each-way on this,' I said to George.

But then it started to rain.

'Don't go too silly,' I warned, knowing the horse wasn't too good in the wet.

Our Jug ran third.

We came back to Sydney and I got Gavan Duffy, a top Queensland jockey and another great mate, on him because I was riding something else in the race. He was at short odds and won. We took him to Brisbane for the Queensland Cup.

'You should have $100,000 on this, George,' I said.

George stayed home but his wife, Andrea, came to Brisbane with me. I told her to keep going around the bookmakers and put on as much money as she could, right up until I jumped out of the barriers.

'Can I have $2000 on number 4, Our Jug?' she would timidly ask a bookie.

'You can have it again, love,' the bookie would say back.

'Okay, how about I have another $20,000 to win? Thank you.'

She got $83,000 on in bets. By the time we jumped, the horse was reeled in to 3 to 1-on favourite. And he delivered.

Despite all of this, I still felt like I hadn't found a really special horse.

'I've ridden some good horses – but I haven't ridden a champion,' I admitted to *Turf Monthly*.

Then, on 12 December, I created history.

I had eight rides for that Saturday meeting at Rosehill – and saluted on six of them, most of them for Brian Mayfield-Smith and a couple for T.J. Smith. The punters were ecstatic, which was a far cry from the scenes at Randwick a few days earlier when I was beaten on the favourite Carlyle Court and they hurled abuse at me from the birdcage as I returned to scale.

Brent Thomson had ridden six winners for Colin Hayes at Balaklava in South Australia in 1983, but my effort was the first time that six wins in a day had been ridden in Sydney since Ted Bartle had done it at Moorefield racecourse – near Kogarah – in March 1930. The likes of George Moore, Billy Cook, Wayne Harris, Neville Selwood and Ron Quinton had ridden five in a day – but not six.

I was 25 years old. Success was coming my way. It was all coming together. The back injury from that fall in Adelaide two years earlier had given me a lot of grief, and it meant I'd missed out on two-thirds of the 1986–87 season, costing me any chance of winning the premiership.

But now suspension loomed as the biggest threat to me winning the title for the second time.

Right on cue, after winning the last at Rosehill on Hot Zephyr in December, I was hauled into the stewards' room. They had charged me with careless riding in the second race. I'd won the first of my six on Tommy Smith's Potter McQueen, but it was claimed I'd shifted inwards when insufficiently clear of Diabolical Liberty.

I was rubbed out for two weeks, meaning I was unable to ride during the Villiers Summer Cup carnival at Randwick over Christmas. A request was put in to see if I could still ride in the big races.

'After consideration, the panel considers the incident serious enough for you to be suspended for the required time,' John Schreck said.

I just laughed and wished Schreck and the stewards a Merry Christmas.

'I'll now be able to have a leg of turkey for you on Christmas Day,' I said as I left the room.

5

Cruising

I will never forget the first words that John Schreck, the chief stipendiary steward for the Australian Jockey Club, ever said to me.

I'd just arrived in Sydney to ride for Nebo Lodge. I was the Kiwi jockey who had just won the Melbourne Cup on a horse by the same name. One of my first wins was at Canterbury.

Schreck didn't say 'Hello' or 'How are you?' or 'Welcome to Sydney'.

He said, 'Don't think you're going to come to Sydney and ride horses like that.'

I knew there and then that he didn't like me – 'He's going to be an arsehole for the rest of my time racing under him,' I thought – and that's what happened. Schreck seemed to have it in for me until he left Sydney to be a steward in Asia midway through the 1990s. Why he didn't like me is a matter for him, but my suspicion is it was because I am a New Zealander. I found that a lot when I first arrived in Australia. Robert Sangster and Bob Lapointe had all those Aussie jockeys to choose from, and they went for me. I found it hard initially to fit in with the other jockeys because I was taking their rides.

And I've never been backward in coming forward. Whether that character trait has been detrimental, I'm not sure. People probably say I'm an arrogant, cocky little arsehole. But who cares? That's me.

Schreck also seemed wary of my relationship with another high-profile racing identity.

One day I was at Chequers – the famous sauna and steam joint in Goulburn Street. I went to pay my bill after spending a few hours there.

'Your bill's been paid,' said the lady behind the counter.

'No, I pay my own bills,' I said.

That's just me. I hate letting anyone pay my way, no matter who it is, because then you owe them a favour.

'I'm sorry,' she said. 'But Mr Freeman has fixed your bill up.'

'What? I don't know Mr Freeman,' I told her. 'Why's he paying for me?'

She was polite but wouldn't say any more and I decided to let it go. But the next day I went back to Chequers and after my session I discovered my bill had been paid again. So I started grilling the staff at the counter when a voice from behind me said, 'Hi Jimmy, I'm George Freeman. The bill's sweet.'

I turned and, sure enough, there was George Freeman.

'I don't mean to be a pest, and I appreciate it, but I don't want you paying for me,' I told him. 'I like to pay my own way.'

I thought he might be offended but instead he shook my hand. He told me he respected that.

'Smart boy,' he said.

'I don't know about that,' I said. 'I'm talking to *you*.'

George Freeman was what you call a colourful racing identity. I'd seen him a few times at Chequers, where he could often be found having a sauna and then a shave. He was always perfectly dressed. He was one of those high-profile people you're lucky to meet through racing. That's what I love about this sport: you meet all different walks of life.

But I treat people as I find them – until they fuck me over. If you go back to them then, you get what you deserve.

As I got to know him, I found George to be an absolute gentleman. And for whatever reason, he took a liking to me, too. He was also an inspiration. He would tell me to keep striving, keep striving, keep striving . . .

'There's a big world out there,' George would tell me. 'It's up to you. What you get out of it is what you put into it.'

Down the track, I rode a few horses for him. He never asked me to do anything that I shouldn't have been doing.

'Just keep winning, son,' he would say.

I was always talking to George about horses. I was talking to him about horses the night before he died from an asthma attack in 1990.

In 1989, Bart Cummings had a fire sale of yearlings when his Cups King Syndicate fell over and he desperately needed to pay creditors. Straightaway George was on the phone, wanting me to pick out some horses for him to buy. He signed a blank cheque and just told me to do my best.

The sale was held at Newmarket, near Randwick, and I stood next to trainers Max Lees and Kerry Jordan. I picked out a nice horse. It cost $126,000.

Then, soon after the purchase, the horse became ill. I phoned George at 8 am on the Sunday.

'Mr Freeman, that horse has died,' I told him. 'The good thing is I insured it.'

'What?!' said George. 'Meet me for a coffee tomorrow.'

When we met, I explained the situation.

'Because you spent so much money, I decided to insure it on the hammer,' I said.

George tried to give me the money for the insurance payout, but I refused to take it. I just thought I was doing the right thing.

'You are the most honest person I've met,' he said.

George wasn't too worried about money.

Soon after that, I was on Kerry Jordan's horse Hunter in the Metropolitan Handicap at Randwick. It was a Group 1 race over 2600 metres.

'He's going very well,' I said to George the night before the meeting.

The horse won. George backed it. It made up for the disappointment of the yearling dying.

I was never embarrassed to be seen with George. On one occasion, I was sidelined because of suspension and he asked me to sit in the stands and watch some of his horses at the trials.

At that time, I was still a bit naive. I didn't know of his full reputation. So I sat in the grandstand with him and suddenly the newspaper photographers at trackwork turned their lenses on the two of us and started clicking off shots.

CRUISING

'I saw you with George Freeman,' Schreck said to me later.

'He asked me to sit and watch some horses with him,' I replied matter-of-factly.

The insinuation was that I shouldn't be seen with George. That it wasn't a good look. Which is ironic because George told me he was quite close to Schreck.

It was clear to me very early on that Schreck was never consistent when it came to me. He looked at my rides differently. It seemed to me like anything he could get me on – farting, burping, let alone knocking a horse down – he was all over me. When you are making the newspaper every week, everyone wants to take you down.

Towards the end of the 1987–88 season, I made a lot of headlines – because I was flying.

And then, out of nowhere, I had my head chopped off.

*

Cruising was a lovely looking horse: big, black, with a white blaze, but one of his eyes was half white. That was the mongrel in him. That was the madness. He was one of those horses, no matter what you did, that made you look bad.

The late Teddy Doon – bless his heart – was an ex-jockey from the 1960s and he rode a lot of trackwork for Brian Mayfield-Smith. He had the job of galloping Cruising. There are generally two markers around the track that you have to gallop between during trackwork sessions. Cruising would jump and run in, run out. He was one of those horses who looked as if he would deliver on the track but would always do something to get beat. Basically, he was a prick to ride.

The horse was also a special for missing the start. Always. In one of his trials, he ducked under the barrier and got stuck there. They eventually got him out, treated him for an injured back, and he had to be re-trialled some time later. He looked like Phar Lap on that occasion – but he was far from it.

When he lined up for the Toyota Welter (1200 metres) on a rain-affected track at Rosehill on 8 June 1988, he brought my career to a grinding halt.

He bombed the start. It was always the way with him. He then ended up behind a couple of horses, because he was hanging in (veering towards the inside rail). I tried to get him out but he wouldn't come out and kept running in behind them. It looked like I was trying to get him in behind the other runners in the field, like I was pulling him back.

Then finally I hooked him wide, trying to get around the field. Cruising, which had eased in betting from 5 to 2, to 4 to 1, finished third, three-quarters of a length behind the winner, Secret Flash.

Now, I'll be the first to admit that the ride did not look good. I've always said that it looked smelly. But Schreck threw the book at me: I was charged under Australian Rule of Racing 135(a) which says 'every horse shall be run on its merits'. In other words, the claim was that I necked it.

It didn't make sense. I had the best job in Sydney, so why would I want to neck a dirty dog like that?

'Why would I stop this mongrel from winning?' I asked Schreck. 'He couldn't win anyway.'

Schreck adjourned the matter and a date was set for me to front the stewards again.

It capped off what should have been a great day. I had landed a treble but I'd had a massive run-in with

Brian Mayfield-Smith after the hearing. He was filthy with me because I had taken some gear off Freedom Rings in another race.

'I'm the trainer,' he said. 'What gives you the right to take off any gear from any of my horses?'

I'd won three races for him, and he was still whinging. I was about to get on the scales after winning, handing my whip to Schreck, and Brian was into me.

'Go and get fucked, will you?' I said.

The reporters were aware of the blow-up.

'He's been at me for twelve months,' I said later. 'Things have been getting worse. I ride the odd shocker like everyone else, but towards the end he wouldn't even watch a video with me to let me explain what happened.'

I had no idea how much worse it was going to get.

After I was charged, I did some investigating. I knew that Cruising had been crook. He was always being treated for something. I discovered he had been at the chiropractor for his back, but then I also learnt he was being treated for sesamoiditis – sore feet, basically – and that explained why half the time the horse would hang in, and the other half he would hang out. I also came to know that he'd been treated two days before the race, which was never disclosed to the stewards.

The worst thing was I felt like I was on my own. Nobody at Nebo Lodge would help me out. Not Brian Mayfield-Smith. Not Bob Lapointe. None of them. I knew the ride looked bad, but in my own mind I knew I was innocent so I wanted to fight it the whole way.

The inquiry in late June was nothing but a joke. I asked for a vet to go into the witness stand, but he wasn't allowed. It was comical. As I said in that inquiry, I was laughing because two of the stewards were falling asleep. I was thinking, 'How can they give me time when there are two of them nodding off?'

Schreck outlined five areas where he and his colleagues had doubts about the ride:

From the start of the race [when] your mount jumped awkwardly, you did not endeavour to make up sufficient ground. From about the 800-metre mark to the home turn you failed to allow Cruising to be placed in a more prominent position. Then, after straightening, we consider you did not use enough vigour to get closer to the leaders. Approaching the 200-metre mark, you failed to take a run on your inside between Secret Flash and Hi Ho Fury and you shifted to the outside at the 100 metres and used insufficient vigour to the winning post.

I had a solid comeback:

I did not hold the horse – I'll bet my daughter and my job on it. I'm not here to give a horse a 'run'. I'd be the only one to suffer. My bosses Lapointe and Sangster would sack me on the spot if I did. I make my living out of winning races, and big races. That's what it's all about. Why would I go to the outside on the horse where everybody would see me? All I would have to do was take him to the inside and run up the arse of another runner and make a good job of it.

In other words, if I was going to pull the horse up, why would I do it out in the open, on the outside of the field, like I had, for everyone to see me doing it?

They also ignored a few other facts.

CRUISING

First, Cruising hated a wet track. This was undeniable; Brian had appeared before the inquiry and actually disclosed that he had approached Schreck 'unofficially' on the day of the race and discussed the possibility of scratching the horse because of the deteriorating track.

Then there was the evidence of other jockeys. Mark Lynch said that he noticed I was having difficulties at the 600 metres. Troy Phillips said the bit appeared twisted in the horse's mouth. 'You can't steer 'em without a rudder,' I told the inquiry. I had also been instructed by Brian to keep Cruising back in the field until we got around the home turn.

The main point of contention was that I used the whip in my left hand. I can say that over the last 50,000-or-whatever times I've ridden, I would've used the whip in my left hand four or five times. I'm a right-handed jockey. That's one of the reasons Bart used me so much in Melbourne, because I was effective in the counter-clockwise way of racing. But because Cruising was ducking in so badly that day at Rosehill, I tried to hit him with my left hand.

The stewards rejected the idea that the horse was hanging in, as I was claiming. Brian Killian, one of the other stewards, grilled me after watching a replay.

'Looking at the film, the horse is "off" – does it look like that to you?' When a horse is 'off', it means the horse is unwell or unfit.

'You are questioning it and it doesn't look good,' I replied. 'Blind Freddy can see that. I've got to put it to you why it doesn't look good.'

Schreck then asked if I would've been happier had Cruising been withdrawn.

'From the horse's point of view, yes,' I said. 'And I wouldn't be sitting here.'

None of the facts seemed to matter. We were asked to leave the room as the stewards conferred, and when I came back their verdict hit me like a sledgehammer: a twelve-month disqualification. I couldn't believe it. Brian Mayfield-Smith was equally stunned. He thought I'd cop three months at worst.

The media erupted, but New Zealand newspapers were in my corner.

'It's unbelievable the amount of shit being put on me on radio and television here in Sydney,' I told Mike Dillon of the *Sunday News*. 'The race has been shown on television with the incidents highlighted. I was judged guilty before I was even charged.'

I appealed the next day and was given another stay of proceedings but decided not to ride.

'I don't think I would be too popular with the punters if I was beaten on five favourites,' I told Max Presnell from *The Herald*. 'I'm keen to get it over and done with as soon as possible.'

It didn't matter. The Racing Appeals Tribunal knocked the appeal on the head after fifteen minutes of deliberation.

'That's it,' I said outside the hearing. 'I'm not going any further. My people did their best. I did my best. But I'll be back in 1989. I haven't pulled up a horse in my life and I wasn't going to start in an eight-horse race. I may not ride in Sydney, but I will be riding in Australia.'

A reporter asked what I would do during my disqualification.

'Play tennis, golf, relax. What else is there to do?' I said.

It wasn't the end of it completely. I took the matter to the NSW Industrial Court, for one last roll of the dice. The appeal was again dismissed. I could've taken it further to the Supreme Court if I wanted but decided to let it go.

It was clear to me that there were a bias against me because I was a Kiwi. There had been bias against all the New Zealand jockeys – and horses – around that time.

'Even the local Sydney jockeys admit the Kiwis get screwed twice as hard for the same offence,' I told Anthony Sullivan from the *Sunday Star*. 'But it's not just me. Shane Dye and Bruce Compton both got six months, Poetic Prince was relegated from the Caulfield Guineas when he wouldn't have lost a race in a million years if he was an Aussie horse. And both Kiwi and The Filbert got scratched when their trainers thought they were fighting fit.'

The thing that disappointed me the most was that I never got the support of the people I was working for. The whole thing had turned into a dogfight because I knew there were records at Nebo Lodge that said the horse had been treated for a number of issues, and it had been given various substances, and I wanted to use those records as part of my defence.

But the stable wouldn't release them. Why? That's any-one's guess.

There was a lady in the office who wanted to help me. She was the only one. When I went to her one day, she said that the records I was after had now disappeared.

Lapointe was great on many levels for me when he first convinced me to come to Sydney, but he didn't take a side. Brian Mayfield-Smith just dogged me. He didn't want to know about it. We blued about the whole thing. I didn't ask him to appear at the appeal, because he'd made it clear he wasn't in my corner.

I think Brian was a great trainer. One of the best I've ridden for, or seen. To achieve what he achieved, with all those horses and all that pressure, and to knock T.J. Smith off the mantle after all those years, was something special. But it took him a long time to mellow. He just wanted everything done his way. And I don't know if I was ever his first choice of jockey.

The Cruising saga was the end for me and Nebo Lodge.

We had to get out of the house at North Parramatta, but we stayed in the area. I wanted to keep fit, so I started training with the Parramatta Eels rugby league team alongside the likes of Peter Sterling, Brett Kenny and Ray Price. I was a Parra fan because I lived in the area.

The suspension also gave me time to help at home. My daughter, Nicole, was born with hip issues, and it meant I could devote my energy to her.

'When my little daughter was born she had clicky hips – no socket,' I told Roy Masters in an interview in *The Herald*.

I made a promise to the bloke upstairs that if He got my daughter right, I'd do something about it. A top orthopaedic surgeon treated her and now she is 100 percent. When I got the disqualification, I had time to make good on the promise. I went to hospitals and the feeling I got from seeing all those kids in wheelchairs . . . We planned for months to have a big money-raising function for Camperdown Children's Hospital. Last week, 450 racing people turned up and we raised $160,000.

As the day approached for me to make a comeback to racing, the phone rang. It was Bart Cummings.

'They're idiots,' he said of all those who had given me no support. 'I'll have ya.'

But it was clear to me from the moment the stewards delivered their verdict: there might have been only one rulebook but it was never consistently applied across the board. The rules applied to some jockeys but not to others. My cards had been dealt – and I was going to pay for it for the next 30 years.

I should also add that Cruising, with a host of other jockeys on top of him, never won another race.

6

Getting Off The Canvas

I loved riding at Flemington. I loved riding at Flemington for Bart Cummings.

In the minutes before the 1991 Lightning Stakes, the master trainer's instructions were very clear. He wanted me to trail the field on Shaftesbury Avenue, a big, strapping chestnut horse which was one of the sprinting stars of Bart's stable.

'Don't you let him go,' Bart said. 'I want you to get him off the bit, so he has a look.'

'Has a look?' I asked. 'Look at what?'

'Get him to look at everything. So when I run him up the straight next time, he won't be going mad.'

Bart had the horse set for the Newmarket Handicap in two weeks time. It would be run up the same stretch of turf, the famous Flemington straight, but over 1200 metres – an ideal distance for him. The Lightning, at 1000 metres, was too short.

'I reckon he'll still win, Mr Cummings,' I said.

'I wish it was 1100 metres,' Bart said. 'Be patient, get there late.'

If the race was at Moonee Valley, with the short sprint for home after coming around the corner, the horse wouldn't have been any chance. But this was Flemington and that long straight gave him time to wind up. It gave me just enough time, too.

As we came down to the last 200 metres, eight runners were spread right across the track. The ninth runner was buried in behind them. That was Shaftesbury Avenue.

Suddenly, the split opened. It was more like half a split. I just drove the horse into it . . . and won by a lip, beating Bureaucracy (ridden by Mick Dittman) and Lightning Bend (with Wayne Harris on board). The race was far too short for my horse, and we got there late, just as Bart said, but we got there.

That was Shaftesbury Avenue, one of the handful of very good horses I was lucky enough to ride in the early 1990s when I came back from suspension.

Discarded by Nebo Lodge and having spent twelve months on the sidelines, I was determined to do it on my own. The Cruising debacle had taught me who my friends were in racing, and on that score I could count them on one hand. I'd been deserted by those who were supposed to protect me, to look after my best interests, and in the end they counted for nothing.

From now on, I was going to specialise as a freelance jockey, targeting the big carnivals. 'You get nothing for winning the premiership,' I told *Turf Monthly*. 'The real money is to be made by riding Group winners at the major carnivals. That's why I am a carnival jockey now.'

I resumed riding on 24 June 1989. The headline on the backpage of *The Sunday Telegraph* signalled my return: 'JIM'S BACK – with a near spill and two trips to the stewards' room.'

My first ride back from suspension was on a two-year-old called Party Mood. I was sandwiched between runners at the 200 metres. 'It was a scary couple of seconds, because I thought I might crash,' I said afterwards.

I was cleared of any blame in the subsequent inquiry, but I was back in the chief steward's sights only half an hour later for my ride on Our New Horse in a handicap race.

'We're delighted to have you back but we have to record a severe reprimand against you,' Schreck said.

It was like I had never been away.

*

If there was one man who compared to Mr Cummings, it was Mr Smith.

Tommy Smith – better known as T.J. – dominated Sydney and Australian racing for decades. In the 1950s he prepared one of the greatest in Tulloch, he won Melbourne Cups with Toparoa and Just A Dash, he trained legends like Gunsynd and Kingston Town.

T.J. wasn't much taller than me. He had a squeaky little voice. It was like talking to a mouse. Like Bart, he was immaculately dressed. Like Bart, he was very witty and had plenty of one-liners in his back pocket. He was great fun to be around. But above all, his horses were a pleasure to ride. Because, like Bart's, they were so well prepared. They were fit, on the speed, and you only had jump them out, be in the first three and do exactly what the boss told you to do.

Bart and Tommy were freaks because they could just pick out horses that could win. When you know the horse underneath you has ability, you don't have to gas them. They'll give it to you anyway. You're just a passenger then. You're only pointing them in the right direction, and they will take you there. You can't get them to lift, because they are there anyway.

The one thing I will say about Tommy is that he would never give you a spray in front of the owners. He'd pull you aside and tell you at the track the next day. You didn't want to be on the wrong side of him because you knew what was coming. If you had ridden one of his horses badly, you wouldn't be getting a second chance. You wouldn't be on the horse next start.

Tommy started putting me on his horses as soon as I moved to Australia. I rode a couple for him in Brisbane, and now and then in Sydney as I established myself.

Early on I rode a two-year-old for him in a 1000-metre race at Randwick. At the 800-metre mark, there was a crossing, so there was a small gap in the rail. The horse I was riding was the favourite. Malcolm Johnston, his regular rider, was on the second favourite, another one of Tommy's.

My horse jumped out from a wide barrier and began well enough. But when we got to the 800 metres, it tried to duck out through the gap in the rail. Meanwhile Malcolm's horse jumped and led and won – easily. I was only a kid. I came back to the enclosure shitting myself.

'Sorry, Mr Smith,' I said. 'I couldn't steer it. It tried to run out the 800-metre gap.'

'That's all right, son,' he said. 'I backed the other one.'

Here I was thinking I'd ruined a favourite for the great T.J. Smith, but he wasn't too worried about me, he was more than okay with the result. He was too clever, Tommy.

GETTING OFF THE CANVAS

It was through Tommy that I first met his daughter, Gai Waterhouse. In the early 1990s, she became a regular face at the track. We saw her more frequently from 1992 after she was finally given her trainer's licence and Tommy started getting more sick.

It would be nice to be given everything. The big kick. But Gai had a lot of pressure on her. She was the wife of Robbie Waterhouse, the bookmaker who had been banned from racetracks because of the Fine Cotton scandal.

But she also had a legacy to carry on. From the very beginning, Gai was very much moulded like her father: tough, ruthless when she had to be and not afraid to stand you down when she had to.

Gai started training at a time when racing, as far as I'm concerned, was at its peak. Ronnie Quinton and Mick Dittman were the leading riders in Sydney. They had a shrewd, take-no-prisoners approach. They were brilliant. I was known as 'The Pumper' but Mick was known as 'The Enforcer'. His brilliance was his strength; how he could read the race. He was also a champion bloke.

But more than anything, it was a period when racing was blessed with great horses and I was blessed to be riding many of them.

In the spring of 1989, I won the Thousand Guineas and the VRC Oaks for Bart with Tristanagh. The following autumn, I teamed up with Doc Chapman and won the AJC Derby with Dr Grace, and I also won the Galaxy for him on Potrero. Later in 1990, I won another VRC Oaks for Bart with Weekend Delight, making it two in a row for Mr Cummings and me.

They were all great horses. But they weren't Rough Habit.

Some horses you get on the back of and you can just feel they have something special. It's the way they move. It's their attitude. The way they carry themselves. They walk with a presence.

Rough Habit, who was trained by Johnny Wheeler, had no right to feel this way. He was small. He wasn't pretty. He had half a white eye and this ugly white blaze down over his muzzle and his right nostril. Les Carlyon once said he looked like someone had spilt a glass of milk over him.

But he was tough. He was Muhammad Ali. He was Mike Tyson. He could get off the canvas whenever you asked. He'd be half dead and still put his head out and win by a nose. Despite his small size and his athleticism, he manoeuvred through the field like he was a truck. He had tremendous speed to let down at the end of the race. He'd do it at 1200 metres or 2400 metres.

And he was unbeatable on a wet track. If there was any rain around, he'd go from 4 to 1 in the betting to fours-on.

Rough Habit had nine campaigns, from Australia to New Zealand to Japan to America. He won eleven Group 1 races in Australia, six of them in Brisbane. He did it against quality opposition – against some of the best horses of all time.

I won three consecutive Doomben Cups (1991, 1992, 1993) on him, and that was against the likes of Naturalism and Mannerism. He won the Caulfield Stakes (1994), defeating Jeune and Paris Lane, horses that had won the Melbourne Cup. He won two All Aged Stakes (1992, 1993) at Randwick. He won the Queen Elizabeth Stakes (1992) against a field that included Super Impose.

He also won two Stradbroke Handicaps over 1400 metres at Eagle Farm. In the minutes before the first one, in 1991,

I walked into the mounting yard and was stunned to see a childhood mate, Dave Smith. We had played in the same Hutt Old Boys team that toured Australia when we were eleven years old. I hadn't seen Dave in fifteen years.

'What are you doing here?' I asked.

'I'm a part-owner in Rough Habit,' he said.

It was the horse's second Stradbroke, the following year, that most of his fans remember the most. He'd won in 1991 carrying 55 kilograms. In 1992 he was lumped with 58.5 kilograms and he was coming out of barrier 20 in a field of twenty. The field also contained $2.25 favourite Schillaci, the champion grey trained by Lee Freedman.

When I think of the race, I hear the call in my head from Wayne Wilson, the veteran Brisbane racecaller. Wayne once told me he thought it was one of his greatest calls:

Two-fifty metres to go and Schillaci is the leader. Barossa Boy is chasing him on the outside and he's looming as a big danger. Schillaci's in front, joined by Barossa Boy. Barossa Boy's hit the lead . . . LOOK AT ROUGH HABIT! Rough Habit's flying on the rails! Rough Habit moved up, grabbed the lead and he's won the Stradbroke! What a performance!

He hadn't just won on the rail. He'd got off the canvas to do it.

People remember that win, but the one that stands out the most for me wasn't a Group 1. It was a welter over 1400 metres in the final race on Caulfield Cup Day in 1992. He was carrying a whopping 62.5 kilograms.

The heavens opened up as we got to the barrier. It was raining so heavily they had to delay the start. I was loving it because I knew he loved it. He was growing a fin and flippers, right before my eyes.

After the start, I was tailed off behind the last horse. The field was going quick, despite the wet. It came down to the final 100 metres and he was still 4 lengths off the lead but he just lifted and won the race in the final stride. You deadset thought he'd run out of the carpark because he'd come home that well.

As we came back to the mounting yard, the crowd went mad. They came out and stood in the pouring rain, getting soaking wet, just to applaud him.

When I went to weigh in, I was 2 kilos heavier. I took my boots off and poured litres of water out of them. That's how much extra weight he'd carried. He should never have won that race. But, like always, he still did.

*

If I have one big regret in racing, it's that I never rode a Melbourne Cup winner for Bart. I should've been part of his fabled twelve wins. I should've been on Kingston Rule in the 1990 Melbourne Cup, but I declined the ride. Hard to believe now, I know.

Kingston Rule was by the famous American sire and former US Triple Crown champion Secretariat, and out of the 1982 Australian Horse of the Year, Rose of Kingston. He was bred in the purple, and a beautiful looking horse too.

And he had Bart written all over him: he was relaxed, he didn't pull or fight you. He was the nearest thing to Kiwi that I had ridden although he raced a lot closer to the speed. He had the same sort of easygoing attitude. He knew it was a big day but he wouldn't let it get to him.

I won on Kingston Rule in the Coongy Handicap (now known as the David Jones Cup) and told Bart that he would win the Moonee Valley Cup, a race that qualifies the winner for the Melbourne Cup.

'Boss, he will piss in,' I said.

Sure enough, I jumped out, put him third spot, looked back, got down in his ear – *Kiss! Kiss!* – and he won easily, untouched. I knew it then. 'Fuck, this horse will win the Melbourne Cup.' I knew he was unbeatable.

'Ride him in the Cup,' Bart told me as I climbed off Kingston Rule's back.

Of course I wanted to. The problem was I had committed to Just A Dancer, the talented four-year-old trained by Graeme Rogerson and owned by my great mate Michael Hibberd, from Melbourne. I'd won the Herbert Power on him at Caulfield, and then he was unlucky when he struck trouble in the Caulfield Cup a week later.

There was no decision to make. I'd told Rogey and Michael that I was riding Just A Dancer in the Cup. And I did. He finished twelfth. Kingston Rule, with Darren Beadman on board, won the Melbourne Cup in 3 minutes 16.3 seconds – a record that still stands today.

I was showing loyalty back then, but sometimes loyalty goes just one way in this business.

Sometimes, it's just about bad luck. Which brings me back to Shaftesbury Avenue.

After winning the Lightning, I was primed to ride him in the Newmarket a fortnight later. Before that, I had to ride Diddy Do It for Rick Hore-Lacy in the Blue Diamond Stakes at Caulfield. The horse fell in the run, and I was catapulted out of harm's way. Or so I thought. As I was laying prone on the turf, the horse – all 500 kilograms of it – kept sliding and went straight over the top of me. Mick Dittman also came down on a horse called Lady Purpose. One of the other runners galloped on his forearm, and took out a big chunk of muscle that was flapping off the side of his arm.

The ambulance came and went straight to Mick. I can remember it because he was lying in the back of the ambulance, squealing like a pig because he had this big gash the shape of horseshoe in his arm.

One of the ambos came over to me. I could barely breathe, let alone speak.

'I need some oxygen,' I gasped.

They took me to the nearest hospital but sent me home because the X-ray showed no damage. They said there was nothing wrong with me. The huge pain in my chest told me differently.

I went home and pumped some Valium into me. I was so sore. I thought every bone in my ribcage had been crushed. Then I woke up at 3 am and it felt like a crane was sitting on my chest.

In the morning, I headed down to the St Kilda baths to get my body in the soothing, warm sea water. I went into one of the cubicles but was too sore to shut the door. It probably saved my life.

The St Kilda football team were also down there, having a recovery session after playing the night before. The team doctor saw me going into the cubicle.

'You okay, mate?' he asked.

'I had a race fall yesterday.'

'You look like you've been hit by a tram.'

As I went to get in the bath, I went white and then I grabbed my chest and almost passed out. The doctor grabbed me and called an ambulance.

Another X-ray revealed that I had fractured my sternum, from the top to bottom. The crack was about five-and-a-half inches long.

A week later, Darren Gauci won the Newmarket on Shaftesbury Avenue.

At Flemington. For Bart.

7

The Boss

PICTURE THIS.

A large man of equal Aboriginal and Lebanese descent, with a bushy moustache, wearing a white linen suit, a large white Texan hat, a red bowtie and shoes, standing at the gate of the mounting yard at Royal Randwick, trying to convince the greencoat attendant to let him in.

Tommy Smith walks past.

'Let him in,' T.J. tells the greencoat, but the greencoat isn't budging.

So I go over to have a word. I've just won the 1993 AJC Derby on Innocent King for Kerry Jordan, even though I nearly went through the rail on the turn before the straight.

'No, he hasn't got a pass,' says the greencoat.

'Mate, he's coming in,' I persist. 'He's getting on the podium with me.'

That's when the greencoat notices that the man's trousers are too short, and he isn't wearing any socks.

'He's got no socks on!' the greencoat declares. 'He can't come into the mounting yard without any socks on!'

I just laugh.

'Mate, don't worry about him wearing no socks – because he's got no underpants on either. He never wears them.'

I grab the man, pull him into the mounting yard and we walk onto the podium and collect the jockey's trophy for winning the feature race – it was the second of my three AJC Derbies. The sockless man is standing right there alongside me. He's been there for me from the moment he came into my life.

Malcolm Ayoub – Boss – has seen everything: he's seen death, he's seen poverty, he's seen success, he's seen it all. I would put him ahead of Bart Cummings, Gai Waterhouse, Tommy Smith, everyone. He's on the top of the tree with my wife and kids and my mum and dad.

In return, he has treated me like I am his son.

It's a bit hazy when we met because we've gone through so much together and the details become blurry with time. Boss says he first spoke to me after I hurt my back when a horse I was riding for Paul Sutherland went under the barrier. I recall the first time I saw him was at Giles Gym, the iconic sauna, steam and hot sea baths that was precariously perched on the north headland at Coogee Beach before it was pulled down at the turn of the century. He was there on the heavy boxing bag, wearing nothing but a pair of speedos, punching away. Then he asked me to come down to the old Holiday Inn at Coogee, where the Crown Plaza now stands, for a rub.

I remember it like it was yesterday. He was wearing a singlet you wouldn't mop the floor with. (He's gone through about 40 of them since I've known him.) A pair of shorts, and his feet were bare.

That won't surprise those who know him, because he was the first bloke to run the City to Surf – the annual 14-kilometre race from the CBD to Bondi – in bare feet. 'I did it under an hour and charged past the Canberra contingent who had a handy stayer called Robert de Castella running with them,' he told me. 'When it got serious he picked me up pretty quick.'

Boss gave me a good massage that day at the Holiday Inn, rubbing me down with emu oil. When it was over, I felt brand new.

'Can I give you a few bob?' I said.

He wouldn't take it.

'I'll help you,' Boss insisted. 'I'll help you.'

I had no idea just how much he would stay true to those words: as a masseur, mentor, father-figure. Without the Boss, I am not where I am today. It's that simple.

To understand why he is so important to me, I have to explain Malcolm's background, and how he came to learn the secret way of fine-tuning jockeys and keep them in the saddle when they shouldn't be.

His father was a Lebanese immigrant who met his Aboriginal mother in the Pilbara region of Western Australia before they moved to Coonamble on the central western plains of New South Wales. Malcolm is the second of seven kids and they are all split down the middle: as much Aboriginal as they are Lebanese.

Growing up was tough. After World War II, they lived on the banks of the Castlereagh River, 3 kilometres out of town. That wasn't a good time for those areas of New

South Wales, with ugly rioting between blacks and whites setting towns ablaze. Once a week his mum and dad would walk into town, with Malcolm on their shoulders, and then walk back with a big bag of groceries. Boss learnt about life the hard way.

In the early 1950s, he started working at the stable of local horse trainer Otto McMahon. He learnt to ride and eventually started doing trackwork, and soon enough started riding in races. When Otto died, he worked for another trainer, Aikey Campbell, and became a leading apprentice for the region.

Then he moved to Sydney to work under Jim Barker, one of those larger-than-life characters in Sydney racing who loved diamonds and cigars.

'He loved showing off the big diamond on his finger but when he punched, it scratched or cut you,' Malcolm says. 'Jim was tough and hard. Like all the stables, it was slave labour but at least you got a feed and he sent money home to the family. If you tipped a horse to the hamburger bloke at Liverpool and he had ten quid on it and gave you something, Jim would whack you on the chin and take the money. He was very possessive.'

It was during those times that Malcolm started going to Giles Gym, which was the place to go for jockeys, footballers and fighters. He watched closely as the old-timers used liniments and creams on racing legends like Jack Thompson and Edgar Brit. By simply observing, he discovered how the body worked, what it responded to, and how to fix it.

'Nothing special,' Boss says now. But he would say that.

With his mum being Aboriginal, he particularly knew the value of bush remedies. She was always using goanna oil.

Or, better still, emu oil, which basically comes straight from the emu itself.

This is where Johnny 'J.J.' Miller comes into the story. Johnny was a champion jockey in the 1960s, having ridden for Colin Hayes in South Australia and also winning the 1966 Caulfield and Melbourne Cups on Galilee for Bart. He won the Sydney Cup on the horse the following year.

Before that, Johnny was riding and living in Western Australia. One day, he had a bad fall in a race in Kalgoorlie and cracked several vertebrae in his back. 'You won't ride for a while,' he was told. He phoned Malcolm, who took one look at him and told him to go straight to hospital.

'I can't go into hospital,' Johnny told Malcolm. 'I've got money to pay off everywhere.'

He was so sore that Malcolm could barely touch him. So he started to gently rub him down with emu oil.

Within a week, Johnny felt well enough to get on a horse and ride around his farm. After two weeks, he felt even better. Three weeks later, he was back riding trackwork.

That's what Malcolm does: he rubs the injury away.

In the barriers, you'll smack your legs, hurt your foot. The horse can rear up and hit you in the head. A couple of times, I've had plates from the horse in front come flying back and hit me in the head, the guts, the ribs. Or you might just be training and you hurt your wrist punching the bag. Injuries are always waiting for you in this sport.

Unless I had a bone break – which can only be fixed with time – Boss taught me it could all be rubbed out. The rest was just mental. You've got to get up and go through the pain barrier.

That's because he's old-school. I'd lie on my table or couch at home and he'd rub me with methylated spirits.

It kept me cool after spending hours in the sauna. Or he'd rub the metho into any cuts I might have.

We'd go to the sauna and he'd rub me down with those big knuckles of his like he was going up and down an old washboard. Or he'd be up and down my guts with Sunlight soap – the yellow liquid, not the green. He'd soap me up and the toxins in it would burn the fat off.

I never questioned it – I just did it. Boss knew. He still knows.

Ironically, I have little feet, so I was always riding up on my toes. The pressure and weight on my toes meant my feet wouldn't get the proper circulation. But my feet are as smooth as a baby's arse, all because Boss has rubbed them for years with emu oil.

His big thing was circulation. He's always said that you need the blood flowing through your veins, to be warm. If you're cold, you're cold for a reason. He had towels to wrap me up. Even now, he goes to the markets and buys jackets and sends them to me in the mail.

'I'm putting it in the mail now,' he's said a hundred times. Anything to keep me going.

That's how it always was with us. He'd never let me down. We'd train at Coogee, or Chequers. We'd train wherever there was a spa and sauna. There's not a sauna in Melbourne we haven't been to. Pad work, sit-ups, he'd stand on my feet and make me do endless crunches. We've never done anything different.

We wouldn't get the weight off. We burnt it off by getting fit. When you haven't ridden for two months, because of injury or suspension, you have to go through the pain barrier and get fit it again. Boss was always there while I did it.

Did I ever think it was all too hard? Yep, every day. But Boss would take that out of the equation. That sort of thinking was a minus. He doesn't believe in minuses. He never let me think like that.

As the 1993 Autumn Carnival approached, it wasn't my feet but my back that was giving me grief.

Boss was coming back and forth from Perth, where he was living at the time. My back had never been right after that fall on Sir Zephyr in Adelaide a few years earlier. After Boss had rubbed me down with emu oil, of course I felt much better.

'If you stay the week, I think we can win the derby,' I told him. 'My feet are getting there, but this back of mine is still twitchy.'

We kept working and working. I kept telling him the same thing: 'If you get me right, I reckon I can win the derby on this horse.'

Tommy Smith once told Kerry Jordan that Innocent King was 'the best stayer in the country; the best three-year-old since Red Anchor'. That was a big call – Red Anchor won the Cox Plate, Victoria Derby and Caulfield Stakes in 1984.

Innocent King had hardly sparkled in his three-year-old spring, winning two restricted races over 1400 metres and 1600 metres at Randwick in October and November. He was unplaced in the Sandown Guineas and was sent out for a spell.

He came back over 1300 metres at Rosehill and won easily first-up. The next month, he finished third to Kingston Bay in the Canterbury Guineas. That's when I got on him, and he smoked them in the Rosehill Guineas. It was his first Group 1 success.

Then he was sent out as the $3.50 favourite in the AJC Derby, the race I'd won in 1990 with Dr Grace.

Coming out of an inside barrier, I had the run of the race, tucked nicely behind the leaders and on the rail. But as the field hit the top of the straight, disaster struck.

Grant Cooksley, who was on the second favourite Kaaptive Edition, ran me into the inside rail. If you watch a replay of the race, I look like I'm about to jump over it. It could've been much worse, because if I had gone down I would've taken a lot of the field with me.

Racecaller Johnny Tapp didn't notice the interference as the rest of the field wound up to make their charge for the $1 million winner's purse:

Innocent King looks to be struggling as they come over the rise followed by Palate and Burst on the extreme outside . . . On top of the hill now, Slight Chance is struggling, she's headed by Air Seattle, Irish Rort, here's Kaaptive Edition coming through in the centre and Palate right down the outside . . .

They were all lining up across the track. Nobody noticed Innocent King on the rail.

Air Seattle wide out joined again by Kaaptive Edition. Slight Chance is battling on . . .

Hold on, Tappy. Here I come.

Innocent King! Innocent King is now bursting along the fence! He's coming home far the better, Innocent King, after looking well beaten. He's come again to win the derby.

I'd lifted it, thrown it over the line, and won. It took me the whole straight to get balanced but I did it.

But the win wasn't just mine, it was Boss's too. And I wanted him there that day because of what we had gone through to make it happen. My back didn't hurt one bit as I was trying to find him after the race.

Boss had bought the white suit he was wearing when he was in Singapore buying horses. I wish he'd bought some socks and underpants while he was there. But it wasn't his go to be at the track. He's not into that scene, with people dressed up and having a good time. He's humbler than that.

I celebrated with him that night. Whenever he was in town, straight after the races, I was with Boss. I'd be with him before I was with the owners. We'd celebrate with our beers, but no matter how pissed I got, or how hungover I knew I was going to be, there was a commitment to give him one more hour at seven o'clock on Sunday morning down at the Holiday Inn at Coogee.

'I'll be up,' he said. 'You be there.'

'Okay, Boss.'

And I always was.

*

Malcolm has hands of magic, but it's his heart that means more to me.

He's one of the most generous people I know. Jim Barker's advice to him when he left his stable was to go into the business of selling horses. 'But not yearlings,' Barker warned. 'It's too tricky.'

Barker gave Malcolm a horse named Mailbox, and he found an owner and the horse won several races in the bush. Malcolm's speciality became finding the unwanted yearlings of the glamour stallions like Danehill, then placing them interstate or in the bush.

When Malcolm moved back to Perth, he received a call on behalf of Tommy Smith, who was having trouble at Tulloch Lodge and needed to sell a few of his horses. For a long time, he was selling about twenty horses a year for

Tommy and then for his daughter Gai Waterhouse. One of the horses Tommy wanted offloaded was Starstruck, who was bought by Johnny Miller's wife, Kay, for $12,000. The horse went on to win the Australian Cup at Flemington.

But the thing with Boss is that as soon as he makes any money, all he wants to do is give it away. He will give anyone his last dollar.

He once sold a horse at Christmas time and got $5000 for it, so he bought some seafood and sent it to the Waterhouses, who I'm pretty sure could've bought it themselves. I've seen him buy chickens and turkeys and give them to families who are homeless or doing it rough.

Thanks to Boss, I've had meat from the same butcher in Randwick for decades. Boss never lets me pay the bill. Even when I've been flying, and had good times, he never let me pay him back.

That's why I say I've never had a poor day with him. He's been like a father to me. He's been the best friend I've ever had. I'm dreading the day I don't have him, and there have been some close calls over the years.

Malcolm has struggled with asthma his whole life, which developed into emphysema in the 1990s. When he lived in Sydney he was in housing commission on Gardeners Road at Mascot, on the way to the airport. He was very sick then. I would stay with him a lot when he was sick. Many a night I had to call ambulances to take him to hospital.

Then he got very, very sick. He was rushed to the Prince of Wales Hospital in Randwick and the doctors feared the worst. The emphysema became so bad that it was difficult for him to walk. For the next two months, I'd go and see him, get him out of bed, buy him the papers, do whatever he needed me to do.

Malcolm recalls it likes this: 'Every night, every day, Jimmy was there to see if I needed anything. He was always on the doctors' backs, making sure they were on top of what was going on.'

After two months, the doctors didn't know what to do. He was as grey as a ghost.

'Malcolm isn't making much improvement here,' they said. 'We have to make a decision about whether he stays here or goes back to Perth. We fear we can do no more.'

His family decided to fly him back to Perth. He was sent home because the doctors didn't think he would recover. If I'd have lost him, it would've taken me a long time to get over it. It would've hurt me that much.

But we didn't lose him. He got into the swimming pool, walking up and back, up and back. He slowly found his way back to the gym. He'd put on a lot of weight from the drugs that had been pumped into him to keep him alive.

Even then, he was always there for me. When the big carnivals came around, the call would go out, and he was there the next day.

I love my mum and dad, but he's up there with them because he's been alongside me as much as anyone. I love Boss.

8

Jockey Tapes

THE PHONE RANG AT 3.30 AM. IT WAS FRIDAY 7 APRIL 1995 –
the day before the $2 million Golden Slipper. I had a genuine
chance to finally win the race because I was booked to ride
Lee Freedman's Flying Spur.

I was already out of bed, about to make my way to trackwork.

The voice on the other end was Shane Dye, a fellow
Kiwi jockey.

'You're all over the paper!' he said in a huff. 'The shit's
going to hit the fan.'

'What do you mean?' I asked. 'What are you talking
about?'

'You better get a lawyer,' Shane said. 'Chris Murphy will
help you . . .'

My head started spinning there and then. And it didn't
stop spinning for another three years. The shit that was

about to hit the fan was the scandal that came to be known as 'Jockey Tapes'.

As soon as I got out the door, I found a newspaper. I nearly fainted. The headline was plastered all over the front page of *The Sydney Morning Herald*: 'Revealed: how Sydney races are fixed'. I scanned down the page. Something about 'leading jockeys' setting up and fixing races and dealing with underworld figures. It was done in collaboration with a man charged with drug importation referred to as 'Mr C'.

The story was written by Kate McClymont, and her story, in full, read like this:

A major investigation by the Australian Federal Police (AFP) has uncovered a huge race-fixing organisation involving several of the country's leading jockeys and some of Sydney's biggest race meetings.

Tapes made by police of about 4,000 hours of conversations between leading jockeys from May 1993 to August 1994, transcripts of which have been obtained by *The Herald*, have revealed that alleged conspirators in drug importation bribed jockeys in three cities – mainly in Sydney, but also in Adelaide and Brisbane – in one of the most extensive race-fixing scams Australia has seen.

The AFP has referred the allegations to the Organised Crime Squad of the NSW police because it is a State matter rather than a Federal one.

According to the tapes, ten jockeys, including two of Sydney's leading riders, were involved.

The jockeys were also involved in getting syndicate members to place bets on mounts they were riding, in breach of the Australian Jockey Club's rules of racing.

The revelations present a major early test to the Carr Government.

Yesterday, *The Herald* approached the new Minister for Racing, Mr Face, for a comment on the allegations of race-fixing. Mr Face's office said he would not comment and had not yet been briefed on the details of the tapes.

But the AJC's chief steward, Mr John Schreck, said after obtaining details of the tapes that he would consider an inquiry.

The 'Jockey Tapes' indicate that the race-fixing occurred at major Sydney meetings and often there were several races on the one day in which horses were not allowed to run on their merits.

The tapes suggest that two current senior Sydney jockeys – Jockey 1 and Jockey 2 – participated in race-fixing with an alleged drug boss, Mr C, who is now in prison awaiting trial for drug importation.

According to the tapes, Mr C, who headed the alleged drug syndicate, met jockeys before race meetings to collect 'the mail', or information, on which horses to back on that day.

Sometimes the fix was not organised until the horses were waiting to go into the barrier. One of the two senior jockeys would then give a pre-arranged signal to nearby syndicate members, who then would rush to bookmakers to put $50,000 on the relevant horse minutes before the race was due to start.

The transcripts show that the jockeys also arranged for other people to place bets on their behalf.

According to the AJC's racing rules, a jockey or apprentice may be punished if 'he bet or have any interest in a bet on any race' and that 'the rider of every horse shall take all reasonable and permissible measures throughout the race to ensure that his horse is given full opportunity to win or to obtain the best possible place in the field'.

These racing rules were broken on almost every day of the week.

The conversations on one day alone last year indicated that at three Sydney meetings in a row – Saturday, Tuesday and Wednesday – the jockeys were involved in organised race-fixing.

At 5.35 pm on a Tuesday, Mr C called Jockey 1, who asked Mr C if he had been present for the last race, as he had Jockey 2 and three other jockeys organised to fix the race and the horse came in at six to one. Mr C said that unfortunately he had already left.

Mr C: . . . You had (Jockey 2), did you?

Jockey 1: I had four of them for me . . . I looked everywhere for you.

Mr C: Yeah, I wasn't there, mate. I left dead-set because you know if I hadda thought I woulda . . . stayed.

Mr C said that if he had known, he would have put $50,000 on the horse.

Jockey 1 says he talked to the jockeys at the start and they agreed to go ahead with their plan and that he explained to the jockeys that sometimes he did not see Mr C.

Mr C agrees that he will pay Jockey 2 anyway (he later tells a friend he's got to 'cough up' $1,000 for each of the jockeys).

He then complains that he lost $30,000 on one of Jockey 1's horses the previous Saturday and asks what went wrong. Jockey 1 says he does not know what happened but promises he has something for the next day (Wednesday) and Mr C says that's good, he'll put $50,000 on.

The line then drops out.

At 5.40 pm, Mr C calls one of the alleged syndicate members and asks him for a number for Jockey 2. (*The Herald* has previously contacted Jockey 2 on the number given.) Mr C tells his mate that he just got a call from Jockey 1 saying 'that it was all f---ing sweet. He was searchin' for me in the thing. He had (Jockey 2) sweet and he had three others sweet for (name of horse) started at six and seven to one.'

Mr C calls Jockey 2 at 5.56 pm. Mr C swears that he had already left the racecourse and that he 'never had one cent on it, mate'. He promises Jockey 2, 'I'll do whatever ya's want me to do'. They talk about meeting the next day before the races and Mr C says: 'Just a nice few bob here and there, it's f---ing lovely, isn't it?'

Jockey 2 agrees.

Mr C calls Jockey 1 back . . . and complains once again about the fact that they left the races before the running of the second-last race because they had not received any 'mail'. Jockey 1 says: 'Three of us gunna get our heads together – me, (Jockey 2) and (names another jockey).'

Mr C volunteers a fourth jockey but Jockey 1 says he has got a big mouth. He'll shut up if you mention my name, Mr C says. Jockey 1 says they were going to come up with a horse the next day that would be at the good odds of four or five to one.

Mr C: But it just shows you what can be done. It's terrific when that can be done.

Jockey 1: Listen, I'm, as I've told you from the day one, I'm with you a hundred and f---in' ten per cent.

Mr C: Well I'm with you too, (Jockey 1).

Jockey 1: Yeah.

After they settle on a prospective horse at the next day's meeting, Mr C says he will put $40,000 or $50,000 on and that he'll give Jockey 1 $20,000 to divide between the four jockeys.

Mr C: You know that's not a bad little day's effort . . .

Jockey 1: Yeah.

Mr C: It may as well be in your pocket than all those other pockets, or even the bookies' pockets.

Jockey 1: Exactly.

He later tells Jockey 1 he will also 'throw 10 on' for him.

A check by *The Herald* with the race results shows that everything went according to the jockeys' plan. The horse they had discussed won the eighth race and there had been a betting plunge on it just before the race started.

Things appeared to go well for Mr C and he was winning hundreds of thousands of dollars a week.

Jockey 1 did not return *The Herald*'s calls. Jockey 2 told *The Herald* that while Mr C had spoken to him on the phone, he never talked about or accepted money to fix a race.

After hearing the transcripts, Jockey 2 said: 'I'll tell you what it is. It's some bloke with a bit of money, people bulls----ing to him, trying to get some of his money.'

When asked about a conversation where he arranges for Mr C to put on a $500 bet for himself, Jockey 2 replies: 'If I'm rigging a race and he's putting $500 on for me and $500 for him, that's tipping a horse. That's not rigging a race. For $500, who is going to do anything?'

Jockey 2 said that every jockey he knows had arranged

for people to pay them for tips. He also said that since a jockey was not allowed to bet 'he might say to the bloke, you put this bet on and say you gave it to me after the race. And that's what happens.'

That story brought my life undone.

Fixing races? That was ridiculous. I have never fixed a race in my life. It was garbage talk, as 'Jockey 2' said, that happens in racing all the time. Blokes saying they did this and that. I know it didn't sound good but whose conversations would if you just looked at the transcripts of what has been said?

McClymont had left messages for me to call her, but I had no idea what it was about. I didn't know who Kate McClymont from *The Herald* was. I'd never heard of her before. Why would I call her back, when I didn't know the reason she was calling? I dealt with the racing reporters, nobody else.

I hadn't been named in the story, but they didn't have to. It took about five minutes for everyone in racing to know 'Jockey 1' was me. Everyone was saying, 'It's Jimmy'. The talk was that I'd pulled the races up, I was setting them up, I was doing this and that. 'Jockey 2' was known to be Kevin Moses.

The way it read, it looked like Kevin and I were great mates. We were far from it. He was always a prick to me because I got the job at Nebo Lodge ahead of him. He was filthy from the day I got to Australia. But he's never been a thorn in my side – he's just been another jockey out there who I had to beat. I reckon I've had three or four meals with Kevin my whole life. He hasn't been a mate – he's been a competitor.

Shane Dye told me to meet him that morning at Chris Murphy's apartment, just off Pitt Street in the city. I was there, along with Kevin, Shane and Gavin Eades, who was also said to be on the tapes. Murphy said he'd handle it all, and then read us transcripts of some of the tapes.

I was so confused. I wasn't entirely sure what I was being accused of. My head was spinning. I think I was in shock. 'What the fuck is going on?' I kept asking. I was in the dark. I didn't know what was going on, but obviously the others did.

I knew who 'Mr C' was. He was Victor Spink. I'd first met him at the races. He was a lovely bloke, like dozens of people you meet through racing. I'd seen him in the members' stand mixing with owners and trainers.

I got to know him better through Shane Dye. He'd called me one day in 1994.

'Can you help me?' Shane asked.

'Help you how?' I asked.

'I've been doing my arse with this bloke,' he said. 'I've been tipping to him bad. I can't find him a winner. I owe him money. I have to get square with him and I'm having no luck . . . Can you help me pick a winner for him?'

The last time I had spoken to Victor was six weeks before the story broke. I had no idea that he was in jail, let alone that he had been accused of importing drugs. I also had no idea that he had been talking to this network of jockeys. It was suggested that all these jockeys were talking, like there was a big network. There wasn't. But there was one common denominator: Shane Dye.

The longer that Friday went, the more my life turned upside down.

I was ordered by Schreck, and then another steward, Tom Carlton, to appear at an AJC hearing at their offices at Randwick at 10 am. Murphy told me not to attend. I phoned to tell the stewards that I would be there at 11.45 am. Soon after, Murphy advised the AJC that I would not be there at that time. I was told a hearing would then be held at 3 pm. Murphy again told them I would not be present.

That's because I was standing on the steps of the Darling-hurst Court House, the big sandstone building on Oxford Street at Taylor Square.

Murphy wanted me to get a Supreme Court injunction on the basis that it was illegal for the AJC to use the police tapes under the *Commonwealth Telecommunications Interception Act*. He also wanted my name suppressed. As I recall it, Murphy had written an affidavit, and got me to sign it.

But it all meant absolutely nothing. I waited there all day and nothing happened. I was never called into the court. I went and asked the judge to see if I could be excused to go to the AJC hearing at 3 pm.

'You're going to sit out there, son,' I was told. 'Wait until you're called.'

It was laughable. I couldn't go anywhere. I was in no man's land. I sent a barrister and a solicitor to the AJC to represent me.

I couldn't believe what was happening: I'm all over the paper. I'm on a live chance in the Golden Slipper the next day. And here I am on the steps of the Supreme Court. I'm in hell. I'm just gutted because I know I'm getting shafted. I'm not getting a fair hearing.

At about 6 pm, I was still sitting outside the court. One of the stewards, Bob Nicholson, appeared from nowhere, walked up and handed me an envelope.

'What's this?' I asked.

'I have to stand here while you open it,' he said.

So I did. It was a notice from the AJC saying I had been disqualified from racing for six months for 'failing to attend an inquiry as directed'. I used Nicholson's mobile phone to call John Schreck.

'I've been at the court,' I explained. 'I want a stay of proceedings to ride in the Golden Slipper. This is unfair.'

I remember what he said next. His exact words.

'You've got no right to a stay of proceedings,' he said. Then he hung up.

I swear on my life that's exactly what happened.

Kevin Moses had appeared at the AJC inquiry that day. So, too, had two other jockeys who had been called to appear: Glen Boss and my brother, Larry.

The next day, the Golden Slipper was held without me. Johnny Tapp called the race:

Our Maizcay clear with a hundred to go. Millrich, the filly, coming after him quickly. And getting between them Flying Spur . . . Look at Octagonal jumping out of the ground. Flying Spur hit the front. FLYING SPUR WINS THE SLIPPER FOR GLEN BOSS!

I wasn't watching. I was at Coogee Beach with Malcolm, my career and life never feeling more uncertain.

*

The media went after me. I felt like Princess Diana. It was a frenzy. The dogs hadn't eaten for a week and they hounded me and ate me for the next month. Photographers and cameramen were hiding behind trees near my place in Coogee. Some were sitting in parked cars. Others would be in shops, taking photos from across the road. No matter where I went, they were there.

I understand that media people have do their job to the best of their ability. They want to sell newspapers, and Kate McClymont did a good job selling newspapers that day. If I'd got a dollar for every paper sold that day, I could've retired. I don't think there's ever been a jockey who's sold as many newspapers as me.

I'll tell you how big it was. It was so big that I took Super League off the front page. The battle for rugby league between Kerry Packer and Rupert Murdoch had dominated the news for months. And I took it off the front page – and Murdoch owned the paper! In the end, I was sick of looking at my own head.

The whole thing was sending me mental. Shane was telling me one thing, Murphy telling me another, and it was going to cost this and that . . . There were politicians saying heads were going to roll. They all had an opinion about it. And then there was Schreck wanting answers.

It was little me on my own, dangling on the vine and everyone was spearing me from all directions. I was in a total headspin.

I want to make it very clear that I was not squeaky-clean, under the strict rules of racing. I had tipped to Victor Spink, and talked to him about horses and how they were travelling. To the letter of the law, this wasn't allowed.

But if jockeys say they don't tip to others they are kidding themselves. There wouldn't be a jockey who doesn't. Someone is always telling someone something. Any number of high-profile people might ask you for a winner. I've had people who look like a hobo ask me for a tip, and then learn later they had $4000 to win on it. I talk to people about horses, which is my profession. People ask me for winners and tips.

It doesn't always mean it's for financial gain. There's tipping and there's saying, 'Back this horse and have $10,000 on it. This thing can win. I just have to ride it good and it will win.' Half the owners I won for over the years never gave me a sling. I mean, I know plenty of jockeys who have been mates with bookmakers and very influential people who gamble a lot of money. As I say, the rules apply to some people but not to others.

Yes, I had talked to Victor Spink. I don't deny that. Yes, I had told him to back horses. No, I did not tell him to back them for me. No, I didn't know how much he was having on them. It was no different than what anyone else was doing.

But the things that I was being accused of – like setting up races – were just outrageous.

Unlike these days, when matters like the More Joyous episode drag on for weeks and weeks, things moved very quickly with Jockey Tapes. One of the stewards came around to my place in Coogee and told me to appear before the inquiry on Sunday. It was to be held in the old stewards' room at Randwick.

The stewards were restricted in what information they had. They weren't allowed to be given any of the information from the cops because Victor was being held in custody on his charges and was still to appear in court. As Schreck started to probe, it was obvious he and the stewards were trying to find out what was going on as much as I was. Until I heard the tapes, I couldn't remember a lot of what I had said to Victor.

Schreck was waiting in the stewards' room, front and centre, with his deputy, Ian Paterson, and his little gophers all around him. I didn't have legal representation. I'd brushed Chris Murphy.

I was to be the last in the room that day. Shane went first, then Kevin Moses and Gavin Eades. Schreck questioned Shane about his knowledge of the 'Jockeys Tapes', and Shane told the inquiry that he had no idea if I was Jockey 1 'because I have had no dealings with him'.

That was a surprise to me. I wonder why they didn't check his phone records to verify that statement.

The inquiry also heard how Shane had received a $10,000 loan from Victor when he was at the casino. Victor transferred the money straightaway and Shane paid him back soon after.

Finally, it was my turn to appear. I walked through the media circus out the front. It was clear that I was already guilty and had to prove my innocence. I'd been painted guilty straightaway – by the media, then the stewards, then the government. They needed a head – and I was the biggest head they could go after.

The stewards wanted to establish how well I knew Victor.

Schreck: Who introduced you to him?

Cassidy: It was one day walking out of Canterbury, I think it was, and I was just walking out through the members, past the bookmakers' stands, proceeding to leave the track and he just walked up to me and said, 'How are you going? Blah blah'. And I just sort of met him through there. But I had seen him at the races prior to that. I didn't know who he was until he introduced himself to me on the day. But as I say, I had seen him at the races in the members, dressed up in a suit and that many times.

Schreck: We have all seen him at the races. The contact between you and him was initiated by him?

Cassidy: Yes.

Schreck: Did you ever become matey with him?

Cassidy: He did call into my place one day, but that was through . . . I didn't know that he was coming. I hadn't contacted him or asked him to come or anything. Actually, I didn't even know how he got my address. He just knocked on the door one day and my wife Helen was home and I was with the kids in the swimming pool . . .

Schreck: What was the reason for that visit?

Cassidy: To be honest, I don't know. I let him come in. I didn't object to him coming in and he just came in and raved on about horses, in the respect of how much he was losing and this sort of thing. I just said, 'Well everyone loses on the races'. I said, 'You win some days and you lose others'. And that was really the end of the conversation.

Schreck: So you didn't have any reason to suspect that he might have been involved in criminal activities?

Cassidy: I had no idea. Had I known that, they are the first people you stay away from, probably more so in racing anyway. But I had no idea.

Schreck: Did you know what line of business he was in?

Cassidy: No, I didn't have a clue. You meet people at the races and I don't ask people, especially if they are in the members'. I don't let any Tom, Dick or Harry come running up to me out of the public when I am leaving the course and say, 'Give me a ring' or do this. As I said, I had seen him with what are supposed to be the right sort of people at the races. As you said yourself, he was always well dressed and I didn't ask him what he done. I never did.

That was the problem. I have always treated people as they treat me. I've done that my whole life. It's who I am and how I was raised. Do you ask everyone you meet, 'Are you a drug dealer?' No. These are people at the races. You can't just brush everyone. That said, I can tell you from that moment onwards I never tipped to a single soul again.

Then Schreck turned his direction towards what had been discussed on the tapes – and specifically what had been raised in *The Herald*'s story that had caused this shitfight and had everyone gunning for me.

He wanted to first talk about the last race at a Warwick Farm meeting on a Tuesday. The horse was Raging Planet, trained by Kerry Jordan. It had drawn barrier 16, it carried 56.5 kilograms, sat three wide with no cover the whole way, and it fell in and won. I mean, how you sit three deep and rig a race is beyond me.

Schreck even agreed. 'I think I'm at liberty to say this,' he said. 'Mr Paterson was in charge of the meeting and he has looked at the film hundreds of times; I have looked at the film dozens of times, and I have said to the police, as far as I can see, there is nothing wrong with the race. I acknowledge that . . . You rode it hard to get it home. It wouldn't have taken much stopping. A lot of other jockeys would have got beaten on it.'

This was the race when Victor wasn't there, and said he would've had $50,000 on it if he had been. As anyone who knows anything about racing will tell you, there is no way the bookies would've let someone have $50,000 on a race at a Tuesday meeting at Warwick Farm.

Schreck: Mr Spink says: "'Yeah, I wasn't there, mate. I left dead-set because you know if I hadda thought I woulda stayed". Mr C said that if he had known he would have put $50,000 on the horse.' Fifty-thousand on a horse at Warwick Farm on a Tuesday would buy the field, wouldn't it?

Cassidy: It would be impossible to do that, wouldn't it?

Schreck: I would have thought so. If you put $50,000 on something on Tuesday at Warwick Farm, it would be 10–1 on I would've thought . . . Before the Raging Planet race, did you in fact talk to any other jockeys?

Cassidy: No, I didn't.

Schreck: One hundred per cent deadset?

Cassidy: One hundred per cent. Why that was said was this bloke, when he got my phone number, all he done was hassle me. As I said, the day he turned up at my place that I did let him come in, all he came in and moaned about was, 'I have done $40,000 on this and $50,000 on that'. I didn't know how much he was betting, until he said something that day. I still don't know how he was betting. You would have more of an idea how he was betting than I would. I never asked him. He never put anything on for me.

I was getting aggressive because I was under siege. And it was clear they didn't believe what I was saying because they were going around and around about what had been said on the tapes. I believe they didn't entirely know what they were trying to find out.

Schreck: If we get back to . . . the other riders. Decent men have been accused of being part of a conspiracy, haven't they? Reading this transcript, if anyone sees it they will think, 'Well, they had four of them so that could have been Kevin Moses, McLellan, Boss, Seymour, Olsen, Duffy, Killen, Whitney, your brother Larry, Falvey or Privato' . . . They are all [the other jockeys] in that race, and so four of them have been labelled as being part of the conspiracy, by people reading this story?

Cassidy: I assume so, yes.

Schreck: So . . .

Cassidy: It is just garbage talk . . . He was always saying that he was going to do this and do that, and in the end I said, 'Look this thing will win' . . . I didn't know what the man was having on horses. He was driving me mad and all I was trying to do was help the bloke out in the same respect. I thought if he backed a winner, all he ever talked about was losing money and I thought if he backed a winner he will leave me alone . . . All he ever done, I reckon, was talk bullshit to me, because he was always going to have this money, $50,000 on this and $30,000 on that, and I never seen any of his money. Then he always talked telephone numbers.

That happens with every punter I have ever known. When the punter doesn't win, he's had a shitload on the thing that hasn't won. When the punter does win, he's missed the best price. Or, like Victor that day, he wasn't there.

I admit that what was said did not look good in the cold light of day. A hundred per cent. But I can't be any clearer: I have never stopped a horse from winning. I've never been guilty of that in my own mind. I don't give a fuck what the racing industry or public thinks. I've never pulled a horse.

And if I did, why would I fix a race with any other jockey? I've never had that thought. Yes, everyone is trying to get an edge; getting a quid here or there. But I would never do it.

All I was talking to Victor about was exactly as I said in the inquiry: bullshit. Race-talk garbage. It was absolute bullshit. When I said that I needed $1000 to pay each jockey, it was all gibber. It was the same about 'signals'. Again, all bullshit.

People think it's all fixed. You smile, put the whip in the left hand, put it in the right hand . . . *Is that a signal?* Please. People make all these assumptions. You adjust your goggles . . . *There's a sign! There's a sign! He moved his goggles!*

Victor was calling me about horses, and I was just talking shit to him. If you examined any person's phone conversations, without knowing their context or how it was said, it could be incriminating. I didn't know that it was being taped by the Federal Police.

Schreck: This particular day, when they say that you 'talked to jockeys at the start and they agreed to go ahead with their plan and that he explained to the jockeys that . . .'

Cassidy: I didn't talk to any jockeys at the start. I was just talking garbage to the bloke. One day he is there, he says he has won so much. I don't know whether he just backs my horses, or whose horses he was backing. I don't know that. In the end, I was just talking bullshit to him. One week he is there, and he was had $50,000 on something, and all I ever heard about was him losing. I never seen any of his money. He never give me any money.

Schreck: None at all? You never got anything out of him at all?

Cassidy: I have never got one cent out of the bloke. All he ever done was either always winning or losing. But all I ever heard about was the losing.

Schreck: Never bought you a car or Mrs Cassidy a gold watch or anything?

Cassidy: Definitely not. My wife . . . The association I had with him, my wife wouldn't even be able to describe him. Our relationship with him is nil, bar when he was ringing me on the phone.

Schreck: He is not the sort of person you would say was a close associate or a friend?

Cassidy: Definitely no. He was more of a hassle to me than anything. As it has turned out, he has been an enormous hassle . . . As I said, he always used to talk this and that and I thought, 'I'll get something out of you' and I got nothing out of him because all he used to do is back losers. That's what he used to say . . . I didn't know that his phone was being tapped, I didn't know that people were following him. All I have done is tried to get something out of a bloke . . . As I said, 'Oh yes, they are the four blokes in tow, blah blah' and he wasn't even there. Like I was only talking, well stuff you. I have got to get something out of you. And we got nothing out of him.

This is where I had broken the rules of racing: by tipping for financial gain. In other words, giving some information about the prospects of your horse for the exchange of cash.

There hasn't been a jockey in the world that hasn't. But I wasn't getting anything out of Victor.

One of the few horses I did successfully tip to him was Nurmi – the horse at Canterbury that Victor said he was going to have $50,000 on after missing out on Raging Planet the day before. The horse won. Schreck again told the inquiry there was nothing smelly about the race.

Schreck: I have seen the film of that and again it is a film that should be shown to apprentices – how to win on a good thing. You came round the home turn, balanced it up nicely like a professional jockey should, and let it get flattened out and then let it go and it runs home. It is a classic piece of film of a good jockey, a good man at his job, at work. I do not know whether people can find anything wrong with that race or not . . . Did you get anything out of the Nurmi race?

Cassidy: No.

Ian Paterson then became involved.

Paterson: How many winners do you think you tipped him?

Cassidy: I think I would be flat out tipping three winners.

Paterson: We have two here: Raging Planet and Nurmi.

Cassidy: I wouldn't have tipped him any more than that. As I said, most of the things I tipped were getting beat. In the end, I thought at least he will get off my back. These two will win and he will get something and I will get something and he'll leave me alone.

Paterson: Did he ever give you a reason why he did not pay you for Nurmi?

Cassidy: No.

Paterson: Did you hound him?

Cassidy: No, I never hounded him. If you are tipping a winner, people are going to give you something or not give you something, but he was doing that much . . .

Paterson: You hounded him over Raging Planet. You came up with this scenario here for Raging Planet to try to get something out of him?

Cassidy: Yes.

Schreck: I think what Mr Paterson is getting at is that you tried to work him – to use your words, bullshitted him – over Raging Planet?

Cassidy: Yes.

Paterson: Did you have any intention of giving Kevin something out of it? Out of Raging Planet? If you eventually got something out of him?

Cassidy: No, I didn't get anything out of him.

Paterson: Yes, but you tried to. You said, 'I've got to pay all the other boys. There's four of us we've got to pay'?

Cassidy: I was trying to get something out of him . . . I had not promised any of the other jockeys anything.

Schreck: But that was the scam.

Paterson: That was the scam you put to Mr Spink, wasn't it? 'I've already promised these . . . The horse has won. I've got to pay them.'

Cassidy: But I wasn't going to give them anything because none of them knew anything about it.

Paterson: But Kevin did know something about it?

Cassidy: Only afterwards.

When it was finally over and the inquiry adjourned, I left the room. I was shattered. As I walked through the media scrum, I was trying to put on a brave face but I was doing it tough. Really tough. I just wasn't going to show it. I never had a meltdown. I never lost it.

But, on the inside, I was in hell.

The hearing resumed at 5 pm, and the charges were handed down. It was as clear as mud. I was presented with the Australian Rule of Racing 175(a) for engaging in 'improper actions in connection with racing'.

> Schreck: Do you understand the nature of that charge?
>
> Cassidy: I am being charged with organising that race, do you say?
>
> Schreck: No, you are not. And I would like you to be clear about that. We are not suggesting that at all. We are suggesting that you engaged in improper actions in connection with racing, in that from time to time at various places you falsely pretended – do you understand that? – to a person referred to in an article in *The Sydney Morning Herald* of 7 April 1995, as 'Mr C' that horses you were riding won races as the result of an arrangement or a 'fix'. Do you understand that? We are suggesting that you falsely pretended that. We are not suggesting that you arranged or rigged races. No, we are not. Do you follow that?
>
> Cassidy: Yes.

I pleaded guilty to that charge. As I had repeatedly told the inquiry, there was no fix. There was no signal. There was no network of jockeys trying to set up races. It was all bullshit to a bloke whose background I didn't know, who kept telling me how much he was losing on the punt.

In addition to the first charge, I was also facing a second charge from the inquiry, which said, 'that being a licensed person you engaged in conduct prejudicial to the interests of racing'. That one related to asking Kevin Moses to 'corroborate a claim by you that you had given a signal regarding your horse to "Mr C"'.

I pleaded not guilty to that one.

But I was still very confused. Remember, I had no legal representative with me. It was me versus the system. I just kept asking if I was being charged with fixing races, because I knew I had not fixed anything.

> Schreck: On the evidence before us since we have inquired into these allegations since they broke on Friday, we don't allege that you were [fixing races]. If history proves us wrong, we will have to live with that.
>
> Cassidy: I don't think that will happen . . . You know how much I love my racing. I live for my racing.

I will say one thing in Schreck's defence – he had tried to help me through parts of the inquiry, because he could see that the whole thing was so confusing for me. I was baffled and nearly in tears. This was gibber on the phone from a year ago. I only had a vague recollection of what I had said. When the stewards defended my rides on Raging Planet and Nurmi, it almost felt like they were on my side.

Then they dropped a brick on my head.

I was found guilty of both charges, with a disqualification of three years for the first charge and two years for the second. Those penalties were to be served concurrently.

Three years? I thought it was the end of my career. Nobody was ever coming back from that.

*

The transcripts from the inquiry show that Schreck and the stewards never thought I fixed races. But in the court of public opinion I was guilty as sin. *We've finally found the fox that's been killing the chooks!* And it was me.

Racing is not squeaky-clean, by any stretch of the imagination. Anything where there's money and gambling involved – rugby league, soccer, cricket, any sport – there's always a suspicion that something is going on.

But this whole belief that the industry is crook is completely blown out of proportion. How many times do you hear that J. Cassidy got beaten on the $1.30 favourite and it's had every possible chance to win but there's four people out of 400,000 who say I've ridden it dead? So those four must be right? It's bullshit.

But now they had a scalp. It was bigger than the Fine Cotton scandal. That's how it felt. In racing, there are a lot of people who don't get caught for doing something improper. There's a lot of worse rides out there, right now, by a lot of our leading jockeys that are so questionable but they are never questioned about it.

After the disqualification was handed down, the media went into overdrive. We were all going to jail. We had fixed races and there was much more to come. The stewards were even hammered for being 'too soft' and not weeding out the cheats sooner. It was out of control. Super League still couldn't make it onto the front page.

The politicians also slipped the knife in. They set up

a 'mini Royal Commission' headed by the former head of the Independent Commission Against Corruption, Ian Temby, QC. The investigation into alleged race fixing would be run by the NSW Crime Commission.

I spoke to those investigators at the police headquarters in Surry Hills. We went underground into these bunkers, and I was there for two days. That was the first time I heard the tapes. It was weird, hearing my voice. But I knew I had done nothing wrong.

I wasn't worried about jail. I knew I'd done nothing wrong. And, in the end, there were no charges laid against me. Not for speaking to Victor Spink. Not for taking money from Victor Spink. Not for doing anything corrupt. Not one fucking charge. Not even a parking ticket.

Despite this, NSW Premier Bob Carr told parliament that the crime commission had found 'evidence which indicated the existence of a wide network of race-fixing involving at least three jockeys'. He said that he could reveal that jockeys had breached racing rules by 'manipulating betting arrangements for kickbacks and improper rewards'. He said a 'big, beaming smile' from a jockey signalled that a bet should be placed on a particular horse.

Seriously, Bob Carr didn't know what he was talking about. Down the track, months later, I met him at a function in Maroubra.

'Bob, this is Jim Cassidy.'

He shook my hand. The gibberer didn't have a clue who I was. Did not have a clue. But I was the one doing everything wrong, apparently. He wouldn't know which end a horse's head was on.

If I look back on all of it, it reminds me so much of the ASADA scandal from early 2013 when all those politicians reckoned it was 'the blackest day in Australian sport'. Remember how widespread it was supposed to be? There was going to be hundreds of players and coaches involved. It was going to involve drug taking and all these fixed games. How many did they charge? How many received big, long suspensions? Not many.

The thing that was so hard to cop was the three-year disqualification. Kevin Moses was banned for a year. Why was I different to him? Down the track, Gavin Eades also copped a year. Again, why was I different to him? It was a joke.

Ten days later, I fronted the full committee of the AJC to appeal the severity of the suspension. Three years would ruin me.

I engaged Bruce Stratton QC to represent me. There's this widespread belief that jockeys are swimming in cash. He told the committee just how shaky my financial situation was. I had mortgage repayments of $3000 per month on our place in Beach Street, Coogee. I was paying about $1600 per month on two cars. We had the girls in a private school. Sarsha had just turned five and Nicole was seven. I was earning about $250,000 per year, before tax.

'The penalties imposed are terribly, terribly heavy,' Bruce told the inquiry, especially since no races had been fixed.

It didn't matter. The appeal was dismissed.

That hearing angered me more than anything – because I was standing in front of people who weren't squeaky-clean themselves.

There were people on that committee whose phones were never mentioned in the 'Jockey Tapes' scandal, but they were ringing me for information about horses I was riding. I wasn't tipping to them – I was being asked for information. They were asking *me*. They were ringing *me*.

In fact, if the police had checked their numbers they'd have discovered that many of them were calling me on my home number. It wasn't to discuss politics.

When I appealed, in front of those same people, I should've asked for them to be stood down from the hearing.

I didn't because I would have been buried even further. And I was as low as I thought I could get. The lowest point of my life.

9

Exiled

AND THEN, JUST LIKE THAT, EVERYONE RAN A MILE FROM ME.

I was the hottest thing in town. The sad thing from my perspective was that it didn't matter what I said, or how I said it, nobody believed me or wanted a bar of me.

There were a few who did. My family, of course – and that includes Malcolm. George Costi stuck with me. Maxie Lees. A couple of trainers at Randwick, Jim and Greg Lee. Terrific people. Jim and Greg owned taxis and offered me a job driving one. Could you imagine me driving taxis? I'd get belted. Graeme 'Rogey' Rogerson said he'd give me whatever money he could if I needed it.

But racing people mostly deserted me. I was gone. Stamped 'never to come back'.

The others who supported me were the battlers. They stuck with me. The $5 punters at the TAB. They've always backed me. They're the ones who make up racing, not the high-profile people who swan in and out.

I had one last avenue of appeal, through the Racing Appeals Tribunal, but that was dismissed as well. I didn't have the money to pursue the matter through the courts. I had to let it go.

The money quickly dried up. The toughest part was pulling the kids out of St Catherine's at Waverley because I couldn't afford the school fees. I was looking at three years off the track, so we had to really get serious about the situation.

The first thing we had to do was sell our house at Coogee.

'I have my wife and kids, so what more do I need?' I told Phillip Koch from *The Sunday Telegraph* in August 1995. 'The only thing I want back is my racing. I'd live in a tent if I had to. A house is a house and you have to live within your means. I'm still enjoying life. I'll be back better than ever. Tell them to keep looking over their shoulder – because Pumper is on his way back.'

In reality, I was nowhere near it.

We sold the place in Coogee for about $540,000. You couldn't buy it today for $6 million. We had a fire sale of all the stuff we owned – it was a lemon because hardly anyone turned up. Whatever we had at home, we got rid of it.

'It's humbling, but we're happy,' I told Paul Kent in *The Sun-Herald*. 'We've had to scale down. A lot of my mates have taken furniture and things for me so I can hang on to it.'

I gave one mate a heap of stuff – furniture, photos, memorabilia – to look after until I got back on my feet. I went to see him a few months later, but he'd sold it all without my knowledge. Great mate. When things go bad, they really go bad.

But there was one thing that was never for sale – my riding gear.

'I won't be getting rid of that,' I told Kent. 'I need it. I'll be back.'

We moved in with some friends, Marty and Lou Lou. I slept on a fold-out bed. Then we rented a unit because that's all we could afford.

I should make it clear what a disqualification from racing means – and it's not great if you're someone like me who has spent their whole life around racehorses. It's not great if all you know is racehorses. Not only is a disqualified person forbidden from going near a racecourse, at any time, he or she can't associate with licensed people from the racing industry. You are completely shut out, no questions asked.

I had to start thinking about getting a job. We had absolutely nothing. I needed to catch a bus to get anywhere. I ended up borrowing a mate's car to go to work three days a week as a labourer. I got a hundred dollars a day. We did all sorts of things, from putting up fence posts to renovating the old Cricketer's Arms at Balmain.

Another bloke gave me a job pulling houses down. I was doing that for a while and then found out some of the houses were riddled with asbestos. I had no asbestos gear, so I couldn't do that any more. Then I was working on a place at Point Piper, looking down from six storeys high. If I fell, I was dead.

We did it pretty tough. Much tougher than anyone will ever know. If I worked six days in a week, I was getting $600. With that we'd have to pay rent, buy food, put $50 petrol in my mate's car. I'd have to get a bus into town in the morning to pick up my mate's car then go to work and drive back before 6 pm.

It was so tight that sometimes I only had enough money and time to eat twice a day. I was working in 40-degree heat some days, surviving on bottles of water. Often, I didn't take lunch. As long as the kids were fed, that's all that mattered. Whatever I had went to the kids. I'd buy a slab of beer and that would have to last me two weeks.

All I wanted was for the three years to be over. I just wanted to get back to the track and ride and earn. I still followed the races, because it's in my blood. I remember getting a trifecta. I spent $18 and won $4500. That was like winning $400,000. It was the last race at Rosehill. I jumped for joy. The money could not have come at a better time. So even though my disqualification meant I had to stay away from the racing industry, I sat at home watching it on TV, week in, week out. Sometimes, though, I just turned it off – I'd go blank and not watch it for months. I guess it just hurt too much.

But my love of horses never went away. I've always been happiest when I'm working with horses.

Our daughters Nicole and Sarsha started doing a bit of showjumping at Centennial Park.

'Come for a ride, Dad,' they kept saying. 'Get into it.'

That's how I started showjumping. The showjumpers took me in with open arms. They had a lot of money but they were knockabout people. Chris Chugg, who rode for Australia at two Olympics and was a five-time national champion, took me under his wing. So did Marie Hewitt. She was a great instructor.

The showjumping people thought nothing of what had happened with 'Jockey Tapes'. I think they liked some of the publicity. I put the sport in the spotlight for a while because there were photographers and camera crews following me around when I first started.

Showjumping also got me fit again. When you give racing away, you get heavy for the first few months because you're pigging out, eating and drinking like a normal person. Showjumping got me back down to 54 kilos.

It's a tough sport. Horse and rider have to complete the course without knocking down any jumps, and within a set time. It was something totally different and I'd never done it before. The others all thought I was going to be a genius because I had great balance as a race jockey. It was harder than I thought but I put everything into it. I just wanted to be competitive. I loved it because the showjumping people gave me a chance. I was grateful. It was the same with the people who gave me labouring work, because they all kept me ticking over.

On Golden Slipper Day in 1996 – exactly a year after I was rubbed out – I rode in the Australian amateurs showjumping competition at Wyong. I remember I got $15 for a clear round. I came third in the jump-off. The riding fee for winning the Slipper would've been $150,000.

I remember looking around that day and taking it all in. I was riding in the amateur titles. I was so proud. I was healthy. I wasn't riding in a Golden Slipper but I was doing something I loved: I was riding a horse.

Winning that money on the trifecta had allowed me to buy an eight-year-old showjumper called Lord Axel. He used to be a racehorse under the name Have A Guess, though never won a race.

But I loved him. He was my best mate. I went back to being a strapper again: I had to work him, wash him, feed him and put him away at night. I've always been passionate about the horses. They're my life. They're my family. They give me an income, and many thrills. I went to a few shows where they let off fireworks at night and Lord Axel was so frightened I sat in the stables all night to steady him and make sure he was all right.

It was all still new to me but I threw myself into it. We jumped 1.25 metres at one competition, which was a decent height. Walking the courses was great fun. You had to get your strides between jumps right and remember where you were going. Sometimes, I went the wrong way and had a few spills. My horse hurt his leg one day and I was in tears in the middle of the arena. Showjumping had become my life.

Everywhere we went with showjumping, from events in Orange or Bathurst, to Bega or wherever, a lot of people were really good. 'Good on ya, Pump!' they'd shout. They wanted me there. They wanted to buy me a beer.

I had my little white jodhpurs on, my little jacket, my white shirt, and I'd be red-faced and sweating like nobody's business. I'd have a shower, put my horse away, and then we'd have a barbecue and a drink.

The best part of it was that I got to spend time with my daughters. My kids were healthy and happy, and that's all that mattered. When I was racing, I was travelling around to all the big carnivals. Now I could be with them 24/7. It was a special time.

I said publicly around that time that competing in showjumping at the Sydney Olympics in 2000 was a goal – but I was always coming back to racing.

In January 1996, nine months after the inquiry, the head of the NSW Crime Commission, Phillip Bradley, said publicly there was 'insufficient evidence to justify the prosecution of anyone'.

Ray Murrihy had replaced Schreck as the AJC's chief steward. 'A number of people, and I'm not pointing the bone at racing media people, have been left with egg on their face,' he said. 'Some things were said and written that were terribly detrimental to racing.'

Don't worry about racing, Ray. Nobody had paid a heavier price than me.

I knew I was coming back. I was always coming back. I never doubted that for a minute. I was coming back because I loved racing but I was also coming back to stick it up all those people who said I was a crim, that I was going to jail, that I was a dog.

I knew I would have the last laugh. I'm still having the last laugh.

*

My life seems to turn on a phone call. This time it was Jack Denham.

'Jim, I'll help you get back,' he said. 'Come and see me. I can pull some strings.'

'They better be long strings,' I laughed.

Jack was a legend of Sydney racing. He'd trained for Stan Fox at Nebo Lodge in the 1970s, notching up more than a thousand winners and putting pressure on Tommy Smith for the premiership. Jack won it in 1990–91 and 1992–93. He had won the Golden Slipper with Marscay, and the Australian Oaks and Guineas with Triscay. Those horses were owned by Geoff and Berryl White, influential owners who backed Jack and his son, Allan. The Whites were lovely people.

I'd ridden on and off for Jack over the years. He did things his way. When you were working for him, if you didn't do it his way, it was the highway. He was also famous for how much he hated the media. He hadn't spoken to a reporter for decades. He didn't speak to many people at all.

Jack was only about the business of racing, and he was there to help get me back. Not for the glory but because he knew I was a determined little bastard who wanted to fight my way back.

But it was Malcolm who made it all happen.

Boss had been superb through the whole thing. He always has been. He kept pounding away at me. 'You're coming back,' he'd say. 'I'll get you back.'

Whenever he sold a horse, he'd give me some money. At one stage, I needed a car. He sold a couple of horses and came up with $2000. We went to the car yards along Parramatta Road and found this beat-up little red Alfa Romeo. It cost $1500.

'Wind the window down,' he said as we drove down the road.

I did – and the handle broke. I had to push and pull the window to get it up and down.

The petrol gauge, of course, showed empty so on the way home we pulled into the service station and I went to get out but the door was jammed. I had to get out through the window, like I was in *The Dukes of Hazzard*. From then on, if I had to get petrol, I would make sure nobody was at the service station to see how I got out of the car.

It was Boss who kickstarted the process to get me back on a racetrack again. He remembers it like this:

I sat down with a few trainers, and not many of them
wanted a bar of him. 'He's a villain, he's a crook.' I waited

*another six months and then I met with Max Presnell
from* The Herald. *He said, 'Go and get references from six
or seven of the leading trainers, and ask for a permit to let
Jimmy ride trackwork again.' I approached Jack Denham,
because I had been selling a lot of horses for him. Jack was
nominated as the one who should take him in, because he
had a lot of influence.*

An application to return to race riding was lodged in late
July 1996. When news of it got out, the media that had blow-
torched me were starting to back my return. Murray Bell, in
The Daily Telegraph, wrote a story under the headline: 'Time
to lift the ban on racing scapegoat'.

There is some unfinished business in that 15-month-old
saga quaintly known as the 'Jockey Tapes' scandal.
Champion jockey Jim Cassidy is still on the outer –
a disqualified person.

In the cooler climate that now prevails, the Australian
Jockey Club committee should use its discretion and make
the remainder of Cassidy's three-year disqualification
a suspended sentence.

With the heat and emotion having dissipated from the
argument, it should be clear to everyone that whatever the
nature of Cassidy's offences, they didn't merit a three-year
disqualification.

These findings were set against a background of broad
and sensational media coverage, fuelled by Australian
Federal Police transcripts of 4000 hours of legal phone
tapings of conversations involving the suspected crime
figure.

In the midst of blazing headlines, pressure from Parliament House and, we were assured, probable future criminal charges for a number of unnamed jockeys, Cassidy felt the full brunt of racing's embarrassment.

On 27 September 1996, the AJC committee opened the door for me to make a comeback. The disqualification was reduced to a suspension. That meant I could ride trackwork and attend race meetings, but any application to be relicensed as a jockey would then have to be considered by the committee on 1 January 1997.

I still remember walking back into Rosehill to ride trackwork that first time. I loved the early mornings again. I couldn't wait to get out of bed and get there. It was just nice to put the gear back on and be riding. It was like starting my career all over again.

A lot of people had been good but a lot of them also had their doubts. Doubts about my legitimacy and doubts about whether I would make it back. Plenty would've thought, 'Why give him back his licence?' Because that's racing. That's the mentality of racing people: guilty before innocent. That's the sad thing about the game: you have to prove that you aren't corrupt. It's ruthless.

Most of the other jockeys were glad to see me come back. I hadn't really kept in contact with many of them because I'd gone into isolation. I'd fallen off the radar and kept to myself. I couldn't be at the track so I had stayed away. Because I was disqualified, I couldn't mix with licensed people. Not at all. I had been completely exiled.

As 1996 came to a close, I was getting closer to a racing comeback. I would be awake at all hours, thinking about getting back to the track. And it was drawing me back. I could feel it. I couldn't think of anything but racing.

On 23 December, I fronted the AJC committee again. As I walked in, I hammed it up for the photographers, pressing my hands together in prayer and looking skywards.

The story from Ray Thomas in *The Daily Telegraph* the next day read like this:

> Jim Cassidy's period in the racing wilderness came to its anticipated conclusion at the Australian Jockey Club offices yesterday when the committee formally lifted his suspension.
>
> Cassidy, known in the business as Pumper, will be back in action in the Tattersalls Club Carrington Stakes meeting at Royal Randwick on January 1.
>
> Yesterday's AJC committee meeting was a formality to rubber stamp the recommendations of the club's licensing sub-committee.
>
> 'It took all of a minute to finalise,' AJC chief executive Tony King said last night.

I had been given the all clear to make a comeback – just like I said I would. I knew I wasn't 100 per cent innocent. I had broken the rules. I never said I was a cleanskin. But I was always coming back to say 'Fuck you' to those who said I couldn't. I knew I would, no matter what. I had no intention of running away.

*

How do I reflect on the so-called 'Jockey Tapes' saga?

I know that it taught me to be very selective with who I call a mate. As I said in an interview with *The Sunday Telegraph* soon after my return:

PUMPER

The days of me trying to be the good little bloke and look after too many people have just gone. I love giving a helping hand. Always have. I just like people. But . . . well, I reckon I've let some people take me for granted. Now . . . I guess it was a matter of me standing up, waking up. I opened the window and let them go when I lost my licence. Them? Well, you can call them whatever you like – leeches, bludgers, hangers-on, whatever. They know who they are. You don't need to name them. They don't matter. The real people, the supportive people, are the people that have always been there.

I don't want to use the word 'bitter'. I'm only bitter on those who tried to bury me, especially those involved with the AJC who knew that I had not fixed races or even tried to – but who still gave me three years.

For starters, the suspension turned out to be 21 months. *Hang on, I was supposed to be out for three years!* That made me laugh. Was the crime that I was accused of doing worth that in the first place? As far as I'm concerned, there were plenty of headlines but none of it reflected what had really happened. That's what really pissed me off.

I also think there were certain people who were determined to see me buried because of what I knew. There was one particular person who wasn't a squeaky-clean character. I had personally seen his car parked at the house of a jockey. I knew he was having an affair with the jockey's wife. And he knew I knew. I swear on my life I never told anyone, because I knew what the ramifications could be. But I believe it had a bearing in what happened to me.

How do I feel about some of the people involved now? It's been a long time. A lot of water has gone under the bridge.

But I will never forget what Shane Dye did. He never stuck solid. He never stuck loyal. He could have stuck by me but he stood by and watched me go down.

I also want to make it clear I have no ill feelings towards Victor. You get caught up with people and that's what happens. I'll say it again: I treat people as they treat me.

As for John Schreck, by the time I returned to racing, he had taken off to Macau to head their stewards' panel. He then went to Hong Kong, where Shane Dye became a contracted jockey for eight years. Whenever I see Schreck at the races now, I just look at him and shake my head.

I'd also love to see justice dished out to some of those committeemen who sat there and tried to persecute me. Who put me out in the cold. The ones who were calling me for information about horses but were happy to see me placed in exile.

The length of the disqualification never fitted the crime. I have always known what was in the transcripts of those inquiries, but few people had the balls to defend me. It's gone on all this time, all these trainers and owners who think I'm the crook, but they have never known the full truth of it.

Over the years, I have laughed at the inconsistency of it all. How I was rubbed out for that amount of time while others have been slapped on the wrist.

Damien Oliver is a champion jockey and a good mate of mine. In 2012, he admitted that he had put a $10,000 bet on another horse in a race that he was riding in. The horse he backed, Miss Octopussy, won and the horse he was riding, Europa Point, didn't. I'm not suggesting at all that Ollie did anything suspect during the race, but it's definitely against the rules of racing to be betting in the same race you're riding in, especially on a horse you are not riding.

Racing Victoria let Ollie ride through the whole Spring Carnival, including in the Melbourne Cup, even though he had admitted to the bet. After the carnival, he was suspended for ten months but was back in time to ride Fiorente in the next Melbourne Cup for Gai Waterhouse – and win.

If that was me, I would have been given life. I know there was a different set of rules for me. My record shows it. Someone would get suspended for five meetings, I'd get seven for the same offence. It all impacts on your reputation. *There's Cassidy doing something wrong. He's the bad boy . . .*

By the end of my career, the wheel had turned around. I've been a winner my whole career and history shows that. I've kept picking myself off the canvas and kept going my whole career.

In all my years in racing, I haven't seen any other person who's had to do it as often as me.

10

Divine Intervention

I KNEW IT. I KNEW IT THE MOMENT HE WON OVER 1900 METRES at a midweek meeting at Canterbury.

This was the third time I'd ridden him, and he'd won the last start over the same distance at the same track.

But on this day, 16 February 1997, he gave a glimpse to those who knew enough about racing of what he was capable of. He was forced to race three or four wide without cover, churning through more ground than the rest of the field. His action wasn't as good then as it turned out to be, but the determination he'd shown to win – or to not lose – said a lot to me.

Yes, it might've been a restricted race for three-year-olds at Canterbury. Even Jack Denham still had reservations about how good the horse could be.

But I didn't. I knew.

I climbed down off the back of the monster, and the first

person I spoke to was his owner, the fruit shop millionaire Nick Moraitis.

'He's got Caulfield Cup written all over him, Nick,' I said.

That night, I phoned Malcolm, as always.

'I think I've found a freak, Boss,' I said.

'What is it?' Boss asked.

'His name is Might And Power.'

Sometimes you find special horses, and at other times they find you. I'd like to think it was a little bit of both with Might And Power. He took me to places that few jockeys will ever see. He brought me back to life.

My comeback ride after the 'Jockey Tapes' suspension was on New Year's Day 1997, at Royal Randwick. The media was all over me, with cameramen, photographers and reporters shadowing my every move.

'I've already forgotten what has happened,' I said. 'Life doesn't stop and racing doesn't stop for Jim Cassidy. That is something that I've learnt.'

What more was there to say? I wanted to get on with the rest of my life and career. I was sitting on 50 Group 1 races and 189 stakes wins. I had many more to add to that tally. I'd spent enough time thinking about what the whole shit-fight had cost me.

As I made my way from the jockeys' room and out into the mounting yard for my first ride back, the crowd gave me a massive standing ovation. They might've been cheering my return, or just the fact I was on the short-priced equal favourite, Yippyio, in the Thompson Handicap over a mile.

I didn't win but came second. There was polite applause as I returned to the mounting yard, which made for a nice change to what usually happens when you don't win on an equal favourite.

I had five rides that day and could do no better than a couple of second placings. It didn't matter. It was so good to be back at the track. The blood was pumping through my veins. My eyes were sticking out like dog's balls.

There'd been a lot of attention in the week or so since the AJC committee had given me the green light to return. I was under no illusions about how hard it was going to be. I was around 53 kilos, which is close to my usual riding weight.

What was also tough was getting my timing back. That took me a month or so. I had an itchy arse: I kept taking off early on a few horses because I was desperate to ride a winner. On 9 January, the win came when I scored on Mr Rogers at Canterbury late in the day after being nutted on the line in two earlier races.

'The winners will come,' I told the media. 'I can't be greedy. As long as I'm riding them the way they should be ridden, that is the most important thing.'

I had ridden that day while many other jockeys had gone on strike over a pay dispute. I wasn't a member of the Jockeys' Association but I still supported their claim for a pay rise from $100 to $130 per ride.

'But I have an obligation to owners and trainers and to the AJC which gave me the best Christmas present ever [by reducing the ban by twelve months]. I'm not saying the jockeys shouldn't be getting $130. I just don't think the strike was the way to go.'

I wanted to keep riding. Riding winners and sticking it up those who doubted I would ever come back. A lot of trainers and owners had said early on that they would support me, but it took a while to get them onside. Maxie Lees was supportive, as always. And I was lucky having Jack in my corner because he was associated with Geoff and Berryl White, and they owned great horses like Yippyio and Filante. They were great owners and supporters of the racing industry – and of Jack in particular.

It took me about three months before I was flying again. I won the Queensland Guineas by 5 lengths on Yippyio at Eagle Farm in early May, and as the month came to a close I edged closer to 200 metropolitan stakes winners. One more would've put me level with Harry White and equal seventh overall on the all-time list. Shane Dye was ahead of me on the list with 232.

I'm not big on statistics. I'm not a fanatic about them like some jockeys. My best winner was always my last one. But as I said to the papers at the time: 'If I had my time back from suspension, I would be 40 ahead of Shane.'

*

I reached the 200 milestone but I had lost something along the way.

Despite his win at Canterbury that day, Might And Power lined up two weeks later in the Canterbury Guineas (1800 metres) at 14 to 1. He got to the front, and almost had it won, too, before Intergaze grabbed him on the line in a new record for the race of 1 minute 47.99 seconds.

Might And Power kept running past the post. That was the type of horse he was. You couldn't stop him, even then. There had been this rubbish floating around about the horse being trained with the aid of a jigger, an electric zapper in the end of the whip. They were saying that was the reason he was always so hard to stop. It was laughable. As I've said in the past about that rumour: 'I think if you hit him up with a jigger, you would *never* have stopped him. You would have ruined him.'

A week after the Canterbury Guineas, we lined up again in the Rosehill Guineas, this time over 2000 metres. We had no luck in that race, finishing seventh. I tried everything I could to get to the line and the stewards weren't happy. They suspended me for three weeks for causing interference.

It was the worst possible outcome because it meant I couldn't ride Might And Power in the AJC Derby over 2400 metres a fortnight later. Jack replaced me with Brian York, who had moved to Sydney from Brisbane. He'd also won the Epsom Handicap at Randwick the year before on Filante.

Brian rode him back in the field as instructed, and the horse finished fourth despite almost being knocked over. A week later, he won the Group 3 Frank Packer Plate (2000 metres) by 6 lengths. Brian was in, and I was out.

But I still had Yippyio. As the spring drew closer, I was starting to realise more and more what he could do. He was the early favourite for the Melbourne Cup. But in late August, disaster struck. I was suspended for six meetings for careless riding. I would be out until 25 September.

It meant I would be replaced on Yippyio, and there was always the fear that Jack might start putting other jockeys on his top horses.

'I'm on a shocker,' I told the press. 'You have these bad runs sometimes.'

I returned to win the Metropolitan – a Group 1 race over 2600 metres worth $500,000 – on Heart Ruler for Jack. It was going to be an interesting race, because my younger brother Larry was on Gai Waterhouse's horse, Linesman.

Larry was more a rival than a brother as there was a nine-year gap between us. It was hard for us to get close because I came to Australia in 1984 and he didn't come over until about fifteen years later.

I helped him get going in Sydney. I sacrificed rides to give him opportunities. I got him on a good horse called Coronation Day. I wanted to see him come here and succeed, and he did, which was great. For Mum and Dad, it was good because they had three sons who were successful jockeys: Ricky rode winners early on in New Zealand; Larry had the chance to come here and go from strength to strength; and then there was me.

Larry was a good reader of a race and a great tactician, and he achieved something that I didn't: he won two Sydney premierships and I won only one. He was the second best jockey I think I'd ever seen, and it was great that we could compete against each other at the highest level.

But in the Metrop, I got the better of him.

After the race I joked to the media, 'I said to Larry as we went past him, "Cop that and ta-ta".'

Jack was filthy on himself because he hadn't entered Heart Ruler for the Melbourne Cup.

I was filthy because I wasn't going to be on the horse I really wanted to be riding that spring.

*

Might And Power might've brought me back to life, but Malcolm played a big part in bringing me back to life, too.

Of course, Boss knew of the horse. He knew everything.

He also knew everything there was to know about preparing jockeys.

For starters, he taught me how to sauna properly. Most other jockeys will sit in the sauna and giggle and roast themselves like a piece of lamb. They bring their water and sip on it, have a shower, go home. He showed me how to work while I'm in there.

'All these jockeys come here and burn to death,' he would say. 'They go home being tired and rundown. The more work you do, the better you'll be.'

I wasn't much of a sweater but Boss made me sweat. He'd rub the emu oil all over me, cut the top off a plastic bag, put that over my body with my head sticking out and then wrap tape around it so it stayed in place. Then we'd be on the boxing pads. Then he'd throw a ball to me, back and forth, back and forth. Touch my toes, and stretch back. Bend and stretch, over and over. Once we got in a sweat, I'd lose a kilo-and-a-half in the space of 40 minutes.

Malcolm knew more than any other person what was going through my head when I returned to racing. He knew I had a point to prove. He puts it this way:

He was bitter, he was sour, he was angry . . . but he was determined. He wanted to make it work. People don't understand that about Jimmy: he is the hardest worker. I tested him on the boxing pads with Johnny Lewis a few times, and he'd knock most boxers out cold. He can really fight.

From the way I've taught him, training in the steam room in the plastic bag, I'd just warm him up and put the oil and cream on him, throw him the ball, jogging on the spot, bend

155

*and stretch, bend and stretch . . . The fittest people are the
ballet dancers. All they do is bend and stretch.*

*He did all that exercise with me. He had supple,
beautiful skin. He was light, he was strong, tough. He was
so fit. We just flew them all.*

I needed Boss, too. After I got a call in mid October,
I needed his help to strip an additional 2 kilos, to get down
to 52.5 kilograms. I was at home in Sydney when the phone
rang. It was Jack Denham.

'Jack here. Have you got a ride in the Caulfield Cup?'

'Nope.'

'You have now.'

And then he hung up. That was it. As always, Jack never
had a lot to say.

Earlier that month, Might And Power had been expected
to win the Epsom Handicap (1600 metres). Brian York was
reportedly told before the race not to let the horse lead, to
keep him on a tight rein. He probably knew, like I did, that
Might And Power was a horse that wanted to lead. Stuck
back in the field, the horse fought him the whole way and
when the time came to run down the rest of them, he had
nothing left in the tank. He finished eighth. The horse was
too bold and aggressive to race midfield.

He needed to lead – because he wanted to.

Might And Power made his way south for the Caulfield
Cup in the back of the horse float, with Jack's son Allan and
strapper and trackwork rider Brett Grant making sure the
horse was okay. I got there on Thursday then caught up with
Brett on Friday afternoon at Crown Casino.

We went through the field, and how the race could be won.

'If I lead on him, he just wins,' I told Brett.

Brett laughed. 'Jack won't want you to lead on him.'

In the book *A Horse Called Mighty* by Helen Thomas, Brett remembers the conversation this way:

I told him, 'Mate, if you take another hold of this horse in the run, he's in serious trouble – he'll dead set get away from you.' I made a point of saying that, too, because I knew that Jimmy would probably come down on a nice long rein and he'd really get marching with him. And Jimmy would have thought, 'Geez, he's going way too hard, I'll get a shorter hold on him'. Because that's what some jockeys do. When the horses are going too hard, they'll actually go for a quick hold, drag them back under them and then try to get [them] relaxed again. But Mighty, when he felt hand movement, he was off.

Fuck it, I thought, I'm just going to lead. If he's back in the field pulling, he's not going to relax to run the trip anyway. If I can lead on him, he'll get into a nice rhythm.

Jack liked that about his horses: they could all race on the speed – just like Gai's horses do – but they were also tough. Might And Power was just like Jack, because he was such a big, bold horse, he loved the work. He was an athlete. He was like Johnathan Thurston or Greg Inglis. Or, better still, Richie McCaw.

And the horse was huge: about 600 kilograms. He only had to carry 52.5 kilos. For him, that was like carrying a biscuit.

PUMPER

The other reason I wanted to lead was that so much can go wrong at Caulfield. It's the circumference. You come out of the straight, then you have a tight turn, then you run up to the mile and you're half running up the hill. Then you're turning again at the 1400 metres, then you turn again from the 1000 metres. You're turning, turning, turning . . . If you're trapped wide, you're gone because you're turning all the time. But then you can also get stuck in behind them.

So I was leading, no matter what. I knew in my heart if I let him relax out front he would just win.

In the mounting yard before the race, Jack gave me his instructions.

'Tuck him away fourth or fifth,' he said.

'Yeah, okay.'

I never told him I was going to lead.

Then I looked at Might And Power in the parade ring. He was a maniac. The crowd of 35,600 was pumped that day, and he was wound up. He looked like a time bomb ready to explode. I just wanted to get him out onto the course and away from the punters so he would relax.

In the betting ring, Lee Freedman's Marble Halls was the $3.25 favourite. Mighty was out to about $10. But heading up to the barrier, I knew I had it won. He calmed right down.

John Russell called the race for Sky:

Away to a great start in the Caulfield Cup . . .

We're second going past the winning post the first time, with Freedman's Derobe, ridden by Brent Stanley, trying to get around me. 'No way,' I think. 'Fuck this. I'm going.'

We shoot to the lead and we are already humming. I get him into a nice rhythm. I'm not fighting him now. He's come back underneath me. If I was back in the field, he'd be

158

reefing and pulling. He's relaxed. I'm bobbed over his neck, letting him find his rhythm.

As they race up the hill, Might And Power in charge . . .

See that? That's me taking a peek over my shoulder, before the 600-metre mark. I'm going so well. I have so much horse-power underneath me. There is no way they are going to run me down. *Fuck you all. It's time to get rollin'.* Then I kick away.

This leader, Might And Power, making a merry bid for victory. As they straighten up it's Might And Power . . . He's well clear. Might And Power got away four lengths from Always Aloof and Ebony Grosve . . .

I tap the horse with the whip. Just once.

Might And Power is well clear. A hundred and fifty metres to go and he's six lengths ahead . . . Might And Power has bolted in with the Caulfield Cup! He wins by eight lengths!

I get goosebumps whenever I watch a replay of it. Even now. I knew he'd win but I didn't think he'd get there by that much.

As I went across the line, I punched the air but then lowered my head. It was enormous relief. I'd come back and won the toughest mile-and-a-half race in the world. I'd done it while leading from start to finish. I'd dragged myself off the canvas, put my balls on the line, led on him when I wasn't meant to, and won. And I had backed my knowledge of the horse. I'd known in February, after that win at Canterbury, that the Caulfield Cup was the race he could win.

The winning margin, which was actually seven-and-a-half lengths, was the biggest ever seen at the course, and the winning time of 2 minutes 26.2 seconds smashed the race and course record. His final 600 metres was 34.58 seconds. He was unstoppable. No wonder it's the Caulfield Cup that many say is the best that's ever been.

Lee Freedman, who had two horses in the race, said Might And Power's win was 'greater than Tulloch', whose win in 1957 was considered the best performance in the history of the race. As I said later: 'Phar Lap couldn't have beaten me the way I was travelling 600 metres from home.'

After the race, the media swamped me. Two years earlier, they had said I would never return. Others said I was headed to jail. I told them:

> I copped a good kick in the guts for a couple of years. I've bounced back. I've stuck it right up them. I love it. Now it's my turn to stick it up everyone else. Not sticking it up them word-wise, but riding. There's plenty of scumbags out there but my friends stuck by me. I don't worry about the rest of them. Now, all I worry about is my wife, my family and Jack. I don't give a rat's arse about anyone else. They can do what they like, they can say what they like – they always have and always will. I haven't got any sour grapes. My attitude now is I have come back, I have worked, I'm still working and I am still riding winners and still riding big winners.
>
> I was always coming back. I have been put on this earth to kick arse not lick arse. I've been saying that my whole life, not just because I've won the Caulfield Cup. My life has been controversial, I do things differently. I won the Melbourne Cup from last and they said you could not do it. I have come out and won the Caulfield Cup by leading all the way and running a race record. This time last year, I was sitting at home and watching on television.

Then I saw Jack Denham. He was in tears.
'That was a win, wasn't it?' he said.

'Yeah it was, Boss.'

He didn't say a word about me disobeying his instructions at the time, but he did say later, 'Well, you weren't meant to lead on him.'

If I hadn't led, I wouldn't have won. And then nobody would've known who Nick Moraitis was, either. At that stage, Nick couldn't believe his horse could do that. He had no idea he was that brilliant. But I did.

That night, I celebrated in a suite at the Hyatt Hotel with those who had stood by me. We went hard, drinking champagne and beer out of the Caulfield Cup.

But my mind wasn't far away from another cup. When Might And Power went past the finishing post that day, he was still towing me down the track. I couldn't stop him.

I knew then that he could also win the Melbourne Cup.

*

I said *could*. The expectation was that he *would* win it. After the Caulfield Cup, everyone just thought he would go out and lead and win the Melbourne Cup.

I was never of that belief. The Caulfield Cup is a totally different race: different track, different atmosphere, different distance. Suddenly, the pressure was right on.

The media wanted a piece of me, but I just kept my distance and cruised along. I didn't come out and say silly things, because the spotlight was back on me. There was nothing to be gained through that.

Might And Power had to shoulder a lot more than just expectation. I had never thought of him as a Melbourne Cup horse. When I climbed off him that day at Canterbury, I figured he was a 2000-metre horse, maybe 2400 metres.

But the way he kept rolling after the finish line in the Caulfield Cup meant I knew he could run the 3200 metres of the Melbourne Cup that many horses can't.

Straight after the Caulfield Cup win, the horse was given an extra 3.5 kilograms for the Melbourne Cup. He went from carrying 52.5 to 56 kilos. I was worried then. To carry all that weight, over 2 miles, was not going to be an easy task. If I had to get him to relax in the Caulfield Cup, I would have to put him to sleep in the Melbourne Cup.

I knew I would be ready, because I had already made an important phone call. I couldn't win it without Malcolm. I needed him more than ever. He had been in hospital again with emphysema, but he heeded the call and came to Melbourne to prepare me. He worked me longer and harder than he had ever worked me before.

We did most of the hard work at St Kilda baths. The problem was that we were restricted for time, as a whole heap of schoolkids were using the baths for swimming lessons. So we had to pack the work into me while we were there. We'd get there at 2 pm and there would be a sweat, a swim, then a break, then on with the plastic bag and gloves for a hit-out. Boss would then make me swim four or five laps at the end of the session, before I had a cool shower and headed home at 5 pm. We didn't have much time so we just worked harder.

There were certainly a few people who didn't think the horse could win. They said, *It's got too much weight. Can't run two miles, etc.* But all Boss and I had to focus on was getting me as fit as possible.

It wasn't about me losing weight for that ride, because Might And Power was carrying 56 kilograms. It was about being razor sharp.

By the time we got to Flemington on the morning of the race, everything was in place. Boss remembers what he told me a little differently to how I recall it, but it was the same message:

That morning, I had told him that when you have bitterness in you, it's like cancer. He had a lot of bitterness that he needed to get rid of.

I told him, 'Remember all the things that happened two years ago. You had the world, then you had nothing. Go out and win the Melbourne Cup. Show them how good you are.'

Everything he did that day, he did on his own.

The other jockeys were starting to arrive just as we were finishing up. Before we were kicked out of the room, Boss rubbed me down with methylated spirits, like he always did.

The track is full of old tricks and secrets. But metho has a purpose. A jockey spends so much of his life in the sauna that his body dries out. The metho cools and soothes it.

Boss wrapped me in a blanket, and I jumped into the bunk beds near the jockeys' room and drifted off to sleep.

Johnny Letts, Channel 7's horseback interviewer who speaks to the winning jockeys after they've gone past the post, could smell the metho.

'Who's under the blanket?' he asked Boss.

'Jimmy.'

'Don't light a cigarette near Pumper!'

I didn't hear it because I was already fast asleep.

I had two rides on Cup Day. Of my first ride, Max Presnell wrote: 'It was obvious when Cassidy came out to ride Bezeal Bay in an earlier race at Flemington that he was ready to take on the world.' Bezeal Bay won.

PUMPER

In the lead-up to the Melbourne Cup, the news was breaking that the country's richest man, Kerry Packer, was leading a massive betting plunge on Might And Power to win. A series of telephone bets with bookies in Sydney and Melbourne meant he was set to collect about $6 million.

I knew all that before the race. The pressure was now enormous.

I had to relax just like Might And Power had to be relaxed. That was the only way we could win.

He was much fierier racing in Melbourne. He would chop and change stride with the anti-clockwise way of going, trying to find another gear. But it was his high knee action that made him so hard to handle. If you didn't know any better, you would've thought he was trying to jump out of his skin.

To get him to run the 2 miles with 56 kilograms was going to be much harder than with 52.5 kilos. He wasn't really a two-miler. He was going to have one crack at it, and that was in the Melbourne Cup.

When I approached Jack in the mounting yard, he had just one piece of advice.

'Remember, the winning post is at the bottom of the straight,' he said. 'Not the top.'

I knew exactly what he meant.

*

We are heading to the barriers for the Melbourne Cup. He has a little pony alongside him, trying to keep him nice and relaxed and distracted from the massive crowd that's hanging over the fence.

I can't canter him down. If I do that, I won't be able to stop him. He's an athlete. An aggressive bastard. Maybe that's why we get on so well.

I am talking in his ear. I always do that with my horses. If you talk to them, they listen to you. If you take their concentration off doing what they want to do, and have it focused on you, it switches them off.

'Settle down, big boy,' I tell him. 'Settle down.'

He's like a greyhound. Once that cage opens, he will be running.

Greg Miles is the caller for Channel 7:

Off! Might And Power began well . . .

Heading down the straight, with the crowd of 94,000 going mental, Sunny Lane with Brent Stanley aboard is trying to take him on. I'm talking in his ear. *Woo, big fella. Woo, big fella . . .* He's trying to get away, but I can't let him. We're approaching the finishing post for the first time.

As Might And Power, the Caulfield Cup winner, pulling against Jim Cassidy, took the lead with a circuit to run.

Now, I've got him into a nice rhythm. He's calming down. Now we're getting to 1800 metres. Two idiots are standing right on the rail. At the 1800! I come away from the fence so the horse doesn't get spooked.

Might And Power trying to lead all the way, as he did in the Caulfield Cup, leads from Crying Game second, third to Marble Halls . . .

At the 1200 metres, they're all coming to get me. Greg Childs, aboard Crying Game, is trying to take me on. I'm still talking to Mighty: *Woo big fella. Woooooo . . .*

Then he jumps. He's seen his own shadow on the ground. That's how alert he is.

We hit the turn. Here they come . . .

They sweep around the turn where Linesman joins Might And Power. The brothers Cassidy turn around the bend together.

PUMPER

My brother Larry is on Gai Waterhouse's Linesman. He's already using the whip. I'm not. I'm still cuddling, my hands on the horse's neck, saving my run and what's left of him.

But by the time we get to the clocktower, I have to ask him to get going, with all that weight against us.

Might And Power shook off Linesman, though. At the 300 metres he raced away by two lengths with Doriemus challenging . . .

Doriemus. The 1995 winner, with Greg Hall on top and trained by Lee Freedman, who knows something about winning this race, is reeling in Might And Power.

Might And Power in front at the 200, in front of Linesman and then Doriemus on the outside. Might And Power the leader. Doriemus trying hard. Doriemus coming at him. Might And Power and Doriemus. Doriemus getting to Might And Power. They hit the line . . . PHOTO! Ohhhh, nothing between them. Doriemus and Might And Power in a close go . . .

When we go over the line, I don't know. I'm shaking my head. I just don't know.

My thoughts are a mess: I've done all this work. They've taken me on at the 1200 metres. They've taken me on at the 1000 metres. Fuck me. I did all the donkey work and now I've been beaten right on the line.

After the winning post, Greg Hall stands up in his irons.

Greg Hall waves his whip in the air. He thinks he's won!

Usually, a jockey knows. You know if you've got there or not, even by a snotball. But this time, I don't know.

I look at John Letts, who's got the answer to all my prayers in his earpiece.

'Lettsy!' I shout to him. 'What number is it?'

It takes forever for him to reply.

'You've won it!' he shouts. 'You've won it!'

The numbers are in the frame . . . Number three! Might And Power! Might And Power has held on to win the Melbourne Cup by a nose from Doriemus.

Hally just slumps like he's fallen through his underpants and hung himself. Only seconds earlier, you'd never seen a jockey so happy to come second in a Melbourne Cup. He's shattered. Almost speechless. But he is gracious enough to be the first to come over and congratulate me. 'Good on ya, Pump.'

When I won the Cup in 1983, there was pressure. I was the Kiwi jockey on the back of a horse called Kiwi. But it was a $1000 horse, and an 11 to 1 chance. Not many people knew much about me.

This was different. There was so much expectation with Might And Power, because of what he'd done and what I had gone through.

There was nothing more I could've done, and that's what was so satisfying. When I came back to the grandstand, up the laneway lined with flowers, I felt like every bit of blood had drained out of my veins. It was pure relief. But I was spent. As Nick's sons, Stephen and Paul, led the horse back to the mounting yard and we went under the Flemington arch, I clasped my hands together and looked towards the heavens.

That's the iconic image that appeared on the front page of *The Daily Telegraph* the next day. The headline read: 'A tear, a prayer and Mr Packer's $6m win'. Some say it's not a tear rolling down my cheek, but sweat. I don't know. I just know I was very emotional.

I did thank God. I'm not really a religious person, but I knew the Good Man had looked after me for a reason. Maybe He knew I didn't deserve the suspension. Maybe He appreciated that I had got off the canvas – again – and fought my way back.

Nick was speechless. He was asked how he felt.

'How do I feel?' he said as the TV cameras zoomed in on him. 'How do I look?'

Jack wasn't saying anything, to anyone. Ken Callendar wrote in *The Daily Telegraph* the next day that he heard the trainer say to an official: 'Just as well I had that jock on top, he wouldn't have got home with anyone else.'

It had been an enormous training performance from Jack and his son, Allan. They had kept the horse fresh and fit, which was a real effort because he didn't have a run between the two cups.

And I wouldn't have been there without that phone call from Jack a year earlier, telling me he'd help me get back. Jack trusted my ability and had faith in me when others didn't. He'd gone close to winning the Melbourne Cup in 1988 when equal favourite Natski was just beaten by Empire Rose. He'd had all these great horses and jockeys over the years, but he'd never landed the two big cups. Now, I had given him both. But without that phone call that day, you aren't reading this book.

Jack was late to the podium for the presentation but I was already there. It felt so good. A year earlier, I was standing beside a caravan at the showjumping, drinking out of a VB can, cooking sausages on the barbie and having tomato sauce dripping all over my hand. Now I was on the podium at Flemington, on the biggest day of the year.

'I learnt a saying in showjumping in the past eighteen months that you either go hard or you go home,' I said. 'Since this time last year, I've been going hard and I'm not going home.'

I couldn't have stuck it up the doubters any more than I did – but I would never have said that publicly. I couldn't say anything like that, because it had been stuck up me. That was going to do me no favours. I had to be humble. Once you've done it, they can't take it away from you.

The moment I realised that I had won the Melbourne Cup, I thought of a lot of people. I thought about those few people who had stood by me. I thought of my two daughters, Nicole and Sarsha. What nobody could see was the T-shirt I was wearing underneath my silks, with their faces printed on it.

But the first person I thought of was Boss, because we had been there that morning at Flemington, and now all the hard work had paid off.

Boss had never lost faith in me. He kept me going as much as Might And Power.

And where was Boss as I crossed the line? I'll let him take up the story:

After we'd done our work at Flemington that morning, I headed for the airport. The pilots were getting on the plane at the same time I was.

'Where are you going?' they asked me.

Everyone was coming to Melbourne and I was going.

We landed in Sydney, and I noticed it was getting close to the start of the Cup, so I got the cabbie to stop at the Eastlakes TAB at Gardener's Road. I told the cabbie to come in and watch it with me. The place was packed.

'He's going to win this race,' the cabbie said as Jimmy led the field.

The horse was travelling well. People in the TAB were jumping up and down. But when they crossed the line, I didn't know if he'd won it. Then Jimmy turned around and I saw the look on his face. I knew he'd won it before the numbers came up.

I went home, had a cup of tea and slept for hours. I was exhausted.

Jimmy Cassidy reminds me of Mike Tyson. The system took away everything they had ever worked their guts out to get. People had manipulated them for their ability and knowledge. They had the world, lost it, and then tried to get it all back. They learnt.

Tyson didn't make it back.

Jimmy did.

Nick Moraitis called the horse Might And Power because when his granddaughter received her first Holy Communion, the choir was singing about 'the might and power of Jesus Christ'.

I was lucky to find Might And Power. I was lucky to ride him. I rode him brilliantly and I know that.

But someone up there looked after me.

11

Longy

THERE WAS ONE MAN WHO WAS AS IMPORTANT AS BOSS WHEN it came to all the success I had on Might And Power in my comeback year.

I phoned him a week or so before the Melbourne Cup. He was in Sydney. I was already in Melbourne.

'Get down here,' I said. 'I'm going to win the Cup.'

He slept on a trundle bed right next to me in my one-bedroom suite at the Hyatt. I didn't want him too far away. I never do.

Boss makes me supple – but Longy takes away all the pain.

His full name is Duy Long Nguyen but everyone who has had his magical hands on them simply knows him as 'Longy'. From Rupert Murdoch and Frank Lowy, to Keanu Reeves and Elle Macpherson. He's referred to as a masseur but he is more than that. Longy's life reads like a book. A few years ago, one was written about him. I'll get to that later.

The first time I met him was at the start of 1997. The story is almost too good to be true, like most things that Longy has done over the years to keep me in the saddle.

I was sitting there in the spa at Chequers in a world of pain. I'd fallen off at one of the trials on the Tuesday and could barely move. My ribs were screaming. I was certain they were broken.

Terry Hill, the larrikin rugby league player, was there with a man of Vietnamese descent. Terry was playing for Manly at the time, and the man with him had been working for the club under coach Bob Fulton.

Terry could see I was in agony.

'What's wrong with you, Pump?' he asked.

'I've either broken a rib or I've torn cartilage,' I said. 'I have to go to Newcastle tomorrow and ride but I'm no chance.'

'I've got a bloke who can fix you,' he said. 'Longy, this is Jimmy Cassidy.'

'Yes, I know him,' Longy said. 'I'll fix you.'

He started to feel me all over.

'I don't think it's a cracked rib,' Longy said. 'Where do you live?'

'Coogee.'

'I'll meet you at your place in an hour.'

I went home and, an hour later, Longy and Terry arrived as promised.

'Have you got an empty bottle?' Longy asked.

All I had was a bottle of Johnny Walker Black Label, with an inch or two left. I knocked back the scotch while he boiled the kettle and filled the empty bottle with hot water.

He stretched me out on the floor and lifted up my shirt.

'What the fuck is going on here?' I thought.

Then he started to warm his hands on the bottle, making them as hot as the water. His hands were red raw, and he started probing and feeling around my ribs where the pain was.

Then, without warning, he got the boiling hot bottle and started rubbing it up and down my ribcage. I went as red as a tomato. There was fire coming out of my ears.

'*TEZZA! WHO THE FUCK IS THIS BLOKE?! WHAT'S HE DOING TO ME!*'

I was almost crying from pain. Terry just sat there laughing.

'Suck it up! Suck it up!' he shouted back. 'Weak bastard! Weak bastard! Breathe! Breathe!'

'Breathe?' I yelled. 'Breathe? When I get up I'm going to kick you in the head.'

Longy finished and I stood up.

'How does it feel now?' he asked me.

I'd forgotten all about the rib injury because I was now sore and burning all over. He told me to sit down for five minutes.

'Now do some star jumps,' Longy instructed.

'Star jumps? You're kidding me, aren't you?'

He wasn't. 'You can do star jumps,' he said.

I'd hardly been able to move my arms let alone do a star jump. But I tried – and I did it easily. I felt my ribs. There was no pain.

'Punch my hands,' he said, holding up his palms like they were boxing pads.

I punched them. Still no pain in my ribs.

'Get on the ground again,' he said.

He then went to work with the bottle again. It hurt, but not as much as before. Then he made me lie down for about twenty minutes without moving.

'How do you feel now?' he asked.

I couldn't believe it. I felt brand new. The pain in my ribcage that had been so bad I could barely breathe had disappeared.

The next day, I went to Newcastle and rode four winners from five rides.

I tried to pay Longy but he wouldn't take any money. He's never taken any money from me. Not a cent. I gave him a small pendant I received for winning the 1983 Melbourne Cup. He's still got it.

From that day on, we just clicked. He's one of the funniest blokes I have ever met but he's also my brother, and he was just as important to me as Boss when it came to keeping me in the saddle.

Early on, he was hard to understand because of his strong Vietnamese accent. I had to study his lips to work out what he was saying. But the language barrier didn't matter – his hands did all the talking.

Because Longy puts his hands on me and all the pain just goes away.

*

Longy wrote about his life in 2004 in a book called *The Dragon's Journey*. It says a lot that the foreword was jointly written by Rupert Murdoch and Frank Lowy, two of the richest men in the world. It reads in part:

We have had the pleasure of meeting many inspiring people, but few are more remarkable than Longy Nguyen.

His achievements are a lesson to us all — no matter what hardships we face, it is important to keep fighting, to keep believing . . .

We are just two of the hundreds, probably thousands, to say how grateful we are that Longy has succeeded . . . because without his healing intervention we would not be as active as we are. Anyone who has had back problems will know how limiting they can be.

Longy's full name, Duy Long Nguyen, translates as, 'There is only one dragon'. He is one of seven children and his father, who was an inspector-general in the South Vietnamese Army during the Vietnam War, was jailed for eleven years after the Viet Cong took control of Saigon in 1975.

He grew up tough, earning a black belt in taekwondo by the age of ten and then, by the age of fourteen, he started running his own black-market gang.

Longy and his brothers and sisters fled their war-ravaged country in an old river boat. They arrived in Sydney in 1981, having survived attacks from Thai pirates and coming through Japan. He told *The Courier-Mail* in 2014: 'We could have drowned in the South China Sea if a Japanese tanker had not turned up ahead of schedule. I should have been dead many times before.'

During his teenage years, he became a bodyguard for Chinese underworld figures in Chinatown, almost dying when he was shot several times. Soon after his father was released from prison, his mother Teresa was murdered during a break-in on their home in Saigon.

'I've seen death, unfairness and indignity,' Longy has said. 'I've been a gang leader and a smuggler, been to martial arts school and in army camps – I was just a person who had so much energy and feeling and high spirits. Then one day I suddenly matured and resolved the uncertainties in life.'

Then his life changed. He went to Thailand, Hong Kong and Japan to learn about how he could heal people with his hands instead of hurting them.

When he was a young boy, his mother had introduced him to massage. In Thailand years later, monks took him into their monastery and showed him how to heal those who had been badly injured. In Japan, he was taught Shiatsu and went to work on Sumo wrestlers.

'My secret is that I have the ability to locate the twelve energy lines called Meridians and open them up so the lymphatic system gets the blood flowing again,' Longy has said. 'A lot of problems are due to scar tissue, calcification and excess lactic acid, which I break up with my hands. I am a hand healer who works on the body's six hundred pressure points so the Meridians become unblocked and energy floods in. The more natural, the better. My hand is better than a needle, so why should I use one? I'm not God, so I can't fix everything and I'll get an X-ray taken if there is a serious problem. You must never fool around with the human body, especially a bulging disc in the back. I know my limits. If I can't fix it, I won't touch it.'

I don't know what a lot of that means. I just know that it works!

Around the time I met him, he was working with the Sea Eagles, the Manly rugby league team, but he became so well known and sought after that he treated all walks of life. Frank Lowy employed him for about a decade as a body-guard and masseur.

LONGY

When the Hollywood blockbuster *The Matrix* was shot in Australia, he worked on lead actor Keanu Reeves because of his back issues after a motorbike accident. Keanu was introduced to Longy through co-star Laurence Fishburne. There is a life-size model of Keanu at Longy's home in Sydney's west.

He has worked on a whole heap of sportspeople, from the Australian and Queensland State of Origin rugby league teams, to individuals such as Linford Christie, Pat Rafter, Brad Fittler and Anthony Mundine. He was in the corner for Troy Waters when he fought Felix Trinidad at Madison Square Garden.

Longy did most of this work out of his old clinic in Paddington in Sydney. There was a wall in the reception area covered with messages and autographs from those who have felt the magic of his hands.

Elle Macpherson was so impressed after her first appointment, she wrote on the wall: 'Longy, where have you been all my life? You are very special.'

But there is one name above all of them. Above Elle and Keanu Reeves and Linford Christie. I was the first one he asked to sign the wall, so Pumper's name is at the top.

*

I had to pass a simple test before Longy would let me on a horse: if I couldn't fit in a suitcase, I wasn't allowed to ride. That's how flexible I had to be.

He taught how to roll myself up into a little ball; to the shape of a suitcase. He told me to roll myself up like that if I was falling off a horse, because falling that way would protect my neck. I fell a number of times at trials over the years, and I reckon Longy's wise words saved me from serious neck and back injuries.

After that fall in Adelaide on Sir Zephyr in the 1980s, I could never get my back right. Not even Boss could completely fix it. It went on and off for years. Some days it was okay. On others it was so bad that I couldn't move and I was unable to ride on race days.

When I was riding for Nebo Lodge, Bob Lapointe sent me to many acupuncturists and chiropractors, all of them trying to get me right. I had one bloke who was a masseur for the Parramatta rugby league team. We had no luck there. We were so desperate to get it right I even saw this blind miracle worker. He couldn't work any miracles on me.

There have been plenty of miracle men in racing – and other sports – over the years, but I have never met one like Longy. I only got relief with my back pain when Longy came along. I have never had back trouble since I met him.

On one occasion, I broke the big toes in each foot. Foot injuries happen a lot in racing. A horse will crash out into the barrier and rip your boot open and slice your toes.

'I can't walk, Longy,' I told him. 'My toes are broken.'

Two of them were pointing sideways, that's how broken they were.

'Just ice it,' he said. 'I'll be there in two hours.'

He arrived, walked straight up to me and looked at the broken toes. They were almost black from the blood.

'See how it's starting to go black?' he explained. 'All we can do is tape it together and don't let the blood clot. If I get the blood into the toe, it will heal quicker.'

Now, I'm good with pain. I've got an enormous threshold with pain. But when he put my foot up on his knee and grabbed the toe and reefed it forward, then did the same with the other one, the pain was unbelievable. The toes both went jet black because the blood had got into them. He taped them up and I was able to ride.

Shoulders. Ankles. Knees. Hamstrings. Some days he could rub me for more than three hours and I would be so sore I didn't know if I could ride, but somehow he always got me through.

Once when I was racing in Malaysia, a horse I was about to ride kicked out in the mounting yard. The stupid strapper had turned the horse around and I could see it was going to kick but I couldn't get out of the way in time. The hoof just got my back at the base of my spine. If I got the full brunt of the kick, I would be in a wheelchair or I would be dead. I jumped on a plane straightaway and flew back to Sydney, where Longy worked on me for days until I was right.

Just as Boss is big on the steam and sauna, Longy is big on cold water. In the middle of winter, he'd have me in the pool at the back of my place. The water was so cold that you almost had to break the ice to get in. That's how it felt, anyway. Because he would rub me so hard, the cold water stopped the bruising. I'd get out and I could run through a brick wall. Then I'd sleep like a baby.

There were times when I couldn't fit into a suitcase, but I was that desperate to ride he would help me through the pain. At one stage, I missed the best part of a year after undergoing a shoulder reconstruction. I hurt it again a few days before a Golden Slipper. He showed me how to strap it up and I managed to ride.

Injured ribs were the worst to ride with because you are crouching on top of the horse, crunching your body in tight.

In 2011, my ribs were shot but I wanted to ride a horse for Chris Waller called Merchandise.

'I have to ride, Longy,' I said.

'Don't ride.'

'I have to. It'll win. I need to be right for four and a half minutes. Help me to do it.'

That's all I needed: four and a half minutes.

When I arrived at the course, I could barely breathe. I just had to get through one race, over 2400 metres. I won but I was that sore I needed the chief steward Ray Murrihy to help me down off the horse.

Of all the injuries Longy's rubbed away in the time that I have known him, the one that stands out the most came when I thought I was going to die.

I was riding at Rosehill one afternoon and I kept getting these headaches. I couldn't put a cap on. I could barely touch my head. That's how much pain I was in.

I had four or five rides this day. I rode three horses and all the time it was just getting worse and worse. I tried to bend my neck back, sitting on the horse while riding, and I was just getting dizzy. After my third race, I came back and stood myself down.

'I'm not in a good way,' I told Murrihy. 'I'll have to go to the doctor.'

I was sent to North Shore Private Hospital where I underwent brain scans. There were early fears I had a brain tumour, and Mum and Dad came to my bedside fearing the worst. A white mark came up on a scan, but it must've been where I'd banged my head years ago. They checked it all out. There was nothing wrong with it.

But the headaches were still there. They were there for two weeks as I lay in the hospital bed, looking at the ceiling.

LEFT: Ring-a-ding-ding, before Pumper was king. I was eleven years old here and I didn't get much bigger. The All Blacks' loss became racing's gain.

RIGHT: With Mum at Woodville races, aged fifteen. I'd just come second again on El Donte, a sprinter who kept falling short.

The Cassidy stable circa 1981. As I chased my dream on Australian tracks, the only time I got home was for birthdays. This was my eighteenth.

News Ltd/Newspix

I'd been last the whole way in the 1983 Melbourne Cup, but when push came to shove Kiwi was always going to finish first. Here, we enter the frame and start to reel in Mr Jazz and Noble Comment.

Jim Cassidy

As a kid, I'd whip a lounge chair with a tree branch while listening to the radio call of the Melbourne Cup. Dad told me I could win one myself if I worked hard enough. At age twenty, I did.

Not bad for a kid from Lower Hutt. Winning the 1983 Melbourne Cup on Kiwi was the proudest moment of my career to date.

Businessman Bob Lapointe, left, introduced KFC – and The Pumper – to Australia. Along with trainer Brian Mayfield-Smith, we made Nebo Lodge a racing powerhouse in the 1980s.

Not a scene from *The Sopranos* but the Cassidy clan before I won the 1985 Levin Bayer Classic on the great Bonecrusher. From left: brother Larry, sister Pamela, mum Francie, me, brother Colin and dad Blue.

Jim Cassidy

Jim Cassidy

ABOVE & LEFT: The highs and lows of racing. Lifting trophies as Sportsman of the Year one minute, eating like a rabbit to make the weight the next.

RIGHT: There would be few saunas in the country I haven't seen, but the St Kilda baths was always a favourite. Here, I'm trying to get down to 49.5kg to ride Just A Dancer for Graeme Rogerson in the Caulfield Cup. We came eighth.

Geoff Ampt/Fairfax

Jim Cassidy

Rough Habit had nine campaigns, from Australia to New Zealand to Japan to America. On a wet track he was unbeatable and would go from 4 to 1 in the betting to fours-on.

Bruce Postle/Fairfax

'Be patient,' Bart Cummings told me before the 1991 Lightning Stakes 1000 metres at Flemington. 'Get there late.' On Shaftesbury Avenue I took the master's advice and won by a lip.

The loves of my life. Daughters Nicole, aged six, and Sarsha, four. When my career crashed I had to pull them out of private school to sleep on fold-out beds at a friend's place. I sold everything we owned – except for my riding gear.

Australian racing has never seen anything like the Jockey Tapes scandal that broke in 1995. They were the worst days of my life. I'll never forgive how some people cucumbered me.

Anyhow, have a Winfield. I still had my swagger but to be banned from riding and completely shut out from racing hurt like hell.

ABOVE LEFT: During my 21-month suspension, I was welcomed with open arms by the showjumping family who'd embraced my daughters. Here, I'm training at the property of legendary equestrian Chris Chugg.

ABOVE RIGHT: My darling girls, Nicole and Sarsha. I would never want them to be jockeys, but they had the same affinity for horses as their dad.

I'm baaaaaack! Walking into the Randwick mounting yard on New Year's Day 1997, for my first race after the Jockey Tapes exile. I'm about to jump on Yippyio. We finished second.

Vince Caligiuri/Fairfax

A horse like Might And Power comes along once in a jockey's lifetime. He found me and he brought me back to life. And when he won the 1997 Caulfield Cup by eight lengths, I knew he'd be winning the Melbourne Cup as well – because I couldn't stop him.

ABOVE & BELOW: I'd led the whole way and done all the hard work in the 1997 Melbourne Cup. Then 1995 winner Doriemus with Greg Hall on top came along with 300 metres to go and tried to spoil the party.

When we hit the line, I didn't know who had won but Greg Hall thought it was him .
Number three! Might And Power! Might And Power has held on to win the Melbourne

u've never seen someone so happy to come second in the Cup. Finally the call came:
up by a nose from Doriemus.

The moment I realised I'd won the Melbourne Cup, I thought of those who stood by me during my exile. And I thought of my two daughters, Nicole and Sarsha. What nobody could see was the T-shirt I was wearing underneath my silks, with their faces printed on it. No wonder I shed a tear.

News Ltd/Newspix

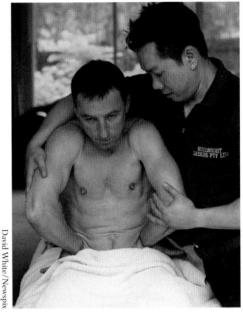

David White/Newspix

Sandra Jackson/Fairfax

ABOVE LEFT: Nobody ever made Might And Power's trainer Jack Denham cry … but I did.

ABOVE RIGHT: I wouldn't have scaled any of the heights I did without Longy Nguyen, whose magic hands rubbed away all the pain. He wouldn't let me ride if I couldn't fit into a suitcase.

LEFT: One of the few times I said 'No comment' after Jack and I had a major fallout over the Banner Headline scandal.

Ray Kennedy/Fairfax

After taking the Caulfield and Melbourne Cups, Might And Power kept going, killing them in the 1998 VRC Queen Elizabeth Stakes, above, at Flemington carrying 60kg and then demoralising Tycoon Lil – and her jockey Shane Dye – in the Caulfield Stakes, below.

News Ltd/Newspix

'Fuck this,' I said. 'I'm calling Longy.'

But I couldn't get in contact him. Longy wasn't in Sydney. He was overseas somewhere with Frank Lowy.

The headaches kept getting worse. I could hardly move. Any time I tried to get up, the pain overcame me.

Longy finally called back. He was in Amsterdam, eating lobster in the suite next door to Frank's.

'Mate, I can't do anything,' I said. 'I'm fucked.'

'I'll be home in two days.'

It was pathetic, really, what happened next. When he arrived in Sydney, I was back home, sitting in a chair. I showed him the scans.

'There's nothing wrong with you,' he said.

I didn't have a headache at the time, because the pain would come and go. He wanted me to do something to bring the headaches on. So I jumped down two steps off the balcony. The headache came on straightaway.

'Turn around,' he said.

He then pushed at the base of my skull and the rush that soon followed was like a burning, tingling feeling. He kept working at a blockage at back of my neck for about seven or eight minutes. When he was done, the headaches had gone.

I was astounded. My mum and dad thought I was dying. I didn't know what was going on. Neither did any of the doctors or specialists who made me undergo all these scans and tests. But Longy fixed it straightaway.

I have two gods: Boss and Longy.

Longy and I have a special relationship. He was always so rapt that I believed in him and I could see what he could do.

PUMPER

Longy puts it this way:

*I have looked after boxers, footballers, track and field
athletes, racing car drivers . . . You name it, I have worked
on them. But none of them could do what Jimmy has
done. When he rode, he was like a monkey on the back
of an elephant. If he makes a mistake, if he has a bad
day, he's dead. He's tougher than any sportsperson that
I have known.*

I don't know about that. But if it wasn't for Longy, my
career would've been over a decade earlier than it was.

12

The Day The Earth Rumbled

I CAN'T REMEMBER THE HORSE, OR THE RIDE, OR THE MEETING. But I clearly remember what I said to Ray Murrihy during a stewards' inquiry one day when he questioned my tactics in a race.

'What are you trying to do here?' Murrihy asked, pointing at the video replay.

'What do you think I'm trying to do?' I fired back. 'I'm trying to win the race. I'm not here to play marbles.'

Even after what I had done on Might And Power, after coming back from the debacle of 'Jockey Tapes', the stench still hung around. Every race I rode was viewed with suspicion.

I was named the NSW Sportsperson of the Year in late 1997 for what I had achieved on the back of Might And

Power. Nobody in racing had achieved that before. It was one of the proudest moments of my career, after everything I had gone through and after everything that had been thrown at me.

But in the eyes of some, it didn't matter.

Ray Murrihy is no John Schreck but he is tough. He had been the chief steward in Brisbane for a long time. Then he came to Sydney to replace Schreck as head of the stewards of the newly named NSW Thoroughbred Racing Board, and from the beginning his toughness was clear.

Murrihy got me for a lot of things I didn't deserve. I was consistently at him, too – not aggressively – but I would stand up for my rights. I wouldn't let anyone push me around. I didn't win many chook raffles with them.

Most jockeys would front the stewards and have their hearings resolved on the day. Not me. Instead, on many occasions, my hearings were adjourned in the afternoon and then my charges would be splashed all over the papers the next morning.

'We're looking at betting sheets,' Murrihy would declare.

'Well, look at them. Look at them as much as you like. I don't bet.'

Heading into the Autumn Carnival in Sydney in 1998, I clashed with Murrihy more than ever.

I also fell out with Jack Denham. It was over separate incidents on his horses Filante and Banner Headline. Only four months earlier, I had won the Melbourne Cup for him on Might And Power. Shows you how long the love lasts in racing.

Filante was a great horse. A real professional. He was a great sprinter/miler who could win from 1200 to

2000 metres. He was a multiple Group 1 winner, one of the superstars of the track around this time.

In early March, he was the 9 to 4 favourite in the $200,000 Chipping Norton Stakes, a Group 1 over 1600 metres at Warwick Farm. When we straightened up for home, my whip got caught in the horse's mane, and I stabbed at his neck with my hands because it was all I could do to give him a hurry up. It was one of those things that happens in the breakneck speed of a race. Filante finished third behind Encounter and On Air.

I distinctly remember that as I handed my whip and cap to Murrihy when I came back to scale after the race, half of Filante's mane came with it.

Then I was hauled in before Murrihy and the stewards, who were all concerned about my whip action.

'Be very careful here,' Murrihy said.

They alleged I had struck Filante in the neck with the butt of my whip on four occasions.

'I don't believe I have, sir,' I said. 'I've roared at him, and I have stabbed my hands into his neck previously.'

Then they asked me if I had been under any instructions from Jack about how I might use my whip.

'No, sir,' was my firm reply.

I knew what they were getting at. And so did Jack when he was called into the room. He was asked for a comment on my whip action on Filante.

'I left it to him,' Jack said. 'I never asked him to use the butt of his whip. I said ride your own race. As if I said to Jim Cassidy to use the butt of his whip. That's got nothing to do with me.'

They kept pushing Jack on the whip action. Before long, Jack was pissed off.

'What are you getting at?' he asked. 'He's riding the horse and it's got nothing to do with me.'

'I don't believe I'm using the butt of the whip,' I said, interjecting.

Murrihy said the whip action created 'a bad connotation'. I knew exactly what he was alleging.

'Are you saying I've got a jigger on the end of my whip?' I asked. 'You can cut the end off and have a look, there's nothing there.'

Murrihy agreed that the whip was in order, but then let the cat out of the bag.

'The connotation is a jigger could have been used at track-work and you're replicating the action,' Murrihy said.

Jack was filthy. He was more worried about his reputation than mine.

'Hang on a minute,' he said, pointing his finger at Murrihy. 'I'm being brought into this. This is definitely an insult to say I am using a jigger. I take exception to it. A very, very dim view.'

The hearing was adjourned but they impounded my whip. Outside the stewards' room, Jack and I clashed. He hadn't supported me at all.

I was angrier than he was. I have never used a jigger. I've never even carried one. There's been plenty of jiggers around over the years – you hit horses with electricity, they run like the wind. But accusing me of using one on Filante was bullshit. I hadn't even ridden him at trackwork. Troy Phillips had ridden him in work that week.

While that inquiry was hanging over my head, another drama was lurking around the corner in the form of a horse called Banner Headline.

It was also trained by Jack. And when push came to shove, he left me out in the cold again.

Banner Headline was an easing equal favourite in the Canterbury Stakes, then a Group 2, over 1300 metres at Rosehill. On instructions from Jack, I settled the horse three back on the rails because he was carrying 58.5 kilograms. At the 700-metre mark, I shifted one off the fence and got in behind Waikikamukau, who was ridden by my brother Larry, and travelling well.

But as we straightened, I struck trouble. I couldn't get out in the clear, because I was boxed in by Kevin Moses on Carry The Star, a 100 to 1 chance. I didn't get a clear passage until late and finished third.

Again, Jack was filthy. Murrihy also thought the ride was smelly, and an inquiry was opened.

Then all hell broke loose.

Two days later, the inquiry into the Filante matter resumed. I was handed a month-long suspension but given a stay of proceedings until the appeal was heard. I was desperate to ride over the autumn because Might And Power was coming back. And I had the early equal favourite Iglesia lined up in the Golden Slipper.

Later that week, on the day before I was due to ride Might And Power in the prestigious Group 1 Ranvet Stakes, the inquiry into the Banner Headline matter resumed.

Jack gave me up cold. He told Murrihy and the stewards that I had 'slaughtered' the ride. The horse only got slaughtered because I was held up behind Kevin Moses and couldn't get out.

'I thought he should have come to the outside at the top of the straight,' Jack told the inquiry. 'He should have come out before he did. Banner Headline looked like he was travelling all right . . . He missed the bus. He let Kevin Moses go around him. Moses outsmarted him.'

I was charged with failing to ensure Banner Headline 'was given full opportunity to win or obtain the best possible placing'. In other words, the stewards were claiming that I had necked it. *Here we go again*, I thought.

'I was straight up with Jack,' I told the inquiry. 'I asked if he thought I was "dead". He said, "No, I think Moses outrode you" . . . I made an error of judgement.'

'There was clear room for you to push Banner Headline up outside Waikikamukau before Carry The Star boxed you in,' Murrihy said. 'Why let a 100 to 1 chance get around you and box you in?'

Fuck this. I felt like I was under attack again.

'Where is a race won?' I shot back. 'Not at the top of the straight. I'm following the horse I thought I had to beat. My horse was having his ninth start this preparation and carrying 58.5 kilograms. He was flat out, I wasn't going well enough to get the run. You can see I'm chasing Banner Headline up. If I come out there, you would rub me out for sure. The rule states that I have to be two lengths clear [of the horse in front]. The last time I did that [came out too early] I got six weeks, and five weeks before that.'

The difference between winning or losing is the risks that you take on the track. Not risks that will endanger lives, but risks that will make you look like a genius if they come off. It's like Jason Day using a four iron when he knows he should be using a six iron. When the risks don't come off, you look like a mug. But when they do, you look like a genius. That's putting your balls on the line. Tell me a great sportsperson who doesn't do this? Who succeeds by playing it safe?

'If Moses stays straight, I get a clear run and my horse wins and it's a brilliant ride,' I argued. 'I have to stand by my judgement and this time I took the wrong option and stayed where I was. In a quick situation, I took the punt but it was the wrong option. Not many times do I take the wrong option, so you are penalising me on an error of judgement?'

Nick Moraitis, of all people, came to my defence. He had backed Banner Headline. He was one of Jack's main owners, and he said he was more than happy with the ride despite having a major bet on the horse and losing. The owner of Jack's most important horse in Might And Power was now standing up for me. What did that say?

Not much. None of it seemed to matter. I was given six weeks. It rubbed me out of the entire Autumn Carnival, taking me off the back of Might And Power in his return and also continuing my hoodoo with the Golden Slipper.

When they told me the penalty, I was gutted.

'I've only been back twelve months working my arse off six days a week,' I told the inquiry. 'I know I've had my fair share of suspensions, but I try and play by the rules. I'm riding for a leading stable and have a good book of rides this weekend with Might And Power. Also, I am riding the equal favourite in the Golden Slipper. Why would I step out of line?'

Outside the stewards' room, I erupted. Jack had just turned on me. He'd thrown me under the bus.

'I know two Jim Cassidys and one is the best rider in Australia,' he said. 'The other one . . . Why didn't you come out? The horse should have pissed in.'

'You double-crossed me,' I roared back.

Allan tried to intervene.

'Fuck your old man,' I said. 'He's a dog.'

'Dad will have a heart attack,' Allan said.

I didn't care anymore. 'I'm having one because he's trying to say I slaughtered it.'

Believe me, there were two Jack Denhams, too. There are two of every trainer you ride for. You're a genius when you win. But when you don't they can be as bad as the punter. Many of them suspect something corrupt is going on straightaway, because many have been involved in suspicious stuff themselves.

By the law of averages, there were a lot more pluses than minuses when I rode for Jack Denham. In fact, the pluses were enormous. That's what pissed me off the most: I won more big races for him than I ever lost. I won them all for him, but it didn't matter. Fuck Jack.

Yes, he gave me a chance when he helped bring me back after 'Jockey Tapes', but I paid him back for all the faith he showed in me with the Caulfield and Melbourne Cups. Yet he still chopped my head off.

I appealed and was given a stay of proceedings, meaning I could ride Might And Power in the Ranvet Stakes the next day. We finished second, and I copped another suspension – this time for careless riding – to be served concurrently with the others I had received.

I had no idea when I might ride the big horse again, if at all. I knew I'd ride again one day for Jack, but I just didn't know when. These things happen in racing. You fall in and out with trainers and owners all the time.

But I knew that things would never be the same between us again.

*

Despite my issues with Shane Dye over the 'Jockey Tapes' saga, I can still appreciate what a great jockey he was – even if he did cucumber me.

He was a fellow Kiwi who came to Sydney in the late 1980s and was as brash and opinionated in the media as I was. And he could back it up because he was a great rider. He went over every race with a fine-toothed comb. He could read a race and he could read jockeys.

And he would take risks. He would take off at the 1000-metre mark if he thought it was the right thing to do. He was good at reading the tempo of a race, like I was. Tactically, he was great.

He was also a confidence jockey. His nickname is 'Billy Idol' because of his resemblance to the 1980s British rockstar with the peroxide hair.

My relationship with Shane then was the same as it is today: I put up with him but I don't trust him. I've never trusted him again after what happened.

Heading into the spring of 1998, Shane had a lot to say about Tycoon Lil, an in-form New Zealand mare who he reckoned would go past Might And Power as the best horse in the country. From memory, he thought she was 'unbeatable'. Talk is cheap in this business if you can't back it up. People only remember who won.

For me, the showdown with Might And Power didn't really matter. After the fallout with Jack, I was dumped as expected and Brian York was back on the big horse.

He won the Group 1 Mercedes Classic (2400 metres) at Rosehill and then the Group 1 Queen Elizabeth Stakes (2000 metres) at Randwick to round out his Sydney campaign. He then went to the Gold Coast and won the Group 2 Hollindale Stakes (1800 metres) before heading to

Brisbane to win the Group 1 Doomben Cup (2020 metres). Mighty was a star – and it hurt to watch him from a distance instead of being on his back.

The horse was then spelled before he returned for the Spring Carnival. Because of his success, he was going to be handicapped out of the Caulfield and Melbourne Cups with too much weight. So the Denhams set him for the Cox Plate, the weight-for-age championship that most trainers reckon is the hardest race in the country to win.

When Might And Power came back, he finished fourth first-up in the Warwick Stakes over 1400 metres at Warwick Farm, but then won the Chelmsford Stakes over 1600 metres at Randwick. Then, in the Group 1 George Main Stakes over the same distance at the same track, something unthinkable happened: he finished seventh.

As the horse was taken down to Melbourne for the Spring Carnival, there was a lot of talk about how bad he had been working. Heading into the 2000-metre Group 1 Caulfield Stakes – now called the Yalumba Stakes – there was a lot of doubt about the horse and whether we had seen the best of him.

Through all of this, I was still an outsider looking in but then some luck fell my way.

Brian York was handed a serious riding charge by Murrihy. The stewards claimed he didn't give one of Jack's horses every chance to win a midweek race at Canterbury. Jack went out swinging for Brian, unlike me earlier in the year. It didn't matter: Brian was rubbed out for three months. And, out of nowhere, I was back in.

The phone rang. It was Jack.

'Want you back on the big horse,' he grunted.

As always, he didn't have much to say. With that, I was back on the big horse.

The Caulfield Stakes was basically going to be a match race between Might And Power and Tycoon Lil. After we jumped, that's how it looked like playing out.

Shane Dye took the mare out early, and parked her in front of me. He got 2 lengths ahead, but at the 700 metres I got within a length. And as I came to the bend and straightened, I drew alongside him, and then powered away.

Might And Power's strapper Brett Grant recalled in *A Horse Called Mighty* how he watched the race from the public area at Caulfield, because he was so nervous:

> When they got round near the 800-metre mark, Jimmy was starting to really stoke the horse up. He's sitting third at that stage, which is unusual being a leader. And they had the big screen there at Caulfield and we were watching on that when I saw Jimmy start to niggle at him.
>
> I said, 'We're gone. We're in big trouble, mate', because he'd never been niggled at. He controlled his own destiny from in front. But he went from being niggled at to jumping straight back up on the bridle, putting pressure on the favourite and then said, 'Good night'. He won by two lengths easing down.

What a freak of a horse. There were 20,000 people at Caulfield that day, and as we came back to the mounting yard, they stood and applauded. For me, it was massive.

'This meant more to me than winning the Melbourne Cup,' I said afterwards. 'It was a must-win. I had butterflies before the race but when I saw him bound into the yard, that was good enough for me. Racing can be a funny game, you've got to take the good with the bad. Today was a good day.'

I had also stuck it up Shane Dye. Tycoon Lil finished out of the placings. He'd said before the race that he was going to take it to Might And Power, and his mare would start Cox Plate favourite.

Now, after that performance, all the pressure was back on us in the Cox Plate. Might And Power was favourite in a race that has been won by all the greats: Phar Lap, Ajax, Rising Fast, Tulloch, Gunsynd, Dulcify, Kingston Town, Bonecrusher, Better Loosen Up, Super Impose, Octagonal and Saintly.

I'd come second on Filante in 1997 to Bart's Dane Ripper, who had Damien Oliver on board. It was the second year in a row that Filante had come second in the race. Despite several attempts, Jack also hadn't won a Cox Plate.

On the Wednesday before the race, I ran into the legendary George Moore in Sydney. George had been T.J. Smith's jockey for many years, winning nineteen times on the back of the great Tulloch. He'd won some of the biggest races in the world, including two Cox Plates. When he retired as a jockey, he went on to be a successful trainer in Hong Kong in the 1970s and 80s. What he didn't know about horses wasn't worth knowing.

I'd had a bit of luck with George over the years. I remember he owned a horse with Tony McSweeny that was trained by George's son Gary Moore. John O'Shea was the stable foreman at the time. The horse got lapped one day but I told George to get on him in his next start at Randwick. It came in from 80 to 1, to about 40 to 1, and the horse won easily.

O'Shea still laughs about it because I think he won a lot of the money.

'I'm riding a champion horse,' I said to George. 'You were a champion jockey. How would you ride him?'

'Just get him into a situation where he can put his legs down,' George said.

On Might And Power, that meant letting him lead, unlike the Caulfield Stakes when he was chasing Tycoon Lil.

Once again, Shane was doing all the talking about how he was going to outride me. I just kept quiet.

'If he's good enough, he should win,' was all I said to the press.

When I arrived at Moonee Valley, the track felt like it was a full house at the Melbourne Cricket Ground. There was about 40,000 packed into the place, with people hanging over the fence, but it felt like a 100,000. They were all there to see if Mighty could add the Cox Plate to his record and make it 'The Big Three' alongside the Caulfield and Melbourne Cups. He was the rockstar. Everyone loved him.

In the mounting yard before the race, I told Jack what I was going to do.

'I don't care how fast I go, I'm leading,' I said. 'If I lead, I'll win.'

Earlier in the day, I had won the Moonee Valley Vase over 2040 metres on Mossman for Clarry Conners. It was the same distance as the Cox Plate. I'd led on Mossman and broke the race record. But I knew Might And Power was 10 lengths better than him. *I'll lead on Mighty and smash the track record*, I thought.

Brian Martin called the race, and it is the call that stands out the most in my whole career:

Set . . . Racing! Tycoon Lil one of the first to break the line. She flew the gate.

Might And Power misses the start just a touch, and is caught three wide. Watch me here as I go around them. I just shove Shane out of the way and lead.

And Jimmy's going towards the front. He takes Might And Power to the lead, turning out of the straight. Might And Power about to cross in front of Tycoon Lil . . .

I'm trying to give him a rest now but Shane's laughing. He'd wanted us to go around him and that's what we had to do. We're doing all the work. They're stalking us every inch of the way.

But I'm not concerned. I know what I have underneath me.

J. Cassidy controls the Cox Plate at the halfway mark at the 1000-metre mark on Might And Power. He's out by two lengths. Tycoon Lil second . . .

We're halfway through and I am riding to break a minute. I know I have them all fucked. I killed them a year earlier in the two big cups by leading from barrier to post. I am going to do it the same way again.

They're filing up the 800 metres and Might And Power, the Horse of the Year in Australia, by two lengths to Tycoon Lil . . .

I'm riding him along, and Shane hasn't moved yet. I have a little look back . . .

Might And Power at the 500 metres. Tycoon Lil under pressure . . .

The mare is under the bat and I've got them all running. They're all chasing me. Good luck . . .

At the 400 metres Jimmy's calling on the big horse . . . Jimmy lets him go on the turn. It's Might And Power, two and three in front from Tycoon Lil. Northern Drake down the outside. Tycoon Lil can't go on. Might And Power in front. He's gonna get it! THE EARTH STARTS TO RUMBLE. Might And Power takes the Cox Plate!

What a call. What a run. I rose out of the saddle in the shadows of the post and punched the air.

Might And Power showed that day what an athlete he truly was, and the time he ran proved it. He won in 2 minutes 3.5 seconds. He beat the Cox Plate record, held by Saintly, the 1996 Melbourne Cup winner, by almost 2 seconds. That's about 14 lengths. Might And Power's record stood until Winx won the race virtually unchallenged seventeen years later.

He also became the first horse since Rising Fast in 1954 to win the Caulfield Cup, Melbourne Cup and Cox Plate in the space of twelve months.

As we came back to the mounting yard, the first thing I noticed was the crowd going mad. The scenes that day were incredible. I trotted him all the way to the top of the straight and they were going wild. As I came back, Nick Moriatis was running up the straight on the course proper, high-fiving everyone.

The media swarmed around me when I got off the horse.

'I've felt pressure over the last two weeks but I think I handle it better than most jockeys,' I said. 'I try to use it to my advantage. But the Cox Plate really was do-or-die for me. I couldn't afford to stuff it up. I rate that as probably my greatest ride. At the very least, it's on par with my two Melbourne Cups. I knew I was on the best horse and I went out there to dominate. They wanted to play stockcars early – but I played back.'

I had given it back to Shane Dye. I'd given it to him in both races. I had been too clever in both of them. I got around him in the Caulfield Stakes, then I shoved him out of the way in the Cox Plate.

'You did the talking early in the week – I did the riding today,' I said to Shane after the dust had settled.

He didn't have a comeback.

At the presentation, I was given a big bottle of champagne and I sprayed it all over the crowd like I was a racing car driver on the podium. It was gold.

Then something happened that nobody would've expected – Jack Denham spoke to the media. He hadn't spoken to the press for more than three decades.

'He just breaks their hearts and he nearly broke mine,' Jack said. 'All I can say is that it's nice to be here this time.'

And then he cried. Actually cried. I'd brought the legendary Jack Denham to tears. That was a proud moment for me, because he's had some champion jockeys riding for him but none had won him the Big Three – Caulfield Cup, Melbourne Cup and Cox Plate – and all on one horse.

But it would only shut Jack up for another five minutes, because I knew before long there would be something for him to moan about.

Without sounding arrogant, those rides on Might And Power also gave me so much confidence in my own ability. I have always prided myself on being a great reader of pace in any race, but particularly in the big-name staying races. A fast tempo can take a lot of horses out of play; a slow one can bring a lot into it. It's assessing form and knowing how a horse will behave. For instance, you might turn up and your horse could be off its head. You have to work out how you will get it to relax. You might have to be closer to the pace, striding freely, and trucking into it when you have to.

Reading pace is knowing how fast you're going. I can feel what gas I have in the tank. I've just got to use it at the right time. And if you've got a great horse underneath you, and there are other big races to win, you get them to win with the least exhaustion and stress possible, because you want to leave something in reserve.

It's also knowing the tempo of the horses around you. Again, that's all feel. You can't really teach it.

As soon as I got off Might And Power after the Cox Plate, I knew he was ready to take on the world. He needed an invitation to race in the $5.2 million Japan Cup, but it was going to be a formality.

Bart Cummings was the best judge in the world and he knew how good Might And Power was.

'He is world-class,' Bart said. 'It's just a matter of going to Japan and picking up the cheque.'

*

Two weeks after the Cox Plate win, Might And Power came out and won the VRC Queen Elizabeth Stakes at Flemington, carrying 60 kilograms. He could've gone to Japan, but in the end Jack and Nick decided to spell him instead.

In early 1999, disaster struck. He was two weeks away from making a return to racing when he suffered tendon trouble during trackwork at Rosehill. It was a shame he broke down – but it was only a matter of time before it happened. That's why Jack and Allan did a good job with him, just to keep him sound, because he was a high-maintenance horse. A horse with that manner was going to break down sooner or later.

He came back for two starts in the spring of 2000 at Rosehill as a seven-year-old, but he finished way back in the field both times and he was quickly retired.

I still see him around. He's become a prominent feature of the Melbourne Cup parade through the city streets each year. He can't help himself, always wanting to charge to the front and lead. He's still a monster, long into retirement.

In the lead-up to the Spring Carnival in 2015, there was a special function at the MCG. He was out there on the cricket ground. I went to walk up to him but the young female strapper stepped in.

'He doesn't really like blokes,' she said.

'He'll like me,' I said.

I stuck my hand out. Might And Power just put his nose down into my palm.

It will be hard when he's no longer around because he gave me so much joy. Whenever I see him, it takes me all the way back to that first day I won on him at Canterbury.

That's the best thing. I picked him out. I didn't ask someone to go find me a good horse – I found him.

Together, we made history.

13

Ring-A-Ding-Ding

A WEEK BEFORE THE CAULFIELD GUINEAS IN 1999, I contacted Paul Langmack.

Rugby league fans will know who he is. He was a Canterbury-Bankstown and Western Suburbs player in the 1980s and 1990s, and post-career has been a larger-than-life character. He had a segment on *The Footy Show* as 'Yesterday's Hero'. The nickname 'Hero' stuck even after Paul got punted from the show.

We first met in the mid-1990s, when he wanted me to sign a hundred posters to sell off as memorabilia. We've been mates ever since.

'Hero, I'm going to ride a great horse in the Caulfield Stakes,' I said. 'If I win, I need a saying.'

'Give me ten minutes,' he said, hanging up the phone.

Ten minutes later, he phoned back.

'I've got it,' he said. 'Ring-a-ding-ding, Pumper's the king!'

'You're a genius.'

The following autumn, I called him again.

'Hero, I need a new saying,' I said.

He needed another ten minutes before calling back.

'Clickety-clack, Pumper's back.'

'You're a genius.'

Then, heading into the following spring, I had more live chances in the big group races so I called him once more.

'Hero, I need another one.'

'How about this?' he said. 'Another group one, Pumper's not done.'

'Okay, I'll write that one down.'

Paul recalls the conversation that followed a few weeks later. 'I can't remember that last one,' I said. 'I'll have to go back to "Ring-a-ding-ding"!'

As I've written earlier in this book, Tommy Smith said if you're a public figure and you need to pay for publicity, you're a mug. I've always tried to be a little bit different to other jockeys and show the public my personality.

I know I'm not everyone's cup of tea and that's fine. But racing is about characters and personalities. They are few and far between. I've always liked being myself, having a laugh with the man on the street and the punter in general admission. They are my people, even if they sometimes abuse you from the other side of the fence because you haven't won on a favourite for them.

I didn't lose too many races on a horse called Redoute's Choice. Sired by the champion stallion Danehill, he was all class. He was every bit a freak as all the other freaks I have ridden. The colt was trained by Rick Hore-Lacy, who was a great Victorian trainer during his time. I had a bit of luck with Rick over the years and I respected his opinion. I'd like to think he respected mine.

So when I rode Redoute's Choice at his first start and the horse bolted in, I knew he had plenty of ability.

'This horse will be something, Rick,' I said.

He was set for the Blue Diamond Stakes – Victoria's richest two-year-old race, over 1200 metres at Caulfield – in February, but I couldn't ride him because I was already committed to David Hayes and his horse Real Jester. I knew there was only one horse that could win that race: Redoute's Choice. He went out and won by 2 lengths.

Come the spring of that year, I made sure that I was back on him.

The first task was the Manikato Stakes over 1200 metres at Moonee Valley, a prestigious Group 1 for the sprinters.

The problem was the horse would be weighted at 50.5 kilograms, which meant I had to get down to about 48 kilos to ride him. Rick told me a month out from the race that he wanted me for the ride. I was going down to Melbourne to win one race, and one race only. I set about making sure I stripped the weight off so it could happen.

The outsider doesn't see what a jockey goes through to make sure he or she can ride. To be good, you have to make sacrifices. And I sacrificed a lot. I missed a lot of things involving my kids and my family to do what I did in racing.

During my career, my main meal for the day would be two lettuce leaves full of cut-up beetroot, carrot, tomato, cucumber, avocado and spring onion. That was my dinner before I went to bed.

Sometimes I would wake up at 1 am and I would be hungry. Starving. But that made me hungry for Saturday.

For race day. That's when the hard work pays off, because I would be focused. That's what Boss taught me: you can't ride good being fat and sloppy. I wanted to be hungry, aggressive.

If my bowels and bladder weren't working like clockwork, my body wasn't working. So I had to be regular. If I was racing the next day, I'd have salad for dinner as usual. And then I'd have two Weetbix with skim milk, crushed in a bowl, and eat them just before I went to sleep because it would flush me out first thing in the morning. If I didn't have the cereal, the food I'd eaten wouldn't come out until later in the week – and that's too late when you're a jockey.

Wasting never worried me during my career. If I wanted to eat, I would. I just knew that I'd have to work harder to get it off. I knew that everything I put in, I would have to burn off. If I had five beers, I knew I had to sweat them out the next day. If I had a leg of lamb, I would have to work twice as hard.

I would've spent half my life in a sauna. There isn't a sauna in Sydney or Melbourne I wouldn't have been in.

I would often sauna on a Sunday for an hour while watching the footy on TV. Or I would sit in the spa at home and watch a movie, just to take my mind off it. When my brother Larry was living in Sydney, we'd sit in the sauna and play backgammon. And it was always much easier when Longy or Boss was around, because we could talk.

But if they weren't, I would heed Boss's advice and do something: jogging on the spot, shadow boxing, unders and overs, working out the sweat. Once my pores were open, I'd start rubbing, getting the fluid out. Keep active. Boss taught me that, too.

I never liked reading the form guide in the sauna like many jockeys because I would drip sweat all over the paper and then get a headache.

You have to be disciplined. You only feel weak if you want to feel weak. I'm not very big but I'm a tough little bastard when I want to be. I learnt that through Boss. When he was there, he'd make me eat because he knew we'd be punching the bag in the morning. He knew we'd train. He knew we'd be in the sauna.

'You can't train hard if you're not eating,' he would say.

It was a tough life, but it was all worth it. It got me a lot of Group 1 winners. It was also my income. It was a long, long time ago that I was kicked off a horse because I couldn't make the weight.

That's why I was always going to ride Redoute's Choice in the Manikato.

For a month, I lived on nothing but celery, lettuce and cucumber. I chopped it all up, put it in a bucket, soaked it in water, and that's all I ate.

The pay-off was Redoute's won the Manikato by a length-and-a-half. I put on 4 kilos that night, most of it in beer.

In the Group 1 Caulfield Guineas (1600 metres) later that spring, there were fourteen runners but there may as well have been just two: Redoute's Choice and Testa Rossa, who was being ridden by Damien Oliver.

Redoute's, who had beaten Testa Rossa by 2 lengths in the Blue Diamond earlier that year, went out as the $2.10 favourite. I jumped and led. I was going to take a sit but I thought, 'Nah. I'm on the favourite, I'll do my own thing.'

He hung off on the corner and Ollie was able to slip through. Instead of fighting him, I held off because I didn't want to be dragging him around the turn. I would lose more ground by fighting him.

Then Ollie got a good length on me and I started shitting myself. That's when I really had to get the horse to lift.

Racecaller Greg Miles called the race:

They reach the two hundred and Testa Rossa [is] sprinting very fast and has taken the lead over Redoute's Choice. Cassidy had to pull the whip . . .

I hit Redoute's Choice up the shoulder a few times. That's all he needed.

It's Testa Rossa clear, though. Redoute's Choice is coming again. Testa Rossa has to fight. REDOUTE'S DIGS! HE LUNGES . . . AND WINS! Redoute's Choice beats Testa Rossa . . . A magnificent Guineas . . .

Ring-a-ding-ding, Pumper's the king!

I got up in the last two strides. What a horse. I had to throw him over the line, but that's the type of brave finish he had in him.

The following year, Redoute's Choice was retired to stud. He stands at Arrowfield Stud in the Hunter Valley and since 2004 he has produced multiple Group 1 winners. Like his sire, Danehill, he has become one of the best stallions in the world.

I'm proud to know I helped him get there.

*

In early 1998, my marriage with Helen ended. It was an amicable split after sixteen years together. We will always be tied together because of our daughters, Nicole and Sarsha. The media had a field day about the divorce but these things happen in life.

They also happen for a reason, because I met Vicki at the dinner party of a mutual friend. Eight months after I moved out of home, Vick and I moved in together and we have been by each other's side ever since.

Later that year, I'd had enough of Sydney. There was a lot of concern about the state of racing in Sydney because of the smaller size of the fields.

When we decided to relocate to Melbourne, it made big news in *The Daily Telegraph*. The backpage headline read: 'WHY I QUIT: Cassidy says Sydney Racing dropped the bit'. This is what I said:

> The horses are better, the trainers offer more opportunities, I get on well with the owners and the crowds are bigger. Melbourne racing is booming. You only get out of racing what you put in and I think I'll get more out of being based in Melbourne.
>
> I have been riding well in Melbourne and I am now in a position to get rides from some of Australia's leading trainers such as Freedman, Hayes, Mayfield-Smith and Hore-Lacy.
>
> Melbourne racing is going from strength to strength. I know Sydney is the place to be with the Sydney 2000 Olympics but as far as racing is concerned I'd rather be in Melbourne. The fields in Sydney are small. Melbourne racing is going ahead and Sydney isn't.

There was a lot more to it than that. The win on Might And Power in the Cox Plate had healed some of the wounds with Jack Denham, but it was never the same again. I'd had my integrity questioned again over another matter. I just thought, 'Fuck them all. I'm out of here.'

We went to Melbourne for a few months and let the dust settle. I rode a few winners but we never liked living in Melbourne as much as we liked living in Sydney so we moved back.

I seemed to make enough headlines whenever I was in Melbourne anyway.

And there were none bigger – or more blown out of proportion – than the drama concerning my ride on Diatribe in the 2000 Melbourne Cup, and then the following year on Inaflury in the Caulfield Cup. If you look at my disciplinary record, you won't find either of these two rides mentioned, but they made plenty of headlines. And mud sticks, even when it's total bullshit.

Diatribe was trained by a legend of the turf – George Hanlon. He was one of those old-timers of the track who I had the utmost respect for. He was a Hall of Famer and a freak very much of the same mould as Bart Cummings when it came to horses that could stay. He got his horses to relax and then finish off. That's why George won three Melbourne Cups with Piping Lane (1972), Arwon (1978) and Black Knight (1984). I rode in my first Melbourne Cup on George's horse Amarant in 1982. In Diatribe, we had the potential to add to his tally.

In the autumn of that year, I got the horse home at 20 to 1 in the Rosehill Guineas over 2000 metres. He raced keen and was at the end of his campaign in the AJC Derby (2400 metres) and finished well back in the field, but he was going to be a sensation come the spring.

Darren Gauci rode him into third place in the Turnbull Stakes (2000 metres) at Flemington in early October, but I was given the ride on him in the Caulfield Cup.

It was a hoodoo race for George, just like the Golden Slipper was for me. He had finished second three times, with Arwon (1978), Our Sophia (1985) and Congressman (1988).

The Arwon loss hurt him the most. He was beaten in a photo finish by Taksan. A reporter said he could still win the Melbourne Cup that year.

'Do you think I didn't want to win the Caulfield Cup?' George shot back. 'An egg in the frying pan is worth two birds in the air.'

When it came to the 2000 Caulfield Cup, George knew as much as I did about what needed to happen. The horse was coming out of barrier 15. He was a backmarker. He didn't want to run on the pace. You had to get him to relax.

'I don't care if you have to go back to last,' George said as we mounted. 'Just get him to switch off.'

Then he left the rest to me. It would need a gun ride to get him home, and I was up for it. I wanted to win it for George.

As the horses were going to the barriers, George fell down some steps and cut his forehead badly. Remember, he was 83 years old at the time. There was all this drama unfolding in the mounting yard but I had no clue about what was happening.

After we jumped, I let the inside runners go ahead and I tucked Diatribe away on the fence, near the rear of the field.

Up front, they were going a hundred miles an hour. Fairway, the 5 to 1 favourite with Damien Oliver on board, led for much of the race. I never left the fence. I wasn't budging, trying to get Diatribe to relax.

At the 800 metres, they all started taking off. I was still buried inside, waiting, waiting, waiting . . .

PUMPER

Greg Miles called the race:

At the 500 metres now and it's Fairway again taking over the running. Fairway the leader from Camerina, and Hill Of Grace has charged through on the outside. They're clear of Pravda coming through . . .

I'm still on the fence, sneaking along the inside. Nobody sees me until the last minute.

Fairway and Hill Of Grace at the two-fifty. They're the two leaders. Diatribe on the rails now . . . One-fifty metres to go. DIATRIBE! DIATRIBE charges along on the inside and Fairway coming down the outside now. Kaapstad Way with a rattling run. But Diatribe is clear. Diatribe in front and Diatribe wins it. George has won it at last!

At last. Another trainer I've won it for *at last*. It was an amazing feeling. To do it for George and also myself, after all the drama that had happened since I won it back in 1997 on Might And Power for Jack Denham . . . No wonder I was emotional.

It was a great lesson in being patient and picking the right moment to make your run. But I had to thread the needle at the top of the straight to make sure I punched through and won.

I knew the horse had the gas. And I knew George had Diatribe right on the day. He really needed to win that Caulfield Cup, because at his age he wasn't going to get many more chances.

When I returned to the yard, it looked like someone had bashed George with a baseball bat. His head was covered in bandages. It was enormous to win the Caulfield Cup for a legend, because in my mind he was up there with Bart Cummings, Tommy Smith and Colin Hayes.

I wore black silks with a big silver fern splashed across the front that day. They were the colours of the owner, John Thompson. He wanted to lick my arse that day. But things were about to go very sour.

*

Diatribe was the second favourite ($7) behind Kaapstad Way ($5.50) heading into the Melbourne Cup. Given the way he finished in the Caulfield Cup, his only query was the 3200 metres. I had to squeeze every last bit out of him to win over 2400 metres at Caulfield. This was going to be a much harder assignment because of the extra distance.

But I knew George would prepare him perfectly. Diatribe was also reasonably weighted at 55 kilograms.

The barrier was also a big concern. Coming out of gate 14, I wanted to get in wherever I could to keep him out of trouble before settling midfield and making him relax.

When we jumped out of the barriers, he came out full of running. But then I was trapped out wide. I was trying to get back across to the fence, but there was nowhere to go. I had no option but to stay out wide. Having done so much work in the run, he had nothing left in the straight and he finished 13 lengths behind the winner, Brew, in eleventh position.

After the race, Thompson was going off in front of a lot of people. He accused me of not trying this and that, and ranted about how I should have found the rail.

I was thinking, *Did you watch the Melbourne Cup through a pair of Coke bottles?* I would've had to interfere with six or seven runners to get in, which could've caused a chain reaction and caused a horse to fall.

George was as disappointed as I was.

'I was in a situation where I could not get in, Boss,' I told him. I would have struck trouble and been pushed right back. I finished up parked three and four deep but with cover down the back and Diatribe relaxed pretty well. But they kept coming from inside me and pushing me wider. Getting towards the 800 metres there was a lot of trouble and I had to ease out further again. I just let him roll forward. He tracked up okay, and then he just plugged in the straight.

George seemed to understand that we didn't have any luck. He could read a race. He wasn't accusing me of anything.

It wasn't until the following Friday, when I was on my mate Michael Hibberd's boat in the middle of Port Phillip, and television helicopters started hovering above, that I got a feeling that something was wrong. Channels 7, 9 and 10 . . . They were all there, trying to track me down.

Then the phone rang. I was told that George, at the insistence of Thompson, had lodged a complaint about my ride.

I didn't understand what was going on. On Cup Day, the stewards had no issues with my ride and there was no inquiry about it whatsoever. But now I was being hauled before them on Thursday to explain the ride. I was filthy.

I spoke to Des Gleeson, the chief steward, and he was sympathetic towards me. He didn't need the drama and allegations about a jockey not trying to win on one of the favourites in the Melbourne Cup.

So I phoned George to find out what was going on. He said it was now in the hands of the stewards, but I got the impression that the owner had just stirred him up.

As for John Thompson, he wouldn't even take my calls.

Stuff this, I thought. When the TV networks came knocking, I was going to defend myself.

'I'm very hurt and disgusted with the whole way the thing has gone about,' I told Anthony Mithen from Channel 9. 'I've contacted Mr Hanlon – he did talk to me for a short time. Mr Thompson refused to take my phone calls. So, naturally, I'm very hurt. Every jockey that rides in the Melbourne Cup – including Jim Cassidy – goes out to win the Melbourne Cup.'

Channel 9 showed mounting yard vision before the race. You can hear Thompson say to me, with George standing right there next to him: 'Get him forward, Jim. He'll get up if he's good enough.' I reply, 'I'm happy. If he stays he wins, don't you worry.'

Thompson was then quoted in the media saying I had gone 'totally against instructions'.

The owner seemed to be the only one who didn't get it. *The Age* reporter spoke to another high-profile owner, John Cappellin, who had put $70,000 on the horse to win $500,000.

'I didn't think it was too bad, as far as I was concerned,' he said. 'Diatribe failed to run the 3200 metres in the Melbourne Cup. The Caulfield Cup is always the best form for the Melbourne Cup, but in hindsight it was probably only Jimmy's exceptional ride that won him the Caulfield Cup.'

At the inquiry, we all sat there and went through the video tape. George Hanlon spoke. Then John Thompson spoke. And then I spoke.

I got up with the pointer and said, 'Mr Gleeson, please. Can we stop the video here and can Mr Hanlon or Mr Thompson tell me where I should have got in?'

It was obvious that if I had moved in, I would've taken down a quarter of the field. Then I told Thompson, 'I don't give a fuck about your Melbourne Cup. I'm not going to kill one of my fellow riders, just because you want me there on the fence. I can't do that.'

In the end, I was cleared of any wrongdoing. I wasn't even questioned by the stewards. They were only following up on the owner's complaint. Thompson came out and made these ridiculous suggestions about jockeys in the future being given their riding instructions in writing, or via video, the night before the race. Maybe we could have mobile phones out there during the race, and he can phone us and tell us what to do. It showed how little he knew about racing.

The Diatribe drama definitely put a dampener on our success in the Caulfield Cup but I wasn't going to let the owner destroy my relationship with George.

George was great, a gentleman. It was just a drama he didn't need. He could read a race and knew about racing. We finished on a good note and this continued all the way until his death in 2010 at the age of 92.

But John Thompson left me high and dry. He said in the acceptance speech after I won the Caulfield Cup that he had reservations about using me again because of my ride in the AJC Derby. Who did this bloke think he was? I'd just won the toughest mile-and-a-half race in the world for him, and he was bagging me. What does that say about him?

I can tell you he was just one of those owners who didn't pay me for my services when it was all over.

A jockey gets a 5 per cent share of the prizemoney that the horse's connections win in any race. But sometimes they get another 5 per cent from the owners. It's declared money. It's not a sling. It doesn't happen in every race, but it does for the bigger ones. To get my services, that was the deal.

That was also the handshake deal I had with John Thompson in the Caulfield Cup but after what happened in the Melbourne Cup he didn't come through. That cost me plenty.

*

A year later, in the 2001 Caulfield Cup, I struck trouble on a mare called Inaflury, the $8 favourite. That caused more headlines than Diatribe, would you believe?

The Caulfield Cup is tricky because, as you head up the hill on the back straight, you don't want to get caught wide. The pace slackens and the chain reaction behind can end a horse's hopes. Inaflury settled at the tail but there was mayhem up front. Damien Oliver checked in front of me. Inaflury had to come out. I couldn't go in. If I hadn't come out, I would've clipped the heels of Oliver's horse in front of me, and then there would've been a catastrophe.

When she saw daylight, about halfway through the race, she took off on me. I couldn't stop her. She raced 4 lengths clear and eventually finished sixth. I was exhausted afterwards because I'd been trying to control her.

The owner, Danny Rose, blew up. Went on like a pork chop. So once again I was hauled into an inquiry at the insistence of the owner, but the stewards could see what was going on. There was no question about my ride. I was struggling to hold the horse the whole race. *Woooooo. Wooo. Fuck.* I changed grip several times, trying to stop her. It wasn't like I was kicking her to go. What am I meant to do?

The owner was unbelievably unreasonable. He threatened to sell up his horses and never be involved in racing again. After the inquiry, he opened up to *The Daily Telegraph*:

I'm not happy with the results and things said in there. I can't call this a kangaroo court – you couldn't do that could you? – but (the stewards panel) already had its mind made up . . . There is too much grey area for me. I'll sell the business and move on to something that you appreciate more, and that appreciates you more. I have 30 horses and I'll finish off the ones that are racing now.

If the owner was like that over Inaflury because she didn't win, what hope did he have in this game? Yes, the Caulfield Cup is a big race and he'd paid good money to get in the field. But that's just what happens in racing.

The trainer, Cliff Brown, also carried on like a pork chop. He couldn't have ridden a gate on a windy day, either.

In my view they were just sore losers. The horse was off its head before the race, the horse was off its head during the race, and the horse was off its head after the race. The clerk of the course had to pull the horse up at the end. She nearly hurdled the mounting yard fence when we got back. I don't know what she had for breakfast but I'd have loved a bucket full of it every week before I went to the races.

Once again, I was cleared of any wrongdoing. But once again the mud stuck.

Ken Callander wrote in *The Daily Telegraph*:

The trouble for Jim Cassidy is he is always trying to live down his past. The whispers, the innuendos, the accusations . . . They all surfaced again after The Pumper's ride on Inaflury in the Caulfield Cup . . . Unfortunately, the headlines create controversy and tarnish Cassidy's reputation; a reputation that has taken a pounding since the little fellow first arrived on our shores.

Here we go again. All this typical racecourse innuendo that a jockey has to cop. Go and watch someone at a pub or club in the TAB area. If the horse they back doesn't win, they screw up their ticket and accuse the jockey of pulling up the horse.

Would I spend that much time in the sauna, in the gym, sweating for hours, if I wanted to neck a horse? There were rumours going around that I was paid $3 million to pull up Diatribe in the Melbourne Cup. If I got paid that, I would've retired the next day. What a load of bullshit.

That's what makes my career so amazing, really. Because all the way along I've been accused of wrongdoing, whether it's big races or little races, and I was able to hang in there and stick it up them.

I was always putting horses into gaps when I shouldn't. I would be taking risks. I did it my whole life, but then you have to put up with this shit. John Thompson and Danny Rose showed exactly what they knew about horses when they complained about two incidents that sometimes just happen in racing.

They also make you appreciate the owners who you do treat you right.

People such as Tony and Frank Mittiga. They owned Gai Waterhouse's two-year-old Excellerator. They always wanted me on their horses. They were great owners to ride for because they were happy and fun. They took disappointments well. For them, it wasn't about the money but the enjoyment of racing.

There were other good owners, too. Ellio Galante, an owner from Western Australia, was freakish when it came to picking out winning horses. I struck up a relationship with a guy called Rob McNulty, and over the past few decades I've gone to Rob every time I've wanted to buy a horse.

Then there was the Muollos, Tony senior and junior, who were straight out of Wellington. I rode Hawkspur for them. I also rode a lot of good horses for Max Whitby, who owned Savabeel, which was trained by Graeme Rogerson. I also loved riding for Keith Biggs and Rod Russell. They met in the early 1990s at a long lunch. Rod showed Keith a valuable footy he had signed by the Hawthorn footballers from the 1989 premiership team. Keith accidentally kicked it onto the roof of a nearby building. They have been great mates since then.

Rod and Keith have been great owners to ride for over the years. Very loyal. The appreciation and joy they share with their friends is something special. You get close to owners like that. You see their kids grow up, and they see your kids grow up.

I first rode a winner for Keith in a fillies race at Canterbury in 1984, but the horse I had the most success with was Dignity Dancer. He won the 'Triple Crown' in Victoria as a three-year-old, taking out the Alister Clark Stakes (1600 metres) at Moonee Valley, the AAMI Classic (1800 metres) at Caulfield, and then the Australian Guineas (2000 metres) at Flemington.

When I rode him in the Classic at Caulfield, I was adjusting my stirrup iron as we went into the barrier. I didn't put the clip in the hole properly, and at the 100 metres when I was getting busy on him, my iron broke. I went to the line with one leg and still got there.

Keith and Rod had backed the horse to win the Triple Crown, which hadn't been done for many years. We celebrated long and hard after we won it.

Late in my career I also rode Sea Siren to victory for them in three Group 1's – the Doomben 10,000, the BTC Cup and the Manikato Stakes.

They were good punters and I told them two months before the Manikato to get on Sea Siren.

'She'll win, boys,' I said.

The boys kept chopping away, and she started $5.50 favourite. And then I won on her. Beautiful.

But with all the best owners the wins and losses didn't seem to matter. It's the relationships that matter more than anything in racing, and the success you can all have together.

For instance, Keith and Rod were part-owners in Doriemus. When they won the Melbourne Cup in 1995 with Doriemus ridden by Damien Oliver, I celebrated with them, drinking out of the gold cup. Two years later, after I had beaten Doriemus by a lip on Might And Power, we were all drinking out of mine.

They are the owners who make racing worthwhile.

14

The Odd Couple

AFTER WINNING THE SILVER SLIPPER AT ROSEHILL IN February 2001, I knew I had the horse to finally win the Golden Slipper. The horse was Excellerator, part-owned by Tony and Frank Mittiga.

I had the ride because the horse's regular jockey, Chris Munce, had been suspended. Chris had won the lucrative Magic Millions race for two-year-olds in early January on Excellerator but now I had slipped on board I didn't want to get off.

'He'll win the Slipper,' I said to the trainer, Gai Waterhouse, after the race at Rosehill.

'No, no,' said Gai. 'I'm not saying who's riding what just yet. But I've got you riding one of them.'

As the Golden Slipper neared, I was desperate to get on Excellerator's back – but Gai had other ideas. She wanted me to ride the horse that came second in the Silver Slipper.

'No, I have another one for you,' she said. 'You're on Ha Ha.'

That's why I don't call her Gai. I call her 'Mum'. I only call her Mum because she's like one. Well, she was to me. What Gai says goes. She's not just my mum around the track, but she's mum to almost everyone who comes in contact with her, especially those working for her. If you've got a sniffle, she'll turn up at trackwork the next day with a nasal spray or cough lollies. She's a hard, ruthless trainer. But she is everyone's mum at the same time.

Through all the years I've known her, riding for her or not riding for her, I would always play up to it.

'Gai, you look gorgeous today,' I'd tell her.

'Oh really?' she'd say.

We had our ups and down, too. But you could have a blue with her and she would bounce straight back.

'That's finished,' she would say. 'Come on, carry on.'

She doesn't hold a grudge. There aren't many like that in racing.

As I've explained, I first met Gai through her father, Tommy Smith, and over the years, from when I first started riding for her all the way through to when I finished, she took training to another level. She will always be the 'First Lady of Racing', no matter what anyone says or thinks of her.

Early into her career, in the early 1990s, she would throw me a bone here and there. She used me when she needed me. Before the 'Jockey Tapes' saga, Gai and her husband, Robbie Waterhouse, took me out to dinner and asked me if I wanted to be the number-one rider at Tulloch Lodge. I knocked it back. After how it all went sour at Nebo Lodge

under Brian Mayfield-Smith, I didn't want to be tied down
to a trainer again.

People have a lot of different opinions about the Water-
houses. I have never treated them any differently to anyone
else I know in racing. Why do you have to bow to people?
I came out of the same place as Gai, and Robbie, and you,
and anyone.

And we all end up in the same place – in the ground. What
you accumulate on the way in terms of wealth means nothing.
What you accumulate in pride and passion and honesty, you
can't buy. I've thought like that all along the way.

I've ridden for some wonderful trainers who are high profile,
and then some who don't have two bob to rub together. I'm
just out there doing my job, no matter who they are.

With Gai comes Robbie. He's been a colourful character
over the years, just like me. He's been *very* colourful, though.
Pretty much everyone – and not just Robbie but a lot of other
people in racing – has to realise that those in glass houses
shouldn't throw stones.

People say Gai is eccentric. I will say she's different, but
I like her. Most people in racing know that she's deaf in one
ear, although I find she's deaf when she wants to be.

'Gai, I've got a million dollars and I want to buy three
fillies,' you could tell her.

'Oh yes, when do you want to buy them?' she would
probably reply.

Every trainer is the same. They're deaf when you tell
them how you plan to ride a horse, but they have a lot to say
if you've given one a sore back.

I'll say one thing about Gai: I've seen her stop and talk to
anyone. At the track, she buzzes around because that is her

personality. It doesn't matter who they are: she will stop and talk to anyone who wants to talk to her.

'Gai! Gai!' strangers will shout from the other side of the fence at the races.

'One moment, I'm coming!' she'll say back.

And she will stop and talk to them. Not everyone in racing would do that.

But there is another one I know who will stop and talk to the punters, just like Gai. John Singleton will buy anyone a beer. I'd like to think I'm the same. It's not big-noting, it's just who we are.

Singo is a multi-millionaire who started off in advertising but now has business interests all over the place, and travels around in a helicopter. He started the Magic Millions yearling sale company with Gerry Harvey and Rob Ferguson, and has bred and raced horses for most of his life.

But he's just an everyday, knockabout bloke who doesn't act like he's anything special. You don't have to wait in line to talk to Singo.

Just like when I rode for Robert Sangster, I was never worried about riding for Singo. I was there to do a job. But it helps that he is a normal person. He enjoys life and he enjoys his racing. He's just fun to be around.

He is also one of the first people I would ever call for advice. He knew that I went bust and lost everything after 'Jockey Tapes'. He's been down and out and always fights back, too. That's why I listen to him.

In the lead-up to the 2001 Golden Slipper, I had a lot to listen to. Singo owned Ha Ha.

Gai and Singo: racing's odd couple.

*

The year before, Singo had already achieved what I had not: he'd won a Golden Slipper.

He did it with a filly called Belle du Jour, who was trained by Clarry Conners and also part-owned by former prime minister Bob Hawke. Singo had given Hawkey a 25 per cent share as a 70th birthday present.

The filly started at $10 on the fourth line of betting, missed the start by 2 lengths, but then reeled in Crowned Glory to win by a nose. Then Singo shouted the public bar for an hour, and the place went mad. The bar is now named in the horse's honour.

Winning the race didn't mean he wanted to win any less the following year. He had another great chance with another filly. We weren't really mates at that stage, but in the week before the race, he phoned me every second day to talk about Ha Ha. *How's she travelling? How's she working?*

I worked her on the Tuesday morning before the race. It was the first time I had been on her back. Until then, Brian York had been her regular rider. He had ridden her when she won a fillies' race at Canterbury earlier that autumn. Excellerator had won the colts race that day.

'The way she's going, I think she'll win, mate,' I told Singo after trackwork.

Gai had never won the race either, and now she had her best chance because she would have five runners: Excellerator ($4.25), Royal Courtship ($5), Spectatorial ($9), Ha Ha ($13) and Newquay ($101).

I wanted to win the race as much as anyone, though. I'd had no luck for so long when it came to the Golden Slipper.

In 1986, I should have won on Imperial Baron but Peter Cook flattened me on the corner – I practically had to put my hand on the ground to push myself back up, and finish third behind Bounding Away.

In 1987, I should have won on Marauding for Robert Sangster but chief steward Schreck had rubbed me out.

In 1988, Tommy Smith wanted me to ride Comely Girl for him.

'I've got a share in Comely Girl and Star Watch, but I want you to ride the filly,' T.J. squeaked.

Star Watch won. I came second.

In 1993, I was on Justice Prevails for John Hawkes, got poleaxed on the corner again, and came second to Lee Freedman's Bint Marscay.

Then came the Flying Spur disaster in 1995 when 'Jockey Tapes' broke the day before the race and I didn't know if I would ride again, let alone win a Golden Slipper.

It was my hoodoo race.

To win any race you need a trouble-free run. It's even more the case with the Golden Slipper. The race was a lot tougher to win back then than it is now. If one falls in the Slipper, six will fall. It will be carnage. The penalties dished out by the stewards are much tougher now, so the race is less helter-skelter than it used to be.

It comes back to the jockeys having some respect for life. Money can't bring a life back. And that's the one thing people have to realise: the money is getting bigger, the stakes are higher for owners, but it depends on the jockeys – not the stewards – to make sure everyone comes back safe. Don't take that risk for the percentage of a big payday, because you have to live with the consequences for the rest of your life – unless you're a ruthless prick. I wouldn't want that on my conscience, even if it was an accident.

Ha Ha came out of barrier 11, but as far as I was concerned I just wanted to keep her trouble-free. I didn't want to get into any argy-bargy trying to get in, and then trying to come out.

After we'd gone a couple of hundred metres, I was in a good spot – and yet I wasn't. I was three deep but I was racing with cover, smoking a pipe. From the 800 metres, I half gave her a squeeze and then, coming to the 700 metres, I just smoked into the race.

Ian Craig was calling for Sky Racing as the field fanned across the track:

Excellerator is coming into the picture now followed by Red Hannigan. Spectatorial joining in and Ha Ha on the outside. Here's Ha Ha in front, inside the 200. Ha Ha hits the front in front of Excellerator, Red Hannigan and Royal Courtship making a late bid . . . But it's Ha Ha in front! And Gai wins her first Slipper!

I sat three deep and still won. There I was thinking Excellerator would be the horse to beat, and Ha Ha beat him home by a length and a half.

In *The Sunday Telegraph* the following day, I wrote a column about how I did it:

Ha Ha settled beautifully for me in the barriers, and I just needed someone to stand her up for that last stride. She showed enough early speed and I was pushing forward but then Mistegic and Justin Sheehan came across and were going forward and I got into a flat spot.

I was trying then to settle two wide but I also had Glen Boss inside me and I was forced to settle three deep. But I didn't panic. I went woo, woo, woo. And she settled beautifully.

She is a real little professional. When she relaxed I thought, 'Don't panic'. Coming to the turn I kept her in a holding pattern. I kept saying to myself, 'Don't panic'.

I have wanted to win this race for so long. So I waited until straightening before making my move. I counted to 10 but 10 came up pretty quickly. It was two, four, six, eight . . . So then I counted again.

I have ridden in enough big races not to get that rush of blood but it can happen. When I straightened up I knew I would be hard to beat, despite being wide.

That's how you win races – when you can sit three wide, stay relaxed and hit the line.

That's magic.

When I came back to the enclosure, the joint was going off. Singo picked me up and put me on his shoulders and then nearly dropped me over the fence. He shouted the bar again, just as he had done the year before. People were running in from everywhere to get a drink.

The stewards called me in because I had waved my whip around before I went over the finish line. That type of early celebration is against the rules of racing. I was fined $200.

'That was for John Schreck,' I told the stewards, referring to what happened six years earlier with Flying Spur.

That Golden Slipper set Gai on the path to win the race six times – the same amount as her father, Tommy. It was the only one I would win, but that was enough.

*

Later that night, I celebrated with Malcolm. As the night went on, I pulled Vicki aside, took the ring off the VB can I was drinking, and asked her to marry me. I'm all class.

A crowd of 40,000 packed into Moonee Valley on 25 October 1998 to see if Mighty could win the WS Cox Plate. To me it felt like 100,000 at the MCG. He led from start to finish, saw off all the challengers, and when he came down the straight it was – according to racecaller Brian Martin – 'the day the Earth rumbled'. I get goosebumps every time I think about it.

Terry Phelan/Newspix

TOP LEFT: The champion stallion Redoute's Choice ... I ate lettuce for a month to ride him at 50.5kg in the Manikato Stakes over 1200 metres at Moonee Valley. I won – and then put four kilos on that night in beer.

Marc McCormack/Newspix

LEFT: You can only hold a grudge for so long, but I never forget. With Shane Dye (left) and Darren Beadman (right) at the Jockeys lunch before the 2000 Golden Slipper.

News Ltd/Newspix

Craig Borrow/Newspix

ABOVE LEFT: The First Lady of Racing. Gai Waterhouse and I had our ups and downs, but I've never seen someone do more to publicise the sport – except for me!

ABOVE RIGHT: I treat people like they treat me. Tony Mokbel treated me well. I didn't know him as the gangster on the run wearing a wig. To me, he was a knockabout bloke who loved a bet.

Darren McNamara/Getty Images

ABOVE & RIGHT: Legendary trainer George Hanlon had come second in the Caulfield Cup three times. In 2000, he had possibly his last chance with Diatribe. In the run, I waited, waited, waited ... and then exploded in the straight to win. When I came back to the mounting yard, we both cried.

Darrin Braybrook/Getty Images

Sean Garnsworthy/Getty Images

LEFT: Damien Oliver is a good mate and a champion jockey. The media would build up our race to The Hundred, but I knew I'd get there before Ollie.

Jim Cassidy

After finally winning the Golden Slipper in 2001, I pulled Vicki aside, took the ring off the VB can I was drinking, and asked her to marry me. I'm all class. We were married on 23 March 2003.

Phil Hillyard / Newspix

Jay Town/Newspix

ABOVE RIGHT: When my youngest daughter Piper pretended to be a jockey coming out of the barriers, she was Chris Munce! But she's always been The Pumper's little princess.

ABOVE LEFT: Larry Cassidy is my brother, but he was also my competitor. When this photo was taken, we were riding both the favourites to win in the 2006 Golden Slipper.

Pat Scala/Fairfax

Nine years after we won the Cup together, Might And Power and I got reacquainted at the Living Legends farm outside Melbourne. A female strapper told me: 'He doesn't like men.' But he still loved me.

ABOVE: Clickety-clack, the Pumper and Bart are back! Winning the 2009 AJC Derby for Bart Cummings on Roman Emperor – 'That was an absolute gem,' Bart told me.

RIGHT: At the Derby presentation, I stood alongside Bart and David Jones ambassador Megan Gale. Bart told me to put my arm around her. She's 180 cm. I'm 150. Can you imagine how that would have gone?

Mark Evans/Newspix

Steve Hart Photographics

Steve Christo/Fairfax

LEFT: Malcolm 'Boss' Ayoub put hot blood in my veins. He's old school, and I never questioned his methods. Here, we work in the steam room at Randwick RSL during the 2009 Sydney Autumn Carnival.

RIGHT: In 2010 with Blue and Francie, my parents, who told me anything was possible.

Jim Cassidy

Michael Dodge/Getty Images

LEFT: Singo tried to kick me off Dear Demi before the 2012 VRC Oaks. Luckily, I stayed on: I won for him and trainer Clarry Conners, who was all smiles after the race.

Saunas. Salads. Starvation. It felt like I spent my career on the scales. It was hard work but if I didn't believe I was one of the best, I wouldn't have done it.

ABOVE & BELOW LEFT: When I got on the back of Zoustar on Derby Day in 2013, he had already been sold for $20 million. I didn't care: I was trying to become only the third jockey in history to reach one hundred Group 1 wins. It felt good to finally get the monkey off my back.

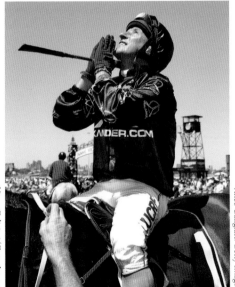

BELOW RIGHT: Chaired off by Chris Waller and co. after breaking The Hundred on Zoustar at Flemington.

ABOVE LEFT: You can never have enough …

ABOVE RIGHT: When I rode against Ron Quinton as a young bloke, I always followed wherever he went – Ron knew where the runs would be. Here we're celebrating my 100th Group 1 win on Zoustar two weeks prior.

The glamour couple about to step out at the New Zealand Hall of Fame awards when I was inducted in 2014.

Vicki Cassidy

Vicki Cassidy

ABOVE LEFT: 'Bruce Lee on the back of a horse.' That's what Longy would call me anyway.

ABOVE RIGHT AND BELOW: Tragedy struck our family in April 2015 when Vicki's beautiful sister Marian died suddenly at the age of 37. As I walked out the door to ride Dissident in the All Aged Stakes, little Piper hugged me and said: 'I hope you win today for Aunty Marian.' I did – my last Group 1 win.

Anthony Johnson/Getty Images

In 2014 I couldn't get a ride on day one of The Championships at Randwick. A week later, I was given the chance on Grand Marshal at 30 to 1 in the Sydney Cup and showed them all The Pumper still had it.

My last Melbourne Cup on Grand Marshal. Frankie Dettori tried to kill me but I've always been a survivor. We finished 21st.

I've enjoyed being the elder statesman of the jockeys' room over the years. It meant a lot to me when they formed a guard of honour before my last race on Oaks Day at Flemington in 2015.

Being showered in good champagne by my mate Glen Boss was not a bad way to farewell the jockey's life.

ABOVE LEFT: The stewards haven't been my best mates over the years. But, in retirement, I'm happy to have a beer with Greg Rudolph and Ray Murrihy.
ABOVE RIGHT: There's been many bosses in my life, but there's one at the top of the list.

ABOVE LEFT: With Vicki and our darling daughter Piper.

RIGHT: Few trainers have stuck with me as much as Graeme Rogerson. Here we are with his wife Debbie.

Jim Cassidy

Jim Cassidy

ABOVE LEFT: Luckily, Piper gets her good looks from her mum.

ABOVE RIGHT: With my dad 'Blue' just before he went into hospital with pancreatic cancer. He fought hard, just like he always taught me. We lost him in June 2016.

Kath Ellis Photography

My whole reason for living, and more important than any Group 1 victory. From left: Nicole, Vicki, Sarsha and Piper.

I've lifted many trophies and been named in the New Zealand and Australian Racing Halls of Fame. But receiving a Legends award at the Hutt Valley Sports Awards after I retired meant the most. Because that's where it all started.

Before that, and then long after, she has been my backbone. I've been lucky that I've had Vicki, Longy and Malcolm in my corner.

The thing that struck me about Vick from the moment I met her was that she didn't care about any of the bullshit that goes hand-in-hand with racing. She told me straight-away that she wasn't big on going to the track.

'You're not going to miss much by not going,' I told her. 'All they will want to know is who made your dress, how much your earrings are worth.'

She's always in the background. Many wives go to the races and want to have their pictures taken for the papers the next day. Not Vick. She's not into the bullshit, the glitz and the glamour. She's been to the races about ten times in her whole life. She'd rather sit at home and watch. She tapes everything, and when I get back from the track we'll watch it together.

Vick prefers to be at home and have everything ready for me when I return. That wasn't the case once or twice, that was every race meeting. And if I had people coming home with me, she had dinner ready for them as well. It was the same when I got up in the morning to ride trackwork: my coffee would be made and my clothes would be laid out. It was like that for decades. She never, ever changes.

Vicki isn't just my wife or my partner but my best friend. I suppose it's hard to love someone that much and also be their best friend, but that's how it is with us. We do everything together. We go everywhere together. If we head out together for a night out, we go home together. Very seldom would I stay out without her.

I'm not making her out to be a saint, but there's nothing she can't do. I've been wild over the years, but she's mellowed me like nobody else ever could.

I've never seen her have a blue with anyone. Which is nice, because I've had plenty of them.

Vicki has brought me many things in my life, but she delivered the most important thing a few years after we were married – another daughter for me, in the form of Piper. And she is as perfect as her mother.

*

Things got humming after that. I landed a few nice rides for Gai and we had a bit of luck in races big and small.

A year after winning the Slipper on Ha Ha, I got back on Excellerator and won the Cameron Handicap and then the Group 1 Epsom Handicap. At around the same time, I won the Group 1 Spring Champion Stakes at Randwick on Platinum Scissors, and then we went to Melbourne and won the Caulfield Classic (which used to be called the Norman Robinson Stakes). In South Australia I won the Oaks on Tempest Morn. I also won the Flight Stakes at Randwick for three-year-old fillies with Lotteria a few years after that.

We didn't always get it right. Carnegie Express was the short-priced favourite heading into the AJC Derby after I had won the Canterbury Guineas on him. If I had been allowed to do my own thing, he would've pissed in. Instead, Gai and Robbie wanted me going forward at the 700 metres. He probably wasn't a 2400-metre horse like the other colt, Don Eduardo, which won by a nose.

When I came back to the enclosure, the punters gave it to me.

'Call in Jimmy,' Ray Murrihy said. 'We'll have a chat.'

In the stewards' room, I explained what happened.

'Larry kept coming back into my lap,' I said.

I was referring to my brother, on the 100 to 1 shot My Tally, who was cramping me in the run. I had to take the horse out and around him.

'If he'd won by half a head, I'd be a genius,' I said as I left the room.

No action was taken.

We all got it wrong that day, because I was prepared to do exactly what Gai and Robbie instructed. I copped a shitload over that ride. She wasn't happy he got beat, but it was her tactics. The owners of the horse transferred to another trainer soon after.

But there were a lot of good times with Gai. Great times. A lot of tough times too. I used to joke that I'm the only one who's old enough to be her boyfriend. She used to try to give it to me. Not in a disrespectful way. I just wasn't prepared to let her control me. I wasn't going to be spoken to aggressively.

We had our ups and downs over the years, but I could say that about almost every owner and trainer I've ridden for. Usually, I've been able to get back into a working rhythm with them again. That's where respect comes. They do their job well, and I do mine.

Gai's mellowed, too. We've always got back together, somewhere along the line.

That said, we didn't speak for about six years over a ride on a horse called Havana Wind in the mid-2000s. Gai and Robbie absolutely baked me afterwards. They basically accused me of not trying on the horse.

I'd jumped off a horse of Graeme Rogerson's to ride this thing of Gai's. The horse of Rogey's was coming out of its preparation, and Gai's horse was coming into it. I led on

Gai's horse and it got beat. She accused me of going too fast and setting up the race for another runner.

I was furious, because I had done nothing wrong. I took great exception to it because I didn't need someone with her profile caning me when her horse needed another run or two.

So I forced the issue, and took her into the stewards and we had it out. We went hell for leather, toe-to-toe. They were accusing me of not giving the horse every chance to win, and I was more than prepared to defend myself over that because I had heard the same rubbish for most of my career.

I want to make it clear that I was the one who pursued it. This time, it wasn't me being questioned – I was questioning her. To me, this was a betrayal. It was totally unfair.

As I remember it, it was very heated, because Gai had a lawyer there and I wasn't having a bar of it.

'She can't say anything, because it's not that sort of inquiry,' I said. 'You're levelling allegations at me. I'm here to find out why you are saying it. Because it's not fair.'

Ray Murrihy was great. I was getting a bit shitty, as I do, because they were trying to cut me up and I didn't deserve it, but he nursed me through it.

In the wash-up, Gai and I went separate ways. I didn't need Gai then. I didn't need anyone. If they wanted me, they wanted me. If they didn't, I didn't give a fuck. I wasn't going to be humiliated and degraded when I was in the right.

Despite all this, we were civil to each other at the races. Even when we weren't talking, we wouldn't disrespect each other. We'd say hello and that was it.

Then, six years after the blow-up, Singo called me. He needed a jockey for the Group 2 Tea Rose Stakes over 1500 metres at Rosehill.

'I want you to ride More Strawberries for me this Saturday,' he said.

'Mum won't put me on that,' I laughed.

Singo laughed back. He loved it when I called her 'Mum'.

'I fucking own it!' he barked. 'You're riding it.'

'Okay, well you work it out with Mum and I'll ride it.'

That Saturday, I was coming out of the jockeys' room at Rosehill and she was coming out of the bathroom. I was just going to keep walking past her and talk to her out in the mounting yard in front of Singo, but she pulled me aside.

'I need to have a talk to you,' Gai said. 'What are we going to do out there? What are we going to say?'

'I'm not going to say anything.'

'How are we going to ride it?'

I just kept walking, sort of brushing her off. I hadn't ridden for her for six years. I wasn't going to pretend that nothing had happened.

We got out into the mounting yard, and she got out her notes.

'What are we going to do?' she asked Singo.

'Where's Jimmy?' asked Singo. Then he turned to me and said, 'What are we going to do, Jimmy?'

'I want to lead,' I said.

'Okay, you're leading. Can it win?' Singo said.

'It can win,' I said.

'Well, I'm having $5000 the win on it for your percentage if it does.'

Gai nearly choked.

'Great, Singo,' I said. 'What price can we get?'

It was $4.60. Sure enough, *bang!* We won. I high-fived Singo when I came back to the mounting yard.

'Thanks, buddy!' he said.

He paid me the next day. I wish every owner was like that.

'Thank you, Gai, the wait was worth it,' I told the reporters at the track after the race. 'They had the chance to beat me but my filly was just too good.'

'A masterly ride on an outstanding filly,' Gai said. 'He controlled the race and turned it into a sprint home.'

'I pushed for Jim Cassidy to ride the filly and he got the job done – us old blokes are hard to beat,' Singo said.

Murrihy was actually laughing. 'The old team's back,' he said.

The last time he had seen us together we were going at each other in front of him.

I never held a grudge against Gai. Whatever I said about her, I would've said to her face. The thing about racing is that everyone has an opinion. All those trainers have an opinion. All those owners have an opinion. They all have a comment, and they all have a snipe. You would leave the trainers' hut in the middle of Randwick some trackwork mornings and you could feel the knives digging into your back. It's just the makeup of people in racing.

But Gai is great for the game. She promotes it for the rich and famous, and she promotes it for the battlers. She was at the top of the tree against the men for a long, long time.

And she will be around for a long time to come. She's not gone.

*

From the moment I won the Golden Slipper on Ha Ha, Singo has been loyal to me. I haven't always ridden his horses for him – he's used other jockeys too – but we have had much success together.

That doesn't mean we haven't had our fallouts. Heading into the Spring Carnival in Melbourne in 2012, he had a good, honest filly in Dear Demi, who was trained by Clarry Conners. She was being set for the VRC Oaks at Flemington, but after my ride on her in the Wakeful Stakes five days earlier I seemed certain to get flicked.

I had no luck in the run. I couldn't go anywhere. I went the whole length of the straight at Flemington, trying to get a split, but I couldn't find one. I didn't really do anything wrong. But Singo was crying afterwards. I had to get the hankies out for him.

He wanted to sack me straight after the race.

'Good luck,' I said and stormed off.

I phoned him the next day.

'I'm riding that filly,' I said. 'She'll win the Oaks.'

'Win the Oaks?' he laughed. 'Bullshit she will.'

Singo said he'd booked Nash Rawiller to ride in the Oaks, but I said, 'No, I'm riding Dear Demi.' So I did.

'Now, I want you to ride her like Kiwi,' Singo told me before the race.

I just laughed.

'That's how I'm riding it: back last and come late. It will win. See you later.'

Dear Demi won and Singo got $600,000.

'I forgive ya,' Singo said, hugging me.

Then he told the reporters: 'I told him to ride it like Kiwi. I told him. I fixed everything from the week before.'

That's Singo. That's the best thing about him. He told me how to ride it. The only thing he didn't do was ride it for me. He's always great fun.

Six months later, we were trying to win the AJC Oaks at Randwick over 2400 metres. I tried to go forward but I couldn't. At the turn, Royal Descent, with Nash riding, was second last and inside me. He had me eight deep going into the straight.

'Go in!' I yelled at him. 'Get on the fucking track!'

Nash went straight back to the fence at the 2000 metres and won the race by 10 lengths. I finished second.

Singo's racing manager, Duncan Grimley, agreed I did nothing wrong, but Clarry abused me when I came back to the mounting yard, calling me every name under the sun.

I said a few choice words back to him.

After the meeting as I was leaving the course in my car, I phoned Duncan. If you get a spray from Duncan, you know you've made a mistake. That's not his style. He's more likely to just walk up to you, laugh and say, 'Jesus, you fucked that up.'

'Duncan, are these blokes for real?' I asked.

He told me to brush it off. But I couldn't.

When I got home, I phoned Clarry.

'Mate, I'm sorry for abusing you,' I said. 'You're not apologising to me, because you would've rung me by now. But I'm ringing you because I abused you. I'm sorry because I like you as a mate and a trainer.'

Next day, we were as good as gold. So was Singo.

People outside of racing might think that this is very dramatic, but that's what the industry is like. There is so much at stake, and it involves so many passionate people from different walks of life that arguments and fallouts will happen. Sometimes the bridges are mended and sometimes they're burnt.

THE ODD COUPLE

One of the most memorable bust-ups was between Singo and Gai, the odd couple. The More Joyous affair was basically a fallout between the owner and the trainer over the health of the horse heading into the All Aged Stakes at Randwick. The media, and stewards, all got involved.

That whole thing was strange for me because they are two prominent people in my life. So I just stayed out of it. I didn't make a comment, I didn't discuss it with Singo, I didn't discuss it with Gai, because it was none of my business.

That's how I am: if it's not my business, I don't interfere. If it's not your business, don't interfere in mine.

I've got enough battles of my own to fight. And Gai and Singo ended up getting back together anyway.

15

Mokbel

THE SPRING CARNIVAL IN MELBOURNE IS RACING'S VERSION of the footy finals. It goes on for the best part of two months, and the Melbourne Cup is the grand final.

All roads lead to Crown Casino at most times of the year, but none more so than during the Spring Carnival. It is where you will find almost everyone in racing, from trainers, jockeys, owners, strappers and handlers, to media personalities, bookies and punters.

It's also where I met Tony Mokbel during the early 1990s.

People hear that name and think the worst. They think of the television series *Underbelly* and all the headlines that came with his arrest in the mid-2000s. I never knew that Tony Mokbel. I only know the bloke with the big, beautiful Lebanese family who was always great fun to be around, whether it was at the races or mostly at the casino. He was a big punter but also a prominent owner of horses.

I will say it right now: he was a person I respected and got along with. We were never best mates, but whenever I came to Melbourne in the spring he was someone who was always great company.

I didn't know him as the man on the run in Greece wearing a wig. To me, he was just a knockabout bloke who loved a bet, who would go to races. He had a really jovial personality.

I never went to Tony's home. I didn't even know where it was. But his family had a place out towards Tulla-marine Airport, and they would ask me to come to lunch every Sunday during the spring. We'd have a big Lebanese barbecue, with homemade lemonade. They were a lovely family, and they were all good to me. Sometimes, Tony wasn't even there but I'd still visit the family.

The whole gang who hung out with Tony were also great to be around. They were referred to as 'the tracksuit gang' in the media. When I knew them, a lot of them had track-suits on. But that doesn't mean you've done anything wrong, does it?

They were good days. They were also enormous fun. I didn't know what Tony did in his life away from racing, but the man I got to know was a good one.

And everyone loved being around Tony. It wasn't just me who was in his company. There were lots of leading trainers, owners and jockeys who hung around him. We were all at different functions together.

If Tony was at the casino, he shouted everyone. There were a couple of times when he did give me money, but that was when I'd lost money at the tables. He helped me out. He helped everybody out.

People out there will say I should be careful who I associate with. I understand that. But as I've said already in this book, I treat people as they treat me. I don't ask them about their background. It's no different with Victor Spink or George Freeman or whoever I've met through racing.

In racing, I've found those people and they've found me, always by chance. I hung around the same type of people in New Zealand, too. That's what racing is: all these different walks of life, different people, and you gravitate to some and leave others alone.

The Tony Mokbel that I knew was no different to me. When I had money, I spent it. When he had money, he spent it. If I had it, I would give it to others to have a bet with and keep the party going. He was the same.

What I can't cop is the hypocrisy in racing. You can't tell me every person you mix with is squeaky-clean. There's always someone leaking something, and every time something was leaked about Tony Mokbel, I always seemed to be right in the thick of it, and it always seemed to be around the time of the Spring Carnival.

On 25 October 2001, a story was published in Melbourne's *The Age* under the headline: 'Tapes link jockeys to drug syndicate'. The story by John Silvester read:

> A group of Australia's best-known jockeys have become embroiled in a police investigation after their conversations with the alleged head of a drug syndicate was secretly recorded by Victorian detectives.
>
> The jockeys were taped providing the drug suspect with inside information on racing. The man has a reputation as being one of Australia's biggest punters.

Racing Victoria stewards have launched an inquiry into the relationship between the man and at least seven jockeys and trainers.

Chief steward Des Gleeson said: 'We have interviewed a number of licensed persons, some on more than one occasion, because of information we have received into their possible relationship with this man. But we can't take it any further at this stage.'

That was the stupid thing about it all. There was nothing further to it. And they hadn't just then launched an investigation, because Gleeson and the stewards had already spoken to the jockeys about it months before. But here it was, splashed all over the newspaper, right on the eve of the Melbourne Cup Carnival.

Straightaway it was written up as 'Jockey Tapes Mark II'. All the fingers, as usual, were pointed at me. I was riding at Geelong on the day the story came out, and all the media converged.

Within a day the story was put to bed because the so-called investigation by the stewards had actually ended weeks before. The story in the *Herald-Sun* read:

Controversial jockey Jim Cassidy yesterday said he did not know if he was recorded on secret police tapes during a major drug investigation.

Cassidy, who is not a suspect in the investigation, would not say if he knew the alleged drug baron who was the principal target of police.

Victoria Racing Club chief steward Des Gleeson said a stewards' investigation of alleged links between jockeys and 'certain persons' had finished.

Mr Gleeson said no evidence had been found of any impropriety or breach of the rules of racing.

Cassidy was one of several jockeys under scrutiny by stewards.

He said yesterday he did not know if he been recorded talking to alleged drug trafficker Antonios (Tony) Mokbel on telephone intercept tapes during a police investigation called Operation Kayak.

'I don't know if I'm on those tapes,' Cassidy said.

He refused to say whether he knew Mr Mokbel.

'I'm not going to say I do know him, I'm not going to say I don't know him,' Cassidy said before riding at Geelong yesterday.

Fuck them.

Why did I have to tell the media whether I knew Tony Mokbel or not? It was none of their business, because there hadn't been any wrongdoing. It wasn't like I was in touch with him every day of the week anyway. The times that I was around him, whether it was lunch or dinner, we weren't hiding away. I didn't know him as an underworld figure. We talked about all sorts of things, including racing.

So the whole insinuation was that I was giving him tips. It was a hundred per cent because of 'Jockey Tapes'. The media just kept throwing it back at me. There was no escape from it. It followed me my whole career. Even when I do guest speaking now, it comes up in one way or another.

There were all those other jockeys hanging around with Tony too. I don't know if they were ever accused of the same things that I was, but it was never printed if they were.

The only other person who seemed to receive scrutiny was Danny Nikolic.

Danny's had many ups and downs, but I got on really well with him over the years. I never had any trouble with Danny. I respected him as a rider and I had dinner with him a few times. I wasn't his best mate but I had respect for him. He was a good, tough competitor. And a good jockey.

In an interview with *Four Corners* in 2012, Gleeson was asked by Nick McKenzie if he had warned me and Danny about associating with Tony:

> Gleeson: We spoke to quite a number of licensed persons, not only jockeys, trainers as well, and advised them to be careful with who they associated with.
>
> McKenzie: Do you think Mokbel was getting inside mail from jockeys?
>
> Gleeson: No, I don't think so. Mr Mokbel won money, he lost money. He was a big player but he wasn't always successful. He lost huge amounts of money from time to time and I think he was an impulse punter as well. But we've no evidence that he was getting information from jockeys, no.

From 2001 onwards, I got hammered all the way because I had known Tony Mokbel.

In 2006, I sat down with Trevor Grant from the *Herald-Sun* a few days before the Caulfield Guineas. We talked about all sorts of stuff about racing, but when he wanted to talk about Tony, I just steered clear of it.

'Mate, I'm not getting into that,' I said. 'I don't see the bloke. I have nothing to do with him. Yes, he was a friend of mine. I've got nothing but respect for him.'

On the day of the meeting, I was all over the front page of the *Herald-Sun*. The headline was: 'MY MATE MOKBEL'.

Trevor Grant, you're a dog.

That bloke just hung me. He had said he wanted to do a story about me, but instead I was all over the front page and making headlines and trouble for myself. All this unnecessary drama, making it look like I had brought racing into disrepute again because of my association with Tony.

As soon as I walked into the racecourse, the stewards pulled me in.

'What's this?!' said Gleeson.

'Hang on a minute,' I said. 'I don't write the headlines.'

I had two rides for Mick Price that day. I couldn't get out of the course quick enough when the meeting was over. From that moment on, those types of stories just made it harder and harder for me to get rides.

If I look back, all this shit over the years cost me so much. People such as Singo, George Costi and the Mittigas kept me going. But other owners and studs dropped off because they thought, 'You're a rorter. You're pulling them up. You're not trying on them.' Please.

Soon after that story, Lee Freedman tried to stick it up me a few times when he spoke at functions. 'He'd be out mowing Tony's lawns,' he supposedly said of me. I had a good laugh because I'd seen Lee in Tony's company a few times.

In fact, I'd seen half the Melbourne racing crowd with Tony. Most of the jockeys knew him but it was always me who was reported as being his best mate. I never raised their names with the stewards or the media. I'm not a rat. I don't go talking about someone else's business. I don't dob people in.

They've done nothing wrong to me, so why should I do something wrong to them?

The same could be said of Eddie Hayson, the big Sydney punter and horse owner who was also a colourful character.

I found Eddie to be a great owner. I never had a problem with him. I loved riding for him. I had a lot of success on a horse called Wanted, which he part-owned with Gary and Gayle Johns, the parents of rugby league stars Andrew and Matthew.

I was also hauled before the stewards after I rode a horse called Interfere, which was trained by Tim Martin, to victory at Rosehill in May 2006.

The horse was well backed and the stewards thought something was smelly about the whole thing, because I led from start to finish.

'I'm normally in here for not winning on one,' I told the inquiry. 'I'm in here now for winning on one.'

I remember Murrihy asked me if I knew what the horses were doing behind me.

'When you give me a helmet with rear-vision mirrors on [it], I'll be able to tell you what they're doing behind me,' I said. 'When I'm in front, it's a bit hard to tell.'

Nothing ever came of the whole thing – just like nothing ever came out of my relationship with Tony.

In 2007, I was summoned to appear before the Australian Crime Commission. They looked at all my phone records. They looked through my bank accounts. They had photos of me with Tony. Photos at his mum and dad's place, arriving and leaving. They wanted to know if I knew anything, or if I was doing anything illegal. If there was something illegal in having lunches and dinners and drinking alcohol and having fun with someone, then I was guilty of that. I hadn't really seen Tony since 2001.

In the end, the crime commission just dropped off. I was never charged. But, sooner or later, something was written and it was all brought up again. They'd wait for a year or two, and then they'd start on me again.

In June 2008, another story ran in *The Age* by Nick McKenzie, who seemed to be after me at every turn:

> One of Australia's leading jockeys, Jimmy Cassidy, accepted bundles of cash from alleged crime boss Tony Mokbel in return for tips about horses he was riding.
>
> Cassidy, a Sydney jockey who has won the Melbourne Cup twice, accepted more than $50,000 from the alleged crime boss in return for a number of winning tips given from 1997 onwards.
>
> An *Age* investigation has found that Mokbel laundered millions of dollars through Australia's racing industry, while paying a small number of jockeys and trainers for tips in an effort to improve his betting odds. Jockeys and trainers are banned from tipping in return for money.

Bundles of cash? That will do me. I would not be so fucking stupid as to start taking $50,000 off Tony Mokbel. He did give me money. If he won at the casino, he'd give me some money to have a bet. But that was it.

As soon as anything ever came out in the newspaper linking me to Tony, the stewards would call me in and question me.

After the story in *The Age*, Ray Murrihy hauled me before the stewards' panel at Racing NSW's offices in Druitt Street.

He grilled me, going over and over my relationship with Tony, and everything that had been written about us over the last eight years or so. I was under attack, and I'd had enough.

Murrihy: In what ways do you say that Tony Mokbel was 'fantastic to you'?

Cassidy: I'll tell you now honestly, Tony Mokbel was a friend of mine. I went to his house. I'd been seen with him. I had nothing to hide. Not one time did I ever say I didn't know him, he wasn't a friend of mine. When he was a friend of mine he was a good friend of mine.

Murrihy: But you knew he had racing interests?

Cassidy: Yes, I did. He had racing interests.

Murrihy: You knew he was a big punter?

Cassidy: Sorry?

Murrihy: You knew he was a big punter?

Cassidy: I knew he bet, yeah.

Murrihy: And wouldn't it seem logical?

Cassidy: If I wanted something off Tony Mokbel, I wouldn't have had to tip winners to him. I didn't take his money. He was my friend. If I ever needed anything I probably could have asked for it or got it, but I didn't because I didn't need it. I went through the 'Jockey Tapes' thing on my arse. I lost everything, sold my house, lost everything. I went working for about $300, $400 a week. They didn't want to write things about me then. Because they've found him [Mokbel] – they let him out. If he was a murderer what did they let him out for? Why did they let him on a racecourse? Same as Victor Spink. You were there. Schreck was there. They were letting him on the racecourse betting up . . .

Murrihy: No, it wasn't in my time.

Cassidy: Well, when Schreck was there he was the same. They were letting him [Victor Spink] on the course. They were giving him badges . . .

Murrihy: If you recall, you were out [suspended because of 'Jockey Tapes'] and I think I met you a couple of times at Centennial Park when I first arrived here and ultimately you came back in 1997 . . .

Cassidy: It was the same thing. All the things that were written about me, same with Schreck. Half the stuff written about me I had told him . . . This is the same. This is twelve years later. I've had a daughter. I've been remarried. I live out of town so I get away from all the scumbags. I don't talk to them. You can have my phone records anytime you like. I've got nothing to hide. I said he was my friend. I said I went there [to his parents' house]. I'd been seen at the casino with him. I didn't ring him up and say, 'Let's go to the casino. I need some money to play with.' I was there playing with my money that I earn, that I pay tax on.

Murrihy: Until what time did this association or friendship continue with Mokbel?

Cassidy: Look, when I found out and the racecourse detectives and Des said to me, 'Look, Jimmy, we're telling you to keep away from the bloke', and then I found out or heard in the grapevine that there were things going on and I stayed away.

Murrihy: What, since 2001, there's been no association since then?

Cassidy: Haven't talked to him, haven't seen him, didn't know where he was. I've had nothing to do with the bloke.

Murrihy: Because that article in 2006 [in the *Herald-Sun*] certainly gives the impression on any reading of it that you were there still supporting the person, having nothing but respect for him.

Cassidy: I'm not going to be saying anything bad against the bloke. Put it this way: he never done nothing wrong to me. He never done anything to my family. He done nothing to my wife. So what am I going to bag the bloke for? If they put me in court today, let alone sitting here, with a noose around my neck, I still wouldn't bag the bloke. They can hang me. Bad luck.

The main part of McKenzie's story was about Bezeal Bay, which I had won on in a minor race on Geelong Cup Day in 1997 – more than a decade earlier!

Murrihy: There was some mention that Cassidy received tens of thousands of dollars from Mokbel. I'll read what it says: 'After his ban ended in 1997, Cassidy returned to tipping, passing on information about horses he was riding to Tony Mokbel or his associates.'

Cassidy: If this dickhead has got this information, why doesn't he bring it forward?

Murrihy: Did you tip him Bezeal Bay?

Cassidy: No. I think that Bezeal Bay that day . . . I can't even remember. You'd be able to look at the betting sheets in Melbourne. I think it was about $1.90 or $1.80 or something.

Murrihy: But the suggestion is Tony Mokbel was laundering drug money and he was happy to assist his chances of winning by getting information from licensed people and by that getting his money laundered.

Cassidy: If I was meant to have got the money off Victor Spink that they said and I was meant to have had the money off Tony Mokbel, I can guarantee you I wouldn't be in this life.

Murrihy: No, but your name, unfortunately, gets . . .

Cassidy: Thrown around all the time.

Murrihy: Thrown around, yeah . . .

Cassidy: All the time.

Murrihy: But I mean, Jim, with all due respect, you don't assist the cause by the article we've referred to coming out.

Cassidy: Yeah, but that's not my fault they print that, sir. Come on. I mean to say, it's not my fault they printed that.

Murrihy: But when this fellow – what's his name? – Nick McKenzie approached you for a comment you said, 'Your paper can go and f . . .'

Cassidy: Yeah, but he didn't tell me he was from the paper. He goes, 'I'm Nick someone. I'm ringing up to get information about Tony Mokbel' and I said that. Yes, I did say that. I said, 'You go . . .'

Murrihy: Well, that probably doesn't behove you as a jockey saying something like that to a . . .

Cassidy: This is crap that's come up twelve years ago. I've had a gutful of it. Look, I've had it stuck up me that far in this game. I'm getting to a stage where I don't really care anymore. I'm out there on my own, minding my own business. I go to the track. I go to the sauna. I come home. I've had a bad run for the last eighteen months and I'm an idiot. I'm still trying to come back and have a go. If I was that wealthy and I didn't have mortgages – you can see my mortgage. You can see my bills, what I draw on my mortgage to try to keep alive at the moment. I'm not crying poor, but if I had that much money I wouldn't even be here. You could have my licence. I wouldn't care anymore. I love what I do. I keep my nose clean. I keep away. But I'm getting to a stage where I've had a gutful.

Murrihy: Yeah, well, let me tell you this. We don't . . .

Cassidy: Half of it's through my own fault, mind you, from knowing the bloke.

Murrihy: Let me tell you this. We don't want to inhibit your ability to earn a living, but also the industry has got to turn on its own reputation and this never assists, does it, this type of exposé and suggestions that probably one of the worst criminals in recent times in Australia has an association with a jockey.

Cassidy: Did [have an association]. Did. Did.

Murrihy: . . . Did, and a further allegation . . .

Cassidy: Let's get that on the record – did.

Murrihy: Did. All right.

Cassidy: Did.

Murrihy: I accept that.

Cassidy: Not any longer.

Murrihy: Well, it's pretty hard. He's inside at the moment.

Cassidy: Well, you can go and visit them.

Murrihy: All right, but this goes on further to allege that . . .

Cassidy: Allege, allege . . .

It was comical. The crime commission asked me about the Bezeal Bay thing. Tony had an old mate of his called 'Max'. That's all I ever knew him as. He's a good mate of Tony's and his family. Good bloke.

He drove me out to Geelong that day in this old blue Holden Torana.

'Who's this driving the Torana?' the police asked me later during their investigation.

'Max,' I said. 'I only ever knew him as Max.'

'Who's this Max?'

'He's my mate. He picks me in his beaten-up old Torana. It took us two days to get to Geelong.'

I go to Geelong for one race and ride Bezeal Bay. I leave and then they've got photos of me getting in this blue Torana.

'Go and have a look,' I told the police. 'He's my friend. He's a harmless man.'

'Was Tony there that day?'

'I'm not sure.'

I mean, the horse was a $1.90 chance. Is he not allowed to back it, just because I rode it?

The whole thing was like the 'Jockey Tapes' scenario. They were suggesting that I was sneaking around, but it wasn't like that at all. I enjoyed Tony's company. I told him how a few horses were going, but that's no different to what you tell anyone at the track. He was no different to Joe Bloggs asking me for a tip. I didn't know that he went and had a $100,000 or $200,000 on horses. Everyone was talking to him. Trainers were associating with him. Owners were associating with him. But once again I was pinpointed.

Are all the people associated with someone with a criminal record questioned, and have their bank accounts examined? That's what they've done to me. If Tony was that bad, why was he allowed on the racecourse?

In 2012, more allegations surfaced. It was reported that an underworld figure had said he gave me $25,000 on behalf of Tony for tips. Do you think I would've forgotten that one? That he'd given me $25K? I would remember that – but it didn't happen.

There was always something written. Every time something was written about Tony, my name would come up. The journos were being drip-fed information from someone and they would then put my name into the mix. They would implicate me or Danny Nikolic.

One report on *Four Corners* on the ABC reckoned I'd received about $100,000 between the 1990s and 2000s from Tony. Well, where is it? The police went through my bank details, through my house, through everything. They didn't find anything.

I considered legal action over all these stories, but who's going to believe me? It would cost me money and how much satisfaction would I get? I know how it works: I would get a story the size of a postage stamp saying it was wrong. It wouldn't be on the front page. You lose your money in legal costs anyway. My hands were tied.

I don't regret my time with Tony and his family one bit. They were good times. They were great experiences. It was just another colourful chapter of my life.

16

The King

THE MUD FROM THE TONY MOKBEL STORIES STUCK. THE RIDES on the leading horses, with the leading stables, dried up.

It was frustrating because I had done so well to re-establish my career and now I'd hit another brick wall.

Heading into the 2009 Autumn Carnival in Sydney, I thought about giving it all away. Publicly, I said I wasn't ready. That I still loved what I did.

But I'd had a gutful of continually running into the brick wall of bad press. The opportunities weren't there. If the media and the stewards had looked at all the other jockeys who had been talking to Tony, I suspect they would not be getting many rides either. Their names were never mentioned. If there was a story about Tony, there was usually a story about me.

So, at the age of 46, I seriously considered walking away for the first time. Instead, I kept hanging in there. It made me more determined.

'Fuck you,' I thought. 'I'm not going away. I won't let you push me away.'

I always maintained that I would finish on my terms. I wasn't going to let this push me out. I owed it to myself to keep going.

The one horse that could help keep me going was Vision And Power, which was owned by Nick Moraitis, who of course owned Might And Power.

Vision And Power had a similar name, but he wasn't in the same class as Mighty. But he was tough. Trained by Joe Pride, it had been a long preparation for the horse heading into the Group 1 George Ryder Stakes over 1500 metres at Rosehill. He'd won four listed races, but couldn't quite get it done in the Group 1 Chipping Norton (1600 metres) and Ranvet Stakes (2000 metres) which he'd previously raced in.

He was a six-year-old gelding and getting a little long in the tooth, but he was like a good mare: when they strike good form, they keep going good. He was on a bit of a purple patch, going up through the grades. Then he stepped up into weight-for-age.

We didn't think he would actually win that George Ryder. We just wanted to give him a good run so he would be competitive in the Doncaster Mile in two weeks time.

He did more than that. I lifted him to win. It was my first Group 1 win since Red Dazzler won the Toorak Handicap at Caulfield in 2006. And I was wearing the pink, white and grey silks that I had worn whenever I rode Might And Power.

'Nick's been a sticker with me, thanks Nick,' I said afterwards. 'It gives me a great thrill to win this Group 1 for him.'

THE KING

A few days out from the AJC Derby (2400 metres) at Randwick on Easter Saturday, I received a call from my racing manager, Matt Privato.

'Mate, do you want to ride Roman Emperor in the derby?' he asked.

'Are you kidding?' I replied.

Roman Emperor was trained by Bart Cummings and part-owned by Malaysian property developer Dato Tan Chin Nam. Together Dato and Bart had won Melbourne Cups with Think Big, Saintly and Viewed. Dato also owned So You Think, the 2009 and 2010 Cox Plate winner and Australian Champion Three Year Old in 2010.

Matt had been listening to 2KY Radio in Sydney and heard Andrew Bensley reveal that Bart needed a jockey for Roman Emperor. Bart had wanted Dwayne Dunn but Lee Freedman had decided to keep his stable rider in Melbourne. I got the ride.

The horse drew a wide barrier and was $15 in the betting. The Peter Snowden-trained Sousa, with Kerrin McEvoy on board, was the $4.50 favourite.

Bart, as usual, didn't have much to say before the race.

'I'll leave it to you,' he said, 'but I don't want you to be too forward, and I don't want you to be too far back. And whatever you do, don't go too early.'

Bart was confident. He hadn't won a Group 1 in Sydney for a decade. When I saw the horse parade, I became very confident, too. He looked magnificent.

I jumped good and I got him running, but I let him have his head. The more you give a horse their head – in other words, just let them run – the more relaxed they usually become. By the 1800 metres, he had gone around them and was settling near the lead.

Coming to the 800 metres, I had Kerrin behind and just outside of me. He kept trying to nudge me back in towards the rail. As we came to the 600 metres, I got the shits. He kept trying to pocket me in. At that point in the derby, you don't want to be coming in; you want to be getting out and mobile.

So I popped out, which popped Kerrin wide, and then I had Bart's words in my ears: 'Whatever you do, don't go too early.'

All of a sudden, I'm there early. Fortunately, I got there without spending a penny.

Mark Shean called the race for TVN:

They turn where Pre Eminence raced up to Roman Emperor. Down the outside, Old Jock's running on. Sousa's into the clear and Harris Tweed is running on as well.

At the 300 metres, I was within a length-and-a-half of the lead, and doing it comfortably. I wasn't asking the horse to do anything. I was just nudging him along. *Get there, get there, get there . . .*

At the 200 metres, I was still cuddling. I was doing a bit, without doing a lot. They were all coming to get me, but I had plenty of horse underneath me. So I asked him to give me something.

It's Pre Eminence and Roman Emperor fighting it out. Harris Tweed and Sousa are after them. But Roman Emperor's got a kick at the hundred. He got away from Pre Eminence and Harris Tweed. Roman Emperor in front. Predatory Pricer's flying as well but ROMAN EMPEROR WINS THE DERBY!

In the mounting yard, Bart was as cool as a cucumber.

'I told you he could win the derby, pretty good horse this bloke,' he said to the press. 'I've had better horses than him, but he can stay. The jockey's not bad either.'

At the age of 81, Bart had just become the oldest trainer to win a derby anywhere in the world. It was his first Group 1 win in Sydney since Allez Suez won the 1999 Epsom Handicap. And it was my first Group 1 winner for him since Shaftesbury Avenue took out the 1991 Lightning Stakes. It was also my third AJC Derby, after winning in 1990 on Dr Grace and 1993 on Innocent King.

Bart explained why he had chosen me to ride the horse. It was the win on Vision And Power in the George Ryder.

'He broke his drought last week so he's an in-form jockey,' he said. 'I needed a jockey who was forceful and good on horses who race up on the speed and there's no better than this bloke. Roman Emperor is by Montjeu and I figured a long time ago that the best way to ride these horses is up on the speed.'

Privately, Bart was over the moon. I'd done exactly everything he asked – I waited and waited, and got there.

As the reporters walked away, he put his arm around me.

'That was an absolute gem,' he said.

When you received praise from Bart, it meant more than when it came from anyone else.

The race was sponsored by David Jones. So at the presentation, I stood alongside Bart and David Jones ambassador and model Megan Gale. Megan is 180 centimetres tall. I'm 150 centimetres. There's Megan, Bart . . . and then there's me. Can you imagine what that looked like?

When it was my turn to address the crowd, there was only one thing I could really say.

PUMPER

'Ring-a-ding-ding is honoured to win for the King! Clickety-clack, the Pumper and Bart are back!'

*

Days later and I was back in a familiar place: in the men's steam room at the Coogee-Randwick RSL Club, bouncing a ball off a wall, wearing a plastic bag, doing whatever Boss told me to do.

I had to get down to 52 kilos if I was going to ride Vision And Power in the Doncaster Mile that Saturday. I told *The Daily Telegraph*:

> It's hard mentally – and physically as well. I'm no spring chicken. I just want to make sure I'm fit and healthy and strong on the day. I'll ride the weight, but I'll admit I'll be doing it a bit tough. Malcolm's my greatest asset in that respect. He keeps hammering me and pushing me and you need that when it gets a bit tough. When I believe I can't win a Group 1 again, I'll give it away. I had a run of almost four years where I hadn't won one. But I never had it in the back of my mind that I wouldn't again. If I had that feeling, I'd give it away. The tough survive in this game. I'd like to think that I'm a survivor.

I had never won a Doncaster. It didn't haunt me as much as the Slipper, but it had always slipped out of my grasp. It was the one race that I couldn't nail.

I was meant to ride Secret Savings for Gai in 1997, but I was committed to ride elsewhere. The ride went to my brother, Larry, and he won. And there had been Magic Flute in 1987 when I missed out on the ride because of suspension.

The George Ryder was always good form heading into the Donnie, but despite that and the low weight Vision And

Power was about $15 in early betting. I told Nick to get on him. By the time we went to the barriers, he was $10.

I settled near the tail of the field but at the 600 metres, I started to sweep right around the field. As we straightened, I was eight wide, out there all on my own.

Mark Shean didn't know who to call:

With two hundred to go, Musket, Vision And Power, Pinnacle, Triple Honour, Largo Lad . . . I don't know where to look . . . VISION AND POWER! VISION AND POWER! VISION AND POWER FOR JIM CASSIDY WINS IT!

That's timing it to the second. I'd held on to beat Black Piranha and Whobegotyou. I was ecstatic. The first person I thought of was Boss, like always. The hard work we'd done at Coogee had paid off.

'I knew it wouldn't stop me if I remained strong of mind,' I said when asked about having to get the weight down. 'I've been sucking on a grapefruit from Moraitis's for a week.'

Now, I had a tricky dilemma: next Saturday was the Group 1 Queen Elizabeth Stakes over 2000 metres at Randwick – should I ride Vision And Power . . . or Roman Emperor for Bart?

'I just hope Jimmy Cassidy doesn't ride the Derby winner Roman Emperor and stays with Vision And Power,' Joe Pride said. 'Jimmy and Vision And Power are one of the great jockey-horse combinations, they just go so well together.'

Before I made that decision, I had to take my daughter Piper to the Royal Easter Show. I spoke to *The Daily Telegraph*'s Brent Zerafa as I rode the merry-go-round:

Lettuce leaves and lentils were replaced by dagwood dogs and waffles as Jimmy Cassidy enjoyed the delights of the Royal Easter Show with his family yesterday.

PUMPER

After a week of heavy dieting and strenuous exercise to strip to 52kg, Cassidy gorged himself at the Show without a worry in the world.

'I have had a couple of dagwood dogs, some waffles, prawns and oysters – basically anything I can get my hands on,' Cassidy joked.

'It has been a pretty hard week, but today was all about enjoying myself with the family and having a good day out. I'll put on a few kilos, but the hard work will begin tomorrow. I'll be back in the gym with the boys but it won't be as tough.'

That's what happens in racing. You don't get too long to celebrate the highs, because you have to keep proving yourself within a few days. Sometimes, the next day.

I told the *Telegraph* that I didn't have a decision to make between Roman Emperor and Vision And Power, because the decision had already been made.

The decision (to ride Roman Emperor) was made after the Derby win, and the decision to run Vision And Power in the race was made last night (Saturday) . . . I am happy with the decision that has been made and it is one that is looking to the future.

It is tough to get solid rides on young staying horses on the up and Roman Emperor is exactly that. The association with Bart is another factor, and you don't pass up those opportunities too often. I'd love to be able to ride them both, but that is the nature of my job.

When I made it clear that I was sticking with Bart's horse, Joe lashed out at me. He told *The Sydney Morning Herald*:

'I'll be lying if I said I wasn't very disappointed in Jimmy,' Pride said. 'He has won six races on this bloke this preparation and to say he's looking forward to next year by riding Roman Emperor is pretty short-sighted. I would want to give myself the best chance of winning [the Queen Elizabeth]. I think Jimmy is not doing that in this race by riding Roman Emperor and I think he will be disappointed on Saturday.'

That's fine. Joe's entitled to his opinion, like everyone in racing. As it turned out, neither of us got it right. Neither horse figured in the finish after Roman Emperor had done a lot of work up front in the race.

Not only did I never ride Vision And Power again after that, but my relationship with Nick Moraitis also started to sour.

I kept riding for him, and kept winning. I had a lot of luck for Nick in some group races on Love Conquers All. And I got Maluckyday home in the Lexus Stakes on Derby Day at Flemington in 2010, qualifying him for the Melbourne Cup, in which he came second to Americain. He would've gone very close to winning the Cup the following year but he contracted pneumonia and almost died. He came back again, and he was a live chance in the 2012 race, but he finished back near the tail of the field.

But while I kept winning consistently for Nick, nothing was coming back in return. He would agree to deals verbally with me but then conveniently forget them. Promises don't pay the bills. There was a lot promised verbally that never came my way. I was winning big races for him and I was on fresh air, which is disappointing.

Many owners have promised me plenty the whole way through my career. A lot of owners wouldn't give you five dollars most of the time. Yet they want to pat you on the back and tell you what a champion jockey you are when you win for them. I'd see Nick at functions, or after I had won, and he would tell the press how great a jockey I was.

It was disappointing because we had a good connection. We shared the experience of Might And Power. And I would like to think I was good to Nick. My record showed that I would win on more than I would get beaten on. And believe me: not all of his horses were Might And Power.

In the last three years of my career, I simply said, 'No more.' In the end, I started barring him. Everyone thinks that he sacked me. But I sacked him. I'd had a gutful of him. That is one thing I want to make very clear: I sacked him.

That said, I am great mates with his son, Stephen. We met through Might And Power and we're like brothers. I have the utmost respect for Stephen, and always will.

But maybe the thing that showed exactly what Nick thought of me was what he said to Singo behind my back. In racing, though, these things always have a habit of coming straight back to you.

When I started riding more for Singo towards the end of my career, Nick called him and said something along the lines of: 'Don't trust Jimmy, he'll let you down.'

He must have forgotten all the winners I rode for him.

*

The mud from over the years, from 'Jockeys Tapes' to my association with Tony, didn't just hurt me in terms of rides. It also threatened to hurt my place in history.

THE KING

You don't race for the accolades. You don't go through all the early mornings and hard work and pain and danger and all the bullshit wanting an award at the end of it. The reward is the good times you have with trainers and owners, as well as the hardworking staff in the background like strappers and handlers, when you pull off a great win. That's the satisfying part.

But sometimes the awards are a great reminder of what you have done. As a jockey who had won two Melbourne Cups, two Caulfield Cups, a Cox Plate and a Golden Slipper, many thought I deserved a place in the Australian Racing Hall of Fame.

Each year, the Hall of Fame nominations would come around and the stories would pop up about how the selection panel had overlooked me again. Nobody would be quoted in the stories, but the journos would write that it was because of 'off track issues'. No one had the balls to put their names to it.

Certain people blocked me every step of the way. I believe I didn't get into the Hall of Fame for all those years because of them. They didn't worry me. They meant nothing to me. But I know who was blocking my induction.

Then, in 2012, I received news that I was being admitted into the Australian Racing Hall of Fame. Charley called me up and started lecturing me on this and that and what was expected of me.

'And I expect you to fuck off. That's what I think of you,' I said. I told him that I was honoured to be inducted into the Hall of Fame, but it was through no help from him. 'I've been inducted for my riding and racing achievements. Not because of you.'

It was enormous to finally get in there, alongside other jockeys such as George Moore, Scobie Breasley, Roy Higgins and Darby Munro. It was also enormous to be a Kiwi inductee. It made all the support from the trainers and owners who have stuck loyal over the years mean so much.

But then, just to sour the moment, I was told about the award presentation only a few days in advance. It was to be held on the Friday night before the AJC Derby. I only found out on the Tuesday about it, so I had no family or friends there. I turned up on my own and sat at the same table with the Inghams, whose family are racing royalty but they weren't my people. It was great to be inducted but the way it was done was not fair. As soon as the official stuff was over, I had to leave because I had to ride the next day. I never got to appreciate what it meant.

In 2014, I was inducted into the New Zealand Racing Hall of Fame, and that was a special night. I was given plenty of notice so I could invite my whole family to attend. I was the last one introduced on the night. It made it more special.

I also like what the New Zealand Hall of Fame says about inductees: 'They are some who were not perfect in character or without controversy. But no one can deny the impact they have all had on an industry which owes as much to the diversity of its participants as to their dedication and striving for excellence.'

One man who is in both the Australian and New Zealand Halls of Fame is Bart Cummings. Relationships come and go in racing. So do people. When Bart died at the age of 87 in 2015, the sport lost a giant.

Bart paid me probably the greatest compliment of my career a few years before his death. He was asked to name his top three jockeys, and he put me there alongside George Moore and Roy Higgins. That surprised me because he had some great jockeys ride for him over the years.

To me, Bart was the King. He was Mr Racing. He knew everything. When I was riding for him in Melbourne, the races were good but his company was better. At dinner after the races, he would sum up a day and then start talking about other aspects of the world. He was a very knowledgeable man.

He also knew a horse better than anyone. I would just watch him watching horses. I'll go back to Kingston Rule and that week before the Melbourne Cup. Bart just had that glint in his eye at trackwork. He just knew.

'He'll win the Cup,' he said quietly but surely.

Bart was an amazing thinker. As soon as he walked out of his hotel room, or onto a track, or anywhere, you could see him thinking. He was just a thinking man. I remember being in Japan with him for two Japan Cups. He would be there at trackwork early, trying to find an edge.

He was the same trainer, right up until the day he died.

Without a doubt, he was every bit as witty and astute until the day he died. My biggest regret in racing is that I never rode a Melbourne Cup winner for Bart. That I never was one of the privileged jockeys to have been a part of his dozen wins in the race. I don't regret not accepting the ride on Kingston Rule, because I had stayed loyal and done the right thing. But it would've been nice to have been a part of history with Bart.

When Bart passed away in August 2015, they held a state funeral at St Mary's Cathedral in Sydney and it was packed with thousands of mourners. I was lucky to have the chance to honour him in another way.

Days after his death, the Australian Turf Club held the J.B. Cummings Ming Dynasty Quality, a Group 3 race over 1400 metres at Randwick. I was on Chris Waller's Metallic Crown. I led from start to finish, fighting back gamely when challenged to win.

Ray Thomas from *The Daily Telegraph* asked me what it was like to have a strong association with Bart, especially when I was his stable rider in Melbourne:

It was such an honour, one of the greatest I've had in racing, to be asked by Bart to ride for him in Melbourne. I was his stable rider there during the 1980s and we won Derbys, Oaks, Emirates Stakes, we won a lot of Group 1 races together and had a lot of success. Bart was one of a kind and that is why it is very special to me to win this race named in his honour.

I also said this of Chris Waller:

I'm some respects, Chris is the new Bart. He hasn't trained a Melbourne Cup or a Golden Slipper winner yet but surely it is only a matter of time. Chris is going in the right direction, it is a magnificent effort to do what he is doing and I'm just glad to be part of the team.

Let me clarify those statements. Chris Waller might be flying now but he's got a long way to go. With all due respect to Chris, he will never be Bart. There will only be one Bart.

My lasting memory of J.B. Cummings will always be when I followed him to New Zealand for the sales. I went to a lot of yearling sales with him, and on many occasions

I just followed him around when he was looking at different horses.

After Bart was finished, I'd get the same horses out and look at them myself. I just wanted to check what they were like: what type of body they had, how big they were, how much they might lengthen in stride when they were racing . . .

I was trying to think how Bart thought. I wanted to see what he could see. Will it develop as a two-year-old? Is it going to be better as a late three-year-old?

Those are the sort of horses Bart was always buying. Big strong, horses, horses that would be champions.

Bart knew a winner. That's why he will always be The King.

17

Pain

OF ALL THE INJURIES I'VE HAD IN RACING, OF ALL THE PAIN I'VE had to go through, the injury that nearly ended it all prematurely came when I was cutting my hedges out the back at home.

I was hacking at a bit of flax when I dropped the hedge trimmer and it almost cut off the index finger, ring finger and little finger of my right hand. The whole three were just sucked right up underneath the trimmer.

I ripped my T-shirt off and wrapped it around my hand, jumped on the motorbike and nearly crashed it driving it up towards the house. I yelled at Vick to get the car and get me to Prince of Wales Private Hospital.

There was every chance that could've been the end of my career. You need those fingers to hold the reins. There was talk from the surgeons about one of the fingers coming off because it was cut down to the bone. But, in the end, they patched me up, I got through it and I could ride again.

That was 2009, and by now a new figure was emerging on the racing scene. His name was Nathan Tinkler.

Nathan was the sparkie from Muswellbrook who struck it rich in mining. He bought the Newcastle Knights and Newcastle Jets, and he also wanted to make a big name for himself in racing. He set up his own racing and breeding operation called Patinack Farm on the Gold Coast.

He was a big bloke and he came with a big reputation for being hot-headed. I found him all right. There was only one time I had words with Nathan.

I rode a horse for him at Warwick Farm one day. The thing was as unfit and as big as Nathan was, so it couldn't win anyway and that's what happened. I was walking back to my car at the end of the meeting and he sent me a text along the lines of: 'If you're going to ride for me like that, you won't be riding for me for very long.'

I got in the car. I was due to ride four horses for him the next day at Hawkesbury, but that was suddenly in jeopardy. I texted him back, which is strange for me because I don't often text. But all it said was, 'Ring me'.

He did.

'Hi Nathan. Jimmy here. Don't say anything, let me speak. I read your text. If you're going send me texts like that, and you won't say it to me instead, you can go fuck yourself. I've got four rides for you at Hawkesbury tomorrow. If you're going to speak to me like that, I'm not riding them. Your call. Don't speak to me like a piece of shit.'

To his credit, he didn't huckle up. I think he respected that I was up front with him. We were okay after that.

I had more luck for Nathan than most jockeys. I rode one at Rosehill for him that was 25 to 1 in early betting, but it was backed into about $3.90. We got it home.

PAIN

In early September 2010, I was on the phone to Nathan's trainer, John Thompson, who had left Bart Cummings's stable to join Patinak Farm. He handed the phone to someone standing with him. It was Nathan.

'I want you to ride Trusting in the Epsom,' he said. 'I think you're the right jockey for the horse.'

Trusting was a big colt but he was frustrating. He often had his mind on other things and he was hard to keep focused on the job. He'd tailed off in the Cameron Handicap at Newcastle, but his second to the glamour mare More Joyous in the George Main Stakes had seen him put up as favourite for the Epsom Handicap – a major Group 1 over 1600 metres at Randwick. Dropping back from weight-for-age to 52 kilograms meant Trusting was going to be hard to beat.

He looked like he was going to win coming down the extreme outside, trying to grab Captain Sonador, ridden by Glen Boss, on the line. He got done by half a head.

There's the pain of losing a big Group 1 race like that, but it was nothing to the pain all over my body. My knees were screaming. They had been giving me hell for years.

My right knee, in particular, had been very painful since a fall at Eagle Farm in 2007. I had been rushed to hospital for chest and ankle X-rays after being thrown from a colt called Bonza Crop, who snapped his near side foreleg shortly after hitting the front 100 metres from the line in a 1200-metre race. Brad Stewart was on Our Magic, and he crashed into Bonza Crop, sending him to the turf as well.

Like every race fall, if you get out of it with a few injuries then you are ahead. Brad was quick to get to his feet but I was treated by ambulance officers for several minutes and then taken to Brisbane's Mater Hospital. The X-rays showed I had broken my right ankle. I needed to have surgery and have a pin inserted.

The ankle came good but my knees gave me grief all the way until I had my last ride. They still give me grief. I've had three operations on both knees over the years, and they were always done by Merv Cross, the legendary orthopaedic surgeon in Sydney who has got countless sportspeople – especially rugby league players – back onto the field over many years.

I remember one time when I went to see Merv.

'Jim, I don't know if you're stupid or like pain,' he said.

'Why's that?'

'Because the whole of your cartilage is hanging off the side of your knee.'

He cut it off, put it in a bowl, and gave it back to me. I never had a reconstruction, but over the course of my career he did clean-outs and tightened things up.

I would always do the right thing when it came to recovery. Vick would pick me up from the Royal North Shore Hospital and on the way home we would buy two bags of ice. I would then get some Vaseline and put it around my whole knee, and then lie in bed with plastic underneath me and stay like that until all the swelling was gone. I'd wake up in the morning with two big bags of water underneath me because the ice had melted.

But it worked, because all of the swelling would have gone.

'What knee did I do?' Merv would ask when I next saw him.

I would always do everything possible to get back to health – so I could get back to work. Nobody sees that side of it. The pain.

PAIN

On the way home from the Epsom, I dropped into a mate's place and he gave me a joint. It was more like half a joint. It wouldn't have been an inch long.

When I got home, my knees were killing me. I jumped in the pool, got out, cracked a beer and smoked the joint. The pain was gone. Beautiful. I went to bed, got up and had a sweat.

Come Monday morning, I was at Warwick Farm and ready to ride. Before the first race, eight of us were randomly drug tested. Not for one minute did I think that anything would come of it. I had completely forgotten that I even had a few puffs of a joint. I didn't think it would still be in my system. I didn't give it another thought.

Two weeks later, I was at the trials when one of the stewards approached me.

'That test you did the other day has turned out positive,' I was told.

'Fuck. Really? I only had half a joint.'

'You'll have to come in and do another sample.'

They needed to take another sample to see if I still had dope in my system or if I was still right to ride. I knew I was okay, but I put my hand up straightaway about returning the first positive.

'I had a choof the other night,' I told Ray Murrihy.

He asked me if the doctor had prescribed it for me to take.

'No,' I said. 'I was in pain and I took it. I smoked it.'

To Murrihy's credit, the hearing into the positive test would not be held until after the Melbourne Cup Carnival. On Derby Day, with rain flogging down, I won the Group 2 Salinger Stakes for Rick Worthington on a horse called Whitefriars, at the nice price of $15.

Then I went out and won on Maluckyday for Nick Moraitis in the Group 1 Lexus Stakes, positioning myself behind Linton after being second last on the turn and then powering down the middle of the track. That qualified Maluckyday for the Cup, but there was uncertainty about whether Nick and the trainer, John Hawkes, would run the horse. Meanwhile, I was already booked to ride John Singleton's horse Once Were Wild for Gai.

'I'll do a bit of talking, I think,' I said after the Lexus.

If I was to ride Maluckyday, I was going to have to get down to 51 kilograms. So I phoned Malcolm.

'What are you weighing?' Boss asked.

'About 54 kilograms. Can we get it off?'

'Sure, but you won't be any use to the horse. You'd have to lose around five kilos to ride him in a decent saddle. Get real.'

I stuck with Singo's horse. With a bottom weight of 51 kilograms, Maluckyday finished second. I finished eleventh.

As soon as the race was over, I headed to the airport and the next day I fronted a specially convened meeting.

Murrihy did the right thing by me. I asked for the matter to be held behind closed doors, without the media being present, and he agreed to that. It took an hour for them to suspend me for three months.

'He's certainly welcome back, once his suspension ends,' Murrihy told the awaiting media. 'Racing is a dangerous profession, as we are all aware, and the rules require riders to be free of any substances. All I will say about Jimmy Cassidy is that he is riding as good as I've ever seen him. I don't think on a day-in, day-out basis there is a better jockey in Australia.'

Of course, it was big news. I made the front page for smoking half a joint. The media coverage was ridiculous but that's me: I sell newspapers. I hope this book sells as well as the papers I've sold over the years.

To be honest, though, I think I got off light. I had been drug-tested for years and I knew the score. I will openly admit that I had a puff here and there. It was very seldom.

But, certainly when I was riding, I never touched it except for that one time when I got caught.

The testing on jockeys is very tough. There are drug tests and breath tests and that is good. It should be done. They've got a couple of jockeys in recent times for ice. There's absolutely no place for jockeys to be riding with that shit in their system, or the influence of any drug. There's too much risk. There's too much danger.

The problem with younger jockeys – or just young people – is that they don't smoke pot. All these young people who are into popping ecstasy tablets and snorting whatever, well, that's not smart.

I wouldn't say drug use is an issue with young jockeys, but I wouldn't say it's not out there. For a lot of them, it's the company they keep and how they handle the pressure of fame and fortune. These successful young jockeys have got the cash flow to have a lot of things that many people cannot.

But it's the path you want to take. I had 30 years of being able to do what I wanted to do. There were more drugs around in my early days. But I never took that path, I was too keen about working.

I understand that it's a tough job, but you have to be able to handle it. You have to handle the stardom and being in the public eye. Michael Walker is a Kiwi jockey who I consider to be a great mate. He's very talented and he's brash and bold like I was. He has talked about letting the fame get to his head and almost throwing it all in. He was one of the lucky ones who managed to drag himself back. Others haven't been able to do it.

I don't know. I might be different. Fame's good, but really, who gives a fuck about fame? I like the peace and quiet. The racetrack is the place to get pats on the back and have people tell you you're a genius. That's enough. There is always time for a party, but plan it and do it right. If jockeys want to play up, then don't do it when you're riding. Don't put other riders' lives at risk because of your night of wanting to have it all.

A lot of younger jockeys would approach me for advice. Brenton Avdulla was one of them. He's improved so much, from being a wild boy to seeing what he can achieve. He's working harder, he's dedicated, and he's really turned his career around.

I don't want to be a hypocrite. I never have been on any subject. But for me the use of marijuana was about pain relief. I'm not into painkillers. I've had race falls and broken ribs, broken hands, and Longy has got rid of the pain. But I won't take a pill. I am not a pill person. If I had a migraine, I'd rather be taking a joint than a tablet.

It was simply and only about pain relief. And believe me, over many years, I had the pain to prove it.

As I've said earlier, Boss made me supple. Longy rubbed the injury away. But sometimes you just had to grin and bear it. You lived with injuries and pain on a daily basis. You lived with it otherwise you wouldn't ride. I just had to turn up. There was no other option.

PAIN

The only time I would rule myself out and would not ride was if I knew my injury wasn't going to do anyone any justice. If it wasn't going to be fair on the owners and trainers, or even myself, I would not ride.

There were lots of injuries over the course of my career. My shoulder was a nightmare for two years. I kept trying to ride with that one, patching it up and trying to ride, but the pain became too much and I had a shoulder reconstruction.

One of the worst ailments I ever had was a hernia that I kept riding with for several months heading into the Spring Carnival in Melbourne in 2003. It was so bad I could stick my whole fist in it. I was putting socks in my hernia and taping myself up so I could continue riding. I bought a hernia belt, which has two knobs on it, and I would wear that so I could stay in the saddle. That went on for three or four months. People would ask me what was wrong, because I was limping around.

'I've got a bad ankle,' I would lie. I didn't want anyone to know I had a weakness.

I got through almost the entire Spring Carnival, but it was tough with this massive hernia sticking out. All the other jockeys were laughing because I bought those stretchy pants that large women wear to hold their guts in. They thought it was hilarious. I wasn't laughing.

Somehow, I managed to get through to Emirates Stakes Day on the final Saturday of the Cup Carnival. I won a two-year-old race for Graeme Rogerson. I came in and I was white with pain. If I could've smoked a joint right there in the mounting yard at Flemington, I would've sucked it down and blown it out my arse – I was in that much pain.

The course doctor said I wasn't allowed to ride. He wasn't that keen on me flying back to Sydney, either. Half my guts were hanging out.

As soon as I could I flew home and had the operation. I was terribly bruised from the waist down. For the next two weeks, I lay in bed and was given pethidine. I was getting hooked on it. I loved having it every day. There was no pain then. I was off my head.

'I don't want any more of that,' I told the doc.

Then I was sent home and they had me on morphine tablets. I flushed them as well.

I was handed a three-month ban from racing for the positive drug test, but I could get it reduced by a month if I underwent counselling. Meanwhile, the time off gave me a chance to really get my body right and also spend time with Vick and Piper over the Christmas holidays. Normally, I was riding around that time of the year. Now I had some time off.

I was now 47 years old, and people were wondering when I would retire. Was this suspension the opportunity for me to finally ride off into the sunset? No fucking way. There was no chance I would ever walk away on that note.

So I did all the counselling that was required of me and I was allowed back in early January. I told Ray Thomas that I wasn't in a hurry to retire. There were two older jockeys, Neville Wilson (who was 64) and Robert Thompson (who was 53), who inspired me to keep going. *The Daily Telegraph* quoted me as saying:

I rode against 'Nifty' Wilson in Melbourne in the 1980s and we are still riding against each other today. The same goes for Robert Thompson, another great jockey. I take my hat off to those people and I look up to them and what they have achieved in racing. If I wasn't keen to ride, I could have walked away ten times before because I've had plenty of reasons to, but I enjoy what I do and still believe I'm one of the best around. If I had to ride bad horses all the time, I would give the game away and you can quote me on that. I'm not into riding bad horses all the time but I know you have to ride the slow ones to get on the good ones. The hard part for me now is controlling the aches and pains but I'll keep going until my body says enough, or when I think I haven't got it, that's when I'll know it will be time to call it quits. But I love riding, I'm good at it and horses run for me. I was born to ride and I assure you of one thing: I'll be in Melbourne for the Cup in 2011.

My first meeting back was at Randwick. And the crowd, as expected, didn't miss me.

I've had a whole career of hearing funny one-liners from angry punters as I came back to the enclosure. In 1989, on the day I won the VRC Oaks on Tristanagh for Bart, a bloke yelled at me from the other side of the mounting yard fence after I had failed to win an earlier race down the straight.

'Who taught you to ride, Cassidy?' he yelled. 'Go back to Sydney.'

'Ask your wife,' I shot back.

The bloke was furious. He jumped the fence and chased me down the lane towards the enclosure. I was still on the horse and thinking, 'Fuck, what am I going to do here?'

He soon ran out of puff and the crowd pissed themselves laughing.

I've copped it my whole career, like every jockey. *You should've retired two years ago, Cassidy!* But you're that fucked after a race, or fucked off, you don't hear it.

The best one I heard was that day at Randwick, when I led on a horse and won.

'Were you in a hurry to get to the winning post because you had the munchies?' one of the punters yelled at me.

I couldn't help but laugh at that one. Soon enough, the pot thing blew over. Now it was time to keep riding winners.

*

Unfortunately, the winners dried up for Nathan Tinkler – and so did the money. He ended up selling his Patinack Farm empire in 2015 because he was crippled with debt.

Not many people felt sad for him, and I can understand why because he owed a lot of them money. But I felt sad about the situation because he had put so much in and it didn't work. It all fell apart.

Nathan came in and went hard and big – obviously too big – and he got handled by a few people along the way. It was a shame what happened because he gave racing a big lift. Then it all fizzled out. People were burnt and it got nasty.

It can happen in racing.

18

The Hundred

'RING-A-DING-A-DING, IT'S TIME FOR PUMPER TO SING!'

It is Derby Day at Flemington. There are 100,000 people there. I have just climbed down off the back of Zoustar, the outstanding colt trainer by Chris Waller that had been sold to the Widden Stud for $20 million just days earlier. I have won the Group 1 Coolmore Stakes over 1200 metres. The result, in my mind at least, was never in doubt, but there had been plenty who were worried after a barrier trial just eight days earlier – and that included his new owners.

But I didn't really care about Zoustar in that moment. All I cared about was getting the massive monkey off my back. He'd been there for months now, and he was getting heavier and heavier with every big carnival that had gone by.

And now I had done it, in front of all those people, at the racetrack where I had experienced my biggest thrills in racing. Finally, I had won my 100th Group 1 race.

The Hundred.

Thank fuck for that.

There had been an obsession with it for months, the closer that I came to reaching triple figures. Only two other jockeys had done it: George Moore, who rode 118 Group 1 winners; and Roy Higgins, who rode 108.

I understood the interest. It was a big thing because it hadn't been done for so long. But it was starting to eat away at my head. I just wanted to get it done with.

The media built up the race to The Hundred between me and Damien Oliver, who was coming into that spring off the back a ten-month suspension for having a bet in a race that he was also riding in. I never thought of it like a shoot-out between the two of us. I knew I would get there before Ollie, because I was on 99 wins and he was on 97.

Admittedly, it took much longer to get there than I had expected. I turned 50 in January 2013, and returned from my traditional end-of-year break fresher than ever. I felt like the twenty-year-old with the bad moustache who first arrived in Sydney all those years ago.

'In all the years I've known Jimmy, I don't think he's been so happy,' Malcolm told *The Daily Telegraph*. 'He's a great jockey, we all know that, and he has confidence in himself like any good sportsman. But, on and off the track, he's so relaxed. It shows in his riding. He's fit and strong and he's as determined as ever.'

Boss was right. I had a beautiful wife and three daughters. I had Boss and Longy in my corner. I felt like I was riding better than ever. The only pressure was the pressure I put on myself. I have never lacked self-belief, but at the age of 50 I felt more than comfortable with my place in the world.

Heading into the Canterbury Stakes meeting at Rosehill in late March, I needed five more Group 1 wins to reach The Hundred. That day, I had strong rides in three Group 1 races: champion colt Pierro in the $350,000 Canterbury Stakes (1300 metres); Foreteller in the $400,000 Ranvet Stakes (2000 metres); and Singo's mare Dear Demi in the $600,000 Coolmore Classic (1500 metres).

I was excited about getting the ride on Pierro, who had won the Golden Slipper for Gai the year before and taken almost everything else since then, with the exception of the Caulfield Guineas (in which he came second) and the Cox Plate (in which he came third).

Coming out of a wide barrier, regular rider Nash Rawiller absolutely slaughtered his chances in the Caulfield Guineas. If I had ridden him in that race, he would've won. I wouldn't have panicked. I would've just sat back and then come storming home. Instead, Pierro hit the lead in the straight but he was run down by All Too Hard, the little brother to Black Caviar, who was owned by Nathan Tinkler.

I got the ride on Pierro for the Canterbury Stakes because Nash was booked to ride More Joyous – also owned by Singo – in the race. After they jumped, I just positioned Pierro perfectly behind the lead of Rain Affair and then peeled out at the top of the straight and won easily. More Joyous came second.

'What an outstanding, outstanding colt,' Gai said after the race. 'The way he just digs so deep. Such a courageous effort. Nothing to be taken away from the mare [More Joyous]. She tenaciously went to the post but Pierro was too brilliant on the day.'

PUMPER

It was the one and only time I rode Pierro, but a couple of years later when I was asked to name the top five horses I ever rode, he was included. He had the determination of Might And Power. I could feel it in the horse. He had that will to win. There was no such thing as running second. He was just an amazing athlete. To do what he did as a two-year-old, and then as a three-year-old, he was a freak.

I was asked to compare Zoustar and Pierro. Zoustar was more brilliant in terms of acceleration, but the other bloke would just wear them all down. His will to win, to never get beat, was something only the rarest of horses have.

Later that spring, Pierro went on to win the George Ryder Stakes. He then finished second to Sacred Falls in the Doncaster, carrying a topweight of 57 kilograms on a bog track at Randwick. He was then retired to stud for a rumoured $30 million.

When you think about the money, you can understand why he was rushed to stud. It's all about money now. But if he had kept racing, he would have had mercy on his doorstep.

I should also say that his owner, Sydney financier Greg Kolivos, is a great bloke. After I won on Pierro that day at Rosehill, all Greg wanted to do was pay me. He couldn't write the cheque quick enough. There's the difference right there between good and bad owners.

Earlier that day in the Ranvet Stakes, I went out on Foreteller for Chris Waller, who was building a great repu-tation in identifying good European stayers and bringing them to Australia. Foreteller was from France, and in the Ranvet he was too strong despite his starting price of $31, mowing down $2.60 favourite Fiveandahalfstar.

Now I was on 97 Group 1's, creeping closer to the magic number.

That was also my first Group 1 win for Chris Waller. When he first came on the scene in Sydney, nobody thought much of it. I would defy anyone who says they knew he was going to turn into the biggest trainer in the country, which he has.

Chris is from Foxton, just north of where I grew up in Lower Hutt. I've heard him say at a few functions and in the press that he had posters of me on his wall as a kid, which makes me feel old. He and his wife, Stephanie, did it tough when they first arrived in Sydney. They struggled, like we all did early on. He was always ambitious, always very dedicated to what he was doing, but did I think he would become the massive success that he is? Well, to be honest, no. I didn't think he would.

Chris's world changed in 2008 when Bob Ingham, one of the pioneers of Australian racing as we know it today, sold his Woodlands Stud racing and breeding empire to Darley Stud for $500 million. Darley is owned by Sheikh Mohammed bin Rashid Al Maktoum, the ruler of Dubai whose Godolphin operation is the biggest in the world. Bob, having downsized, then purchased twenty yearlings and raced them with Chris. A couple of years later, he bought another 40 yearlings.

He's done a good job to build his training operation into what he has, but I hope Chris remembers this game is very tough. You can't ever think you're too big for it, because the rug can be pulled out from under your feet at any moment. Within a second.

The first horse I rode for Chris was long before his current success. It was a stayer called Star Of The Seas over 2000 metres at Rosehill in May 2001. I won that day, but in those early days I didn't ride for him much. When the opportunities came to ride for him, I certainly did. Chris was using everyone then because he didn't have many horses.

By the end of the 2012–13 season, he had gone well past Gai Waterhouse, Peter Moody and Peter Snowden as the country's leading trainer. And at the top of the tree was Zoustar.

The first time I rode the horse, I knew how good he was – and how good he would become. It was a trial at Rosehill and he was just going around for education. I let him go and *wooshka!* He took off like he had been racing for years. Not many can do that straightaway. He was a natural. Then I rode him in his first start – a 1100-metre race at Canterbury – and he won it easily, like the real good horses do.

Heading into the spring in 2013, big things were expected – of Zoustar and of me. Having knocked off two Group 1 races with Pierro and Foreteller, my run at The Hundred had stalled. I'd had good rides in five Group 1's on Slipper Day, but couldn't win on any of them.

Waller's stayer Hawkspur had been in terrible form heading into the Brisbane carnival that winter, but then I went out and won the Queensland Derby on him. That was the 98th Group 1. I was inching closer, even if it felt like it was taking forever.

In his first start after a spell in early September, Zoustar finished fourth in the Group 2 Run to the Rose

(1200 metres), and everyone started to hit the panic button. I wasn't too concerned. He kept getting bumped in the run and had no luck. More than that, he kept wanting to charge in that race. The horse was too fresh and wanted to over-race.

Chris went off half-cocked and suggested he might take me off the horse for the Golden Rose, a Group 1 over 1400 metres at Rosehill. The race was worth $1 million.

I snapped at Chris.

'If you didn't have him that fresh and ready, he would've won,' I said.

Then came the barrier draw for the Golden Rose. Zoustar drew the widest alley in a field of sixteen runners.

Chris phoned me.

'What do you think?' he said.

'Just bet more,' I said.

The horse was $17 in early betting.

'Keep betting until your nose bleeds,' I said. 'He'll win. Keep betting.'

Then I told him how I intended to ride him.

'I'm gonna neck him,' I said. In other words, I was going to hold him right back, leaving the run as late as possible. 'He'll come late and win. He'll be too strong.'

Zoustar missed the start and I went back to the tail of the field. I was three deep but had cover. I just needed to be patient. I knew what sectionals he could run. He could run 10.2 seconds in his last furlong if he had to. He had blistering speed.

I hooked him wide at the turn, and then, over the last 300 metres, I just cruised up to the lead. Mark Shean for TVN called the last stages:

And Zoustar is zooming down the centre! Dissident the leader but Zoustar is about to gobble him up on the outside. Dissident headed by Zoustar, who ran to the lead in the Golden Rose with a hundred to go. Then Sidestep and Bull- point but it's Zoustar!

The reason for the concern over Zoustar was all the hype around the horse being a stallion prospect at stud. They were talking deals in the tens of millions of dollars. The Iskanders, his owners, had only paid $140,000 for him at the Magic Millions sales on the Gold Coast the year before.

They were worried before the race – but I wasn't.

'I was backing the horse's ability and mine – I knew Chris had done his job but the rest was up to me and the horse,' I said after the race. 'I knew if I could nurse him and put him in the race at the 400 . . . I thought I'd count to ten and wait, but I got an itchy arse and said I'm going for home.'

I had a real itchy arse. I was now just one win away from The Hundred.

*

Heading into the Spring Carnival in Melbourne, there was only one horse that everyone wanted to talk about. Zoustar's win in the Golden Rose had seen him put up as equal favourite for the Caulfield Guineas, but Chris was focused on the Coolmore Stakes down the Flemington straight on Derby Day.

We toyed with them in the Roman Consul Stakes over 1200 metres at Randwick, winning by four-and-a-half-lengths. I didn't need the whip. There was already talk about taking the horse to Royal Ascot the following year, and the speculation about what he would fetch at stud was there as well.

Meanwhile, I had the thought of The Hundred eating away at me. The media was becoming preoccupied with it. Every time I went into a Group 1 race on a live chance, the talk wasn't about whether the horse could win but whether I could reach triple figures. Every time I didn't win a Group 1, the more pressure they put on me, wondering when it was going to happen.

The horse most likely to get me there wasn't Zoustar but Chris Waller's stayer, Hawkspur. He was one of the favourites heading into the George Main Stakes (1600 metres) at Randwick that September.

'It is giving me the tingles just thinking about it,' I told Ray Thomas at *The Daily Telegraph*. 'Whether that extra Group 1 win comes tomorrow or not, it will come soon enough and I will be punching the air when I do it. If Hawkspur can win the George Main Stakes I will get emotional because this is something I never thought I would ever achieve – not even in my wildest dreams.'

I finished fourth.

A month later, I was still sitting on 99 Group 1's but Hawkspur was favourite for the Caulfield Cup.

On the Wednesday before the race, I was at Warwick Farm, an hour before the first, on a stinking hot day. The big screen in the middle of the track flashed up the field for the $2.5 million race. They had held the barrier draw in Melbourne earlier that morning. Hawkspur drew 16. He immediately eased in betting.

Someone asked me what I thought.

'Only a number to me,' I laughed. 'It's the number the second time around that matters, not the first time. If I can win the Golden Rose from 17 on Zoustar, I can win this.'

Then I popped my head into the press room.

'If anyone can win from barrier 16, it will be me. I've done it before and I can do it again.'

You've got to give them something to write about.

I was asked what it would mean to finally reach The Hundred. By now, I wasn't thinking about the glory of it but how much I would like to bury it.

'I'd love to get it out of the way,' I told *The Sydney Morning Herald*.

Hawkspur finished seventh in the Caulfield Cup, but his finish suggested to me he would be a chance in the Melbourne Cup. He wanted more ground.

So it was going to come down to Zoustar in the Coolmore. It was all forming into a perfect storm. I was trying to reach my milestone; it could potentially happen on Derby Day, one of the biggest days on the Australian racing calendar; and there was much talk about how the owners, the Iskanders, headed by Sherrif Iskander, were about to sell the horse for millions of dollars.

Eight days before the race, Chris wanted me to trial Zoustar down the straight at Flemington. I got on him at Chris's stables. He said that he'd be watching from the grandstand and would phone me after the trial.

We jumped out from the 800 metres. There was a thing of John Hawkes in the trial, and another prepared by Leon Corstens, and they went like bats. They just flew. They ran the half-mile in 45 seconds. I wasn't out there to do that. I wanted to go out and run a nice half-mile in 50 seconds and let Zoustar have a look down the straight. That's all he was there for. Not a gallop. We weren't there to bust our arse. Save that for race day.

So he came fourth out of four runners by four lengths, and everyone just shit themselves. *Oh no. Zoustar just got beaten by four horses.* But I couldn't have been happier.

Chris phoned me.

'Everything all right?' he asked.

'Yeah, brilliant.'

'How's everything brilliant?'

'How's it not? The horse feels great. He'll win. No drama.'

The next minute, the owners were all calling me. Sheriff Iskander was on my back, wanting to know what was going on. These blokes had never called me in their lives. They were just worried about their 20 million bucks.

So I called Chris again.

'Mate, everything's all right,' I said.

'You sure?'

'Mate, the horse will fuckin' win. He had a good look, I'm really happy with him. If there was one inkling that the horse was going shit, I would've told you and I wouldn't have said it to anyone else. We're eight days out from the race: the rest is up to you. If you get him the way he was this morning, he will win.'

Without sounding arrogant, I've ridden a lot of horses and I know when one is travelling well, and when one isn't. Zoustar was fine. He was flying.

'I rode a horse up the straight at Flemington called Shaftesbury Avenue once,' I said. 'He got beaten six lengths, too, but then came out and won the Lightning. And Zoustar is going every bit as good as he did the day I trialled him.'

But despite what I knew, there was all this talk that the horse was no good. There's no better place for conspiracy theories than the racetrack. Everyone's an expert.

It was reported that prospective studs dropped off after that jump-out, which shows how much they knew. Then, just few days before the Coolmore, Zoustar was bought by Widden Stud for a reported $20 million. The stud had lost Zoustar's sire, Northern Meteor, in July that year from colic. He had only been standing at stud for a few years when he died. Zoustar had the same freakish acceleration as Northern Meteor. He was a perfect replacement.

There was still a lot at stake for Widden and for the Iskanders. There was the $300,000 in prizemoney, but also a $4 million bonus if the horse won.

In the mounting yard before the race, Antony Thompson approached me. He is the studmaster at Widden.

'Jimmy, if he gets beat, can you talk the horse up?' he asked, referring to the press.

'Go away,' I said. 'The horse will win.'

Seriously. This is before the Coolmore. It was so funny, because they were all panicking about the horse for no reason.

They only had to look at the horse to know there was nothing wrong. Zoustar was a magnificent looking colt. He was a good size but not big and chunky. He was very athletic. He looked the part. When he paraded that day before the Coolmore, he walked around the yard with every bit of presence he deserved. He was the best horse in the race and he showed it off. They had the best looking horse at the track that day and they were more worried about saving face.

But I wasn't thinking about the owners of the horse. I was only concerned about getting The Hundred. Ollie was sitting on 97 but had rides in all four Group 1 races that day – he could get there before me. I had one good shot at it with Zoustar.

It was almost exactly 30 years before to the day that I won the Melbourne Cup on Kiwi. And now I was about to create more history.

We jumped and after the field settled I was the widest runner on the track as we came down the straight. I just had to be patient. In my mind – and not for the first time – the clocktower was when I had to get moving. It had been the key to success three decades ago on Kiwi. It was going to be the same with Zoustar.

Greg Miles didn't call me until then:

Here's Zoustar starting to hit top gear. Villa Verde is coming and Not Listenin'tome as well . . . But it's Zoustar with a hundred metres to go. He gets to Sidestep and Jimmy's got his hundred! Zoustar wins by two lengths.

I knew he would win. There was no way in the world he wouldn't win that day. The crowd went mental. When I got off, the enormity of it all sunk in. I told the reporters:

It's hard to describe, I never thought about riding 100 Group 1 winners, and the dream was to ride in the Melbourne Cup and win one. It probably hasn't sunk in, but to be mentioned with Roy [Higgins] and George Moore . . . we're talking amazingly-talented jockeys. It's been hard to do, I've had my ups and downs, but to me they're all great memories, there isn't one bad one among them. It's a marvellous feat. It's been a roller-coaster, but I've hung in there, and never run away from anything. Who knows, I might ride another 10, 15 or 20 yet. My body will tell me. While I keep getting my opportunities, I'll keep going.

Sherriff Iskander bear-hugged me and almost broke my ribs. I should've sued him. Like so many others, he had promised all these things if I won on the horse. *Oh, we're going to do this and that . . .*

But same old thing: in the end, it all came to a raspberry. They didn't give me $10. All I got from the owners was a stud share of Zoustar each year, which means I'm allowed to breed one horse a year from him. But that had nothing to do with what made the horse worth $20 million.

I saw Sherriff Iskander at the casino at couple of years later. He walked up to me but I wasn't interested. Promises don't pay the bills. And again verbal assurances were made but I saw none of it.

'Don't come near me unless you've got what's mine,' I told him.

But none of that could take away what that moment meant for me. It had all come together perfectly: at Flemington, on one of the great days of racing, on the big stage, on a champion horse. The Hundred was just meant to happen then.

It was great that it was for Chris, too. It wasn't like it was a horse in a race where we were just a chance. It was the race that I had to win, for all of us.

It was a relief to get the monkey off my back. It hadn't happened for so long. When you start out, you think about winning one or two Group 1's, and now I had become only the third jockey in history to reach 100, alongside two of the best in George Moore and Roy Higgins.

Roy was great for racing and he had become a solid friend. Our relationship went all the way back to Melbourne Cup Day 1983, when he told me how to win the race on Kiwi. Two days after winning on Zoustar, we were at the Cup parade through the streets of Melbourne and I made him have a photo with me. I kissed him on the head.

Roy died in March the following year at the age of 75 after a short illness. We lost a great jockey, but an even greater man.

19

'Who's The Magic Man Now?'

I'M IN THE WEIGHING ROOM AT RANDWICK SOON AFTER winning the 2015 Sydney Cup on Grand Marshal – the Chris Waller stayer few had expected to win, and that includes the trainer himself.

I pass my whip and cap to Ray Murrihy, the chief steward. Greg Rudolph, his deputy, is also there.

I had barely heard a word from Chris for weeks. I hadn't heard a word from him on the first day of The Championships, the new two-day carnival in Sydney held over consecutive Saturdays in autumn with ten Group 1 races worth $10 million in prizemoney.

I hadn't heard from any trainer. I didn't have a single ride.

But now I've won the $1.6 million Sydney Cup by a snotball ahead of the Waller stable's more-fancied horse Who Shot Thebarman.

'Well done,' Chris says to me.

They are the first words I've heard from him since winning the race.

'Lost my number, did you?' I ask.

'I didn't have the number to the old people's home,' he says back.

That's how much respect Chris Waller had for me that day. He said that to me in front of Ray Murrihy, Greg Rudolph, a few reporters and other officials, in the weighing room after I had won the Sydney Cup on his horse.

He says he had photos of me on his bedroom wall when he was a young kid in New Zealand – and then he says that to me? I rode for more than 30 years. I was riding winners when Chris Waller was in nappies.

'If you don't shut your mouth, you'll be in the old people's home,' I say back to him.

Chris Waller went down a long way in my estimation that day. But it happened at work so I left it at work. That's where it belongs. But I will never forget it, I know that.

They're a funny breed, trainers. Most of them have never competitively ridden a horse in their life. They're frustrated jockeys.

The best ones are usually those who have been jockeys and then gone on to train horses. I think of blokes like the late Maxie Lees from Newcastle. He was one of the best, because he knew what a jockey was going through.

Then you've got the old-school trainers, who are few and far between. Those sort of trainers want the jockey involved. They want to pick your brain for your knowledge. I'm not new to this game. I have an idea. I reckon I could tell a trainer whether a horse needs blinkers or not.

There used to be some respect. Bart Cummings was probably the greatest trainer we've ever seen – and he had more respect for jockeys than anyone. Bart knew he needed you, even if it was just one more time. He would never bury you because of a bad ride because he might need you again.

But now? The modern-day trainer puts the nail in the coffin and bangs it down. The culture has changed. *You do what I say or I don't need you.*

I would laugh whenever a trainer produced a road map in the mounting yard before a race. A road map predicts where horses are going to settle: which ones are on the speed, which ones will settle midfield, which ones will be near the tail of the field.

The trainer will come out and they will have their road map out, talking to the owners. 'Oh, so and so will be third or fourth here . . .'

What a load of bullshit.

'If that doesn't happen, what do I do then?' I would ask. 'What's Plan B, C and D?'

It's a horse race. You make your own luck. You don't need a map. I need a map when I'm lost in the car. If I'm going to get lost out there on the racetrack, I may as well not be there.

Some trainers mellow when they have big powerful stables with endless pits of money behind them, but there's no doubt that the younger generation is just different. Les Bridge wouldn't say half the things the current-day trainers say, and he's a trainer who has been around as long as any of them.

In the end, you just go with it. You can't fight it. A lot of times, I bit my tongue. But sometimes I didn't.

Chris Waller and I would go back and forth. I've said a few things to him . . .

'Fuck, you didn't have that fit,' I might snap.

He'd fire back.

'Well, if you had ridden it properly . . .'

But, as I said, that's work. That's what happens in racing. But Bart and even Tommy Smith would never throw those snippy comments at you. Chris would have a dig at you, so you'd have one back.

It all changed between us within the space of a year. I had won the Coolmore on Zoustar on Derby Day in 2013. Come the following year, he put Joao Moreira on the back of Brazen Beau in the same race and he won. Joao was in and I was out.

At the time, Joao was flying in Hong Kong. He was a Brazilian jockey who came from nothing, a childhood of poverty, to become one of the world's best. 'The Magic Man' is his nickname. He'd recently been riding in Australia and winning some big races, including the Epsom Handicap.

Joao won the Newmarket Handicap on Brazen Beau for Chris in March 2015, and all of a sudden he was hot property. Robbie Waterhouse came out and said he was the best jockey in the world, and could end up as the best that had ever been.

I couldn't do anything about all that. That wasn't my problem. It was only affecting me because I couldn't get many rides for the Waller stable.

I never talked to Chris about it and I didn't really give a fuck. But it is tough when you're turning up and doing barrier trials and trackwork and all of the hard work and then you are suddenly put on the bench while some bloke from overseas who is no better than anyone else here is getting the rides.

It's up to the trainer to tell you if you're in or out. Most trainers won't show you that courtesy. They never talk to you. It's their business, they run it the way they want, and that's fair enough.

But it wasn't always like that. You usually knew where you stood. As I keep saying, it's all changed.

So, come the first day of The Championships, with the Group 1 Doncaster, AJC Derby, Sires Stakes and TJ Smith Stakes all up for grabs, my phone hadn't rung. Instead, I was at home building a chook shed.

When I finished doing that, I sat down and had a few beers and some lunch. And then I settled in to watch the races.

I was in two minds about not being there on such a big day. The upside was I couldn't get suspended. I could also have a beer and eat whatever I wanted. Better still, I didn't have to deal with trainers talking shit all day.

But if I had been there, I knew I would've won at least one race. I would've won on Grand Marshal in the Group 2 Chairman's Handicap (2600 metres). I'd been on him for five of his previous six starts, for two wins. His grand final was the Sydney Cup on the second Saturday of the carnival. This was the perfect lead-up race, and he should've won it, too.

But Chris dumped me and went for Joao instead. He finished third.

If I wasn't to be on Grand Marshal that day, the likelihood was that I'd be punching around shit horses in all the other races. I'd be fighting it out with the ambulance to make sure I wasn't last home. I was better off building my chook shed.

I'll admit I had the shits because I didn't have a ride. I was thinking if this is the way it's going to be from now on, not getting the rides in the big races, there's no use my hanging around. I might have to pull the pin on my career earlier than I was hoping.

The following day didn't give me much confidence about getting a ride for the second day of The Championships. Sunday is usually the day when a jockey starts organising his rides for the following week. Nobody called.

It wasn't until Wednesday that the phone rang. It was Chris Waller.

'Have you got a ride in the Sydney Cup?' he asked in a sheepish voice.

'No. I haven't. Why?'

'You can ride Grand Marshal.'

'Yeah.'

And then I hung up.

I soon discovered the horse would be carrying 52 kilograms, so that meant I would have to waste to get the weight off – including some of those beers I'd drunk after I built my chook shed.

Grand Marshal was an honest stayer owned by Macau businessman C.C. Lai, who was flying in for the race. I knew Mr Lai would not be disappointed, because I was confident of winning even if few others thought it could be done.

I'd been on the horse every start that preparation except the previous week. I knew he could win the race. He was just coming through, getting ready, and the day to go was the Sydney Cup. This was the 150th year of the 2-mile race.

It didn't take me long to realise why I was given the ride at the last minute. Chris had obviously had no intention of putting me on Grand Marshal. He would've had The Magic Man, but then he was booked to ride Dominant, a champion horse trained in Hong Kong by George Moore's son, John. Joao had been the regular rider on Dominant and had won the Hong Kong Vase. So I got the Sydney Cup ride by default.

Grand Marshal was considered a $41 chance to win the race. He was coming up against some very good horses, including Protectionist, the winner of the Melbourne Cup five months earlier. The $1.67 favourite was Hartnell, who was prepared for Godolphin by John O'Shea. He deserved favouritism after impressively winning the Group 1 BMW Stakes over 2400 metres at Rosehill.

But I was confident. Grand Marshal and I had been plodding along, always with this race in mind. Time to press the button . . .

When the field settled, Hartnell went to the front and strode away. I went to the back, just where I wanted to be. That's where I stayed until the home turn. Then I swept wide and started to make my run.

Darren Flindell called the final stages for Sky Racing:

Hartnell in front, he's been popped the question by Tommy Berry as Dominant for Hong Kong strides up with a big challenge. Dominant races up to challenge Hartnell, who's fighting back under pressure. Who Shot Thebarman's getting the rails run. Blake Shinn is scraping through on Who Shot Thebarman and he raced to the lead . . .

But I was coming, right down the middle of the track.

Grand Marshal goes to second. Hartnell's gone but it's Who Shot Thebarman . . .

You can tell by Darren's voice that he thought it was all over. But I wasn't done yet.

Grand Marshal's pulling back the margin. Here's a great finish. Grand Marshal dives at Who Shot Thebarman!

It took forever for the number to come up . . . It was me! That fucked them all. I'd put egg on all their faces.

'Who's the Magic Man now?' I asked when I came back to the winner's gate at the front of the new grandstand at Randwick. I was still on the horse. 'Where's Moreira?'

That was satisfaction for me. And for Vick. I didn't give a fuck that day about anyone else except for me and Vick. We deserved every bit of it. Jockeys don't come out and do what I did that day, and I can say that. After not getting a ride one week and then coming out and winning the Sydney Cup the following week, it was one of my greatest thrills in racing.

I'd done all the work on that horse – I'm still the only person to win on it – yet Chris Waller wanted to take me off him.

He said after the race that he only decided on the Tuesday to run Grand Marshal. That would've been because he didn't win the Chairman's Handicap, when he went for Joao instead of me. He didn't have to give me a reason why he had dumped me, but I know he would be too weak to give me one anyway. As it turned out, I delivered what Joao couldn't.

The Sun-Herald cornered me after the presentation, and I let my feelings be known:

> I could be as good as Moreira. I don't have to be as good as Moreira. They have to be as good as me. I've ridden over a hundred Group 1 winners. I've got nothing to prove to one owner, one trainer, not my wife, not me. My wife knows how good I am. So do my kids. So do I. It comes down to opportunities. If you're sent to Cowra to write stories, how many people are going to read that? If Joao Moreira were here, having to ride the horses I've ridden for the last

month, he wouldn't have ridden a winner. Neither would Hughey Bowman. Neither would've Damien Oliver. And neither would Douglas Whyte. Or Zac Purton. I'm telling you, if you're riding horses at 20 to 1 every day of the week . . . I had to ask the ambulance driver to slow down last week because I nearly ran into the back of him four times.

Chris barely came near me after I won. It wasn't until we saw each other in the weighing room that he said what he had to say about not having the number to the old people's home.

I thought it was a pretty disgraceful thing for him to say. At least it was the one time when he was man enough to say something to my face.

It didn't embarrass me, but it was a bit hard to cop from a bloke who I've been so loyal to. It's not like I've won a few races for him midweek. I won some big races for him. If you look at my last ten Group 1 winners, most of them have been for Chris. I've contributed back to him.

I think after he said it, he realised in the moment what it meant. How am I with him now? I'm a hundred per cent with him. As I said, it's work – and that's where that stuff stays. But I don't forget.

After that race, I walked back into the jockeys' room and they all cheered and hugged me.

Then I went and found Joao. I explained that I wasn't having a crack at him. It was a crack at Chris and his team for forgetting me. And Joao was sweet. That stuff is water off a duck's back for a jockey.

'Good on you, Pump,' he said. 'I hope I am riding as good as you at your age.'

Joao is 'The Magic Man'. Very polished, very balanced, a very good thinker in a race. Horses flow for him. They get into that rhythm I talk about. He'll be in a tight spot and he'll come out of it as passenger, while everyone else is pushing. He goes with the horse.

But he's got a totally different style to me. I'd like to think I was a lot more effective in a tight finish than him and a lot of other riders because I could lift one to win at times when other jockeys couldn't.

Like Grand Marshal.

*

Peter Moody is not like the other trainers. He is old-school. He's like me.

The thing I like about 'Moods' is that he doesn't give a fuck. He's not afraid to say what he thinks. You know where you stand with him, whether you like it or not.

I worked for Pete when he was the stable foreman for Billy Mitchell in Queensland and then for Bart in Sydney. He loves a beer, a smoke and a laugh. I have the utmost respect for him . . . as a Queenslander.

He also had the toughest job in the world there for a while, because he had to train a horse called Black Caviar. Can you imagine training a horse that is always expected to win? The pressure of that was going to send him into an early retirement – in the end it was the cobalt saga which saw him suspended that did it – but the mare finished her career with 25 wins from 25 starts, including the Diamond Jubilee Stakes at Royal Ascot. That shows you what a freak Peter Moody is.

He also trained a very good horse called Dissident. A week after The Championships, we were back at Randwick for the All Aged Stakes, a $400,000 Group 1 over 1400 metres.

I'd had success on the horse in the previous autumn, winning the Group 2 Hobartville Stakes and then the Randwick Guineas a fortnight later. But Dissident was a Melbourne horse, so it meant I had to give up the ride on him.

When Pete brought him back to Sydney for the All Aged, I was back on. He knew that I could get the best out of the horse. He'd called me two months earlier and said he was setting him for this race – and it was going to be the horse's last before being retired. Now a valuable stallion, Dissident was off to stud.

The All Aged, in my mind, was shaping as the toughest Group 1 of the carnival to win because of the quality in the race. The Hawkes stable's superstar Chautauqua was the $3 favourite. Gai Waterhouse had Australian Guineas winner Wandjina in the race, and Joe Pride had the highly rated Terravista.

On the Tuesday, I galloped Dissident on the course proper at Randwick on a wet track. He went brilliantly. I thought if the track dried out a little bit, he would be the horse to beat.

'If he gets footing, he'll win,' I told Pete. 'The only way he'll get beat is if he doesn't get good footing.'

I was super confident of collecting a second Group 1 for the autumn.

But then tragedy struck the next morning. We never saw it coming.

At 4.30 am, the phone rang. Vick answered it and by the look on her face I knew the news wasn't good. To be honest, I thought it was about my dad, who had not been well.

But the news was about Vick's sister, Marian. She had passed away suddenly. Vick dropped the phone and collapsed.

Marian had been out for dinner that Monday night. When she came home, she laid on the couch and fell asleep. Her partner went to wake her up at 9.30 that night to go to bed but she had died. She had a heart attack. She was 37.

How does that happen? She'd been out for dinner and then she's gone. They did an autopsy down the track and found nothing in her system that could've contributed to her death. Marian was a great girl, just like Vick.

I was supposed to ride a few for Singo that day, but he wouldn't have a bar of it.

'I don't want you to ride,' he said. 'I want you to look after Vick and the family. There's another meeting, another jockey.'

But I was always going to ride Dissident. I really wanted to win that race for Vick and for her mum, Lorraine, and dad, Charlie. And even for me. The first week of The Championships, I couldn't get a ride. The second week, I won the Sydney Cup. Now, a disaster had happened. I wanted to go out and give something back to Vick and her parents. It wouldn't bring Marian back but it could give them some happiness.

As I walked out the door that morning, Piper said to me: 'I hope you win today for Aunty Marian.'

'I will,' I said. 'Watch me. I'll win.'

I hugged Vick.

'I'm not going to say I'm going to win if I don't mean it,' I told her.

Before the race, I approached Pete in the mounting yard.

'What do you want me to do?' I asked.

'You go out there and do what you want to do. You know more about it than I do.'

'Well, I'll either lead or be just outside the lead.'

Coming out of barrier 6, I knew I would have to use some gas to get to the front. I was three deep early and had to shorten up Scissor Kick and Shooting To Win to get near the lead. Wandjina, with Damien Oliver on board, had other ideas.

Ollie and I had talked while heading into the barriers.

'You lead or I lead,' I said. 'But don't get into a head-to-head.'

And that's what happened. Ollie led, and I sat just off him.

I needed to do that to win. If the horse had got off the bit and started scrambling, he wasn't going to let down in the straight when I needed him to find another gear.

Coming down the straight, there were four horses lining up to win it: Chautauqua, Wandjina, Terravista with Hugh Bowman on board, and Dissident. Darren Flindell called the race:

It's Dissident and Terravista . . .

Bowman thought he had it on Terravista, but I'm only starting to get going. To get pumping.

Wandjina fights the inside. Chautauqua's got to lift. Lucky Hussler keeps coming. Dissident puts its head in front from Wandjina who won't sit down. Wandjina's coming back at Dissident. Dissident with its head in front . . . CASSIDY WILL GET IT HOME!

Peter Moody deserved all the accolades he received after that race. He'd turned that horse from an honest competitor into a multiple Group 1 winner. He'd retired Black Caviar with a final win. Now he had done it with Dissident.

I took great pride in helping him do that. That's one of the most satisfying parts of racing, when you can take a horse to the next level that others can't. Trainers – the good ones – can do that. But they need the rider to make it happen for them. You can feel the horse improving underneath you. And that's magic.

As I came back to the winner's stall, I struggled to keep it together. I was physically spent because I had to ride the horse so aggressively to win. But I was also emotional because of what had happened in the previous few days. I wasn't worried about myself during that time, but Vick and her parents. It didn't bring Marian back, but it gave them some temporary relief, if only for a few hours.

Vick wasn't there. She rarely goes to the races, but this time it would've also been too hard. When I got home, we both had a cuddle and a cry. She was so proud that I could do it.

We cremated Marian the following Thursday.

Vick is the toughest woman I know. She never let the pain and sadness of her sister's death stop her from being the positive person that everyone knows her to be. Most days I can hear her in the lounge room where Marian's ashes are kept, talking to her sister or having a little cry.

20

The Game

JACK DENHAM NEVER SAID MUCH BUT HE DID SAY SOMETHING to me that stands out.

'The game's fucked.'

Only towards the end of my career did I realise what Jack meant. It stopped being fun years ago. Of course, things are always going to change, in any sport. But racing has become an industry. In the end, it felt like working in a timber mill.

While that might be the case, racing has always been about the people. When we lose one of our own, it hurts everyone. One of the saddest days I ever had on a racecourse was Golden Slipper Day in 2014.

Nathan Berry and his twin brother Tommy were great for racing. Nathan had won more than 350 races, and had won the Magic Millions on Unencumbered in January that year. He had recently based himself in Singapore and his career was really starting to take off when he collapsed out of nowhere at trackwork at Kranji racecourse.

As he lay in a hospital bed in an induced coma, he was first diagnosed with suspected viral encephalitis and later with NORSE syndrome, which is a condition related to epilepsy. Then he died.

It rocked the whole racing industry, especially the jockeys' room. It's bad enough when someone in their 60s goes, but at the age of 23 it is terribly sad.

It affected me in a big way because I had a fair bit to do with both the boys early on. Their birthday is the same day as mine – 21 January. But everyone across the sport was affected, from the strappers and jockeys, to owners and trainers, to everyone who worked at the track, to your everyday punter.

The game might be fucked, as Jack said, but in times of need the racing family comes together. That week was very heavy for everyone but when there are tough times, racing people are there for each other.

Nathan's death didn't make sense. Each time we get on a horse, we deal with life or death. It's a very dangerous industry: you can be winning Group 1's one day, and then lying in hospital the next and fighting for your life. That's the way the game is. That will never change. There is the potential for a jockey to die every time he or she races. But what happened to Nathan had nothing to do with racing, and that's what made it so much harder for everyone to take.

For the younger jockeys, I hoped it made them realise that life is not a rehearsal. You don't get a practice at it. That's what I say to them when they go out and ride. If you want to fall off and break your neck or leg, good luck. But no money can bring back a life.

I talk to Tommy all the time, and I always make sure I ring him on our birthday because I know he will be doing it tough. I wore a blue tie to Nathan's funeral because they were his colours. Afterwards, I cut a bit off and taped it to my locker, right next to a photo of Nathan. I kept it there until the day I retired.

What happened to Nathan should have been a reminder that racing is about people. The further I went in my career, that seemed to be easily forgotten.

A lot of trainers and owners are money hungry, and they don't care what they have to do to make more of it. There is something like 20,000 horses bred for racing each year, and they go through them like jelly beans. A horse will bleed at trackwork, they'll wipe its nose and put a jockey on its back the following week, no questions asked. That horse can jump out and, anywhere in the race, drop dead. That's the game these days.

It's all about money. Look at the Melbourne Cup and all the other great staying races in this country. Apart from Prince Of Penzance in 2015, it's getting harder and harder to find a locally bred horse that will win the Cup. They are mostly from Europe.

Owners and trainers are too impatient to wait and bring one through. You have these staying races for older horses, but they put on a race for two-year-olds called the Golden Slipper. That's worth $3.5 million. Why persist with a stayer when you can jag an early one without having to pay out money year after year?

The industry is changing and I don't really think it's for the better. In Melbourne, the fields are still strong but in Sydney they are getting smaller and smaller. Sydney trainers could help their cause by having less barrier trials. Take their horses to the races to get them fit.

I think Sydney racing will eventually become more like Hong Kong where they race twice a week at two tracks. That would've been the smart thing to do about fifteen years ago: have just the two good tracks, Randwick and Rosehill, and make Canterbury a training facility.

In time, there will be only four big stables in Sydney: Chris Waller; John O'Shea, who is backed by Godolphin; Peter Snowden; and Gai Waterhouse. Chris is winning a lot of races now but he's got half the field in the race so he has to win.

Eventually, how boring will racing become? Just the big stables racing amongst themselves.

And that means the battler will no longer exist in racing. He or she hardly exists now. The odd country bloke will bring a horse to town because there's five runners and the prizemoney goes down to eighth, but the battler is a dying breed.

The game keeps going because of the battler: the strappers and the handlers who do the relentless daily work with the horses, who go to the barrier trials, who are still working when others are in the committee room having a drink.

I never forget those people. Brett Grant, who was the regular trackwork rider and strapper for Might And Power, was one of them. I gave him $10,000 when we won the Melbourne and Caulfield Cups. I looked after him because he was there helping me do it. It's not a one-man show.

THE GAME

They are the unsung heroes of the sport because they are the ones who get up at four in the morning and do all the shit work and never get a pat on the back. Today, they get abused. Gai might tell her staff to have a shave or to not chew gum. I think they deserve more respect. People forget how hard the work is for those battlers – but I never do because I did all that. That's where I come from.

The change in the industry also means jockey numbers will be smaller. The money is still there because the betting turnover has never been greater, but the fields will get smaller and the jockey numbers will decrease. Those who are left will get much richer. The support's not there in field size, so the others will have to go back to the provincials to make a living.

I was blessed to ride against some of the best jockeys of all time. Ronnie Quinton was different to most in the way he thought and the way he picked where the runs were going to be. I would follow Ronnie a lot. If you were behind him, you could see where he was going to get out.

Mick Dittman would force his own runs on his terms. That's why he was called 'The Enforcer'. He was probably the toughest jockey I rode against, pushing you out of the way. Peter Cook would sit like a mouse until the last second and then beat you. He was magic.

Everyone creates their own style. Wayne Harris was one of the most beautiful, polished riders I've seen. Shane Dye got into this thing of riding with his stirrup three holes shorter on one side. A lot of them wanted to look pretty but I didn't give a fuck. I didn't want to look pretty: all I wanted to do was win. I didn't have time to get up and practise in the mirror what I was going to do.

For me, it was all about reading the play and knowing horses. I would often ride with my toe jammed into the irons. I'd smash my feet on the side of the barrier so often that I turned my toe in a little bit. Because I was riding with little boots on, I would sometimes nudge my toe up under the horse's front shoulder. I'd push my toe in there and it would make them lengthen.

There is a lot of debate about how often you can use whips in racing. I know one thing: if they took the whips away altogether, I wouldn't hesitate making a comeback. When the current jockeys hit the horses with whips, they hit them behind the saddle. All horses have different thickness of skin. You could hit Might And Power over the head and it wouldn't worry him. But some are very thin-skinned. It's a matter of knowing how some are going to respond. I won more races by not pulling the stick.

To be honest, I did whatever I had to do to win. And that was pumping them and lifting them. I've had experts who have never been on a horse being critical of my rides. They couldn't fall off their wives. That's how much they know about racing.

I rate some of the current crop of jockeys really highly. I think James McDonald will be the next real superstar – but how long will he stay in Australia?

He will get more and more opportunities to ride for big money in Japan and Hong Kong and even Europe. But if he stays around long enough, he might set all the records along-side Damien Oliver. I think Hugh Bowman is an outstanding jockey, and I can see him racing in Hong Kong for a very long time in the future.

Jack was right in many ways. Now, I can see what he was talking about.

Tracks aren't maintained as well as they should be. There's too much racing in the winter, so the tracks never recover. They should be racing on better surfaces. There are too many race meetings, every day. It puts pressure on owners and trainers to have staff.

Track maintenance takes a back seat to big new grandstands that are barely filled, and if they are it's only on the main days. Why spend all this money on grandstands when people aren't going to the races? How often do these grandstands get full? That money could be spent in other ways.

The change that I have really seen is in the people who come to the races. They don't come for the racing, they come for the party. I used to love it when the punters threw empty beer cans at me when the favourite got beat. They'd give it to you. That would happen at Randwick in the late 80s and 90s.

'You pulled it, you dog!' they would scream.

Now it doesn't seem to mean as much. Most racegoers will watch the Derby or the Epsom and yell and scream but they don't know what they're cheering for. The people who support racing can no longer afford to attend on the big days. It's easier to buy a slab, get half a dozen pies and sit at home. The average bloke can't afford it.

And that's sad because the average bloke on the street is the bloke that I love the most. What I have loved about racing is that I've met so many different people, from the top to the bottom.

But I've always found the people at the bottom are the better ones. The ones at the top think they're better than the ones down the line who are working just as hard. I'd rather have a beer with the person in shorts and thongs and have a good laugh with them than sit around listening to shit from those with a pinkie in the air. I'd rather be with the knockabouts. They're the real people in this game. The others who want to bleed it, for every cent they can get, I could not be bothered with.

Despite all the bullshit I have been through in racing, it's still the sport that I love. I love it as much as I did when I was on the arm of Dad's chair, pretending to win the Melbourne Cup.

I've loved the winning, the competition, the ability to let my riding do my talking. In my game, you can only be good by winning. Run second? Nobody wants to know.

My main thrill was being tactical and beating the others. That was the special part. Getting off the canvas, never saying never. There was never a way that you couldn't win. There was always a way. You just had to find it.

And I liked the challenge: get beaten one day, come out and do it again. I did it for 30 years, as an apprentice and all the way through. That's how I kept going for as long as I did.

But in the end, it got harder. In the end, in my heart, I didn't have a lot of time for the owners and trainers who I had supported before they gave up on me. They wanted to belittle me and that's why I gave it away. I wasn't going to be a has-been. I wasn't going to be referred to as a 'former jockey'. I was going on my terms.

The thing is, I have something to retire to. There's a beautiful wife in Vick, and three daughters who all make me so proud.

THE GAME

Nicole is the eldest. She's been a great daughter. Every parent's dream. She worked hard at school and she also loved her riding. She would've made a great jockey. I'm pleased she didn't go down that line, but she was a talented show rider. I don't know if she would've had that killer instinct and ruthlessness that you need to be a jockey. I'm glad that she didn't.

She is married to a jockey, though, in Zac Purton and they live in Hong Kong. I was sceptical when they first started dating. If it was my choice, I wouldn't want my daughters marrying jockeys – only because of the lifestyle I know they have to put up with.

I know there's a lot of sacrifices that she has to make, but that's her decision. Zac is ambitious, he's out there, he's a very good jockey. He's done remarkably well during his time in Hong Kong. He's made more money there in a couple of years than I have in a lifetime. I just hope he saves it well and looks after it right for my daughter's sake. I hope he's a good husband, and so far he is.

In 2014, Nicole had a baby girl – Roxy – and I am rapt to be a grandfather. Now that I am no longer riding, I can spend more time with her.

Sarsha is my second daughter, and she is two years younger than Nicole. When they were younger and we took the girls to pony club, the pair could not have been any more different. Nicole was always seeking perfection. Sarsh was more like her old man: rough and tough and from the bluff. Her blonde hair would be going everywhere and she would be making everyone laugh. She didn't care what anyone thought.

These days, she's a media representative with the global bookmaking giant William Hill, and she is front and centre in their television campaigns. She is flying.

Then there is Piper, my daughter with Vick.

When she was about eight years old, I got Piper a pony for Christmas. It all came naturally to her, just as it had with Nicole and Sarsha. One day, Piper said something that nearly knocked me over.

'Dad, I want to get in the barriers,' she said.

Okay. So I set up a dummy barrier with a pole coming down off one of the hedges in our backyard.

'I want to jump them out like Chris Munce, Dad,' she said.

My jaw dropped. She must have picked up from watching TV alongside Vicki that Muncey – a great jockey in his own right – was good at getting horses away at the start of a race.

'You can let it go, Dad,' she advised as I led her and the pony around the backyard. 'I'm Chris Munce.'

She never wanted to be Jim Cassidy. She wanted to be Chris-bloody-Munce!

Unfortunately, Piper suffers from hayfever. One day, she took her gloves off and said she'd had enough of riding. Instead, she wanted a pink four-wheel motorbike. I was riding Sea Siren in the Doomben 10,000 that weekend. I told her if I won the race I would sell the pony and buy her the motorbike. I won the race.

'When are you buying me the motorbike?' she asked as soon as I stepped off the plane.

That was the end of Piper's riding career.

It's been great having her come along later in my life. Mentally, that keeps you going. I can spend a lot of good times with her now I'm no longer in the saddle.

THE GAME

Having a father who is a full-time professional jockey isn't easy. He is either spending time in the sauna, or off to track-work, or riding interstate.

Now, I can live a normal life, with them right alongside me.

Epilogue

BY ANDREW WEBSTER

WHAT'S THE DEFINITION OF SILENCE?

Jimmy would probably say it's the sound his critics make whenever he's dragged himself from the edge of retirement, into the sauna, onto the end of Boss's boxing pads, onto Longy's massage table, onto one of Singo's horses, and then shoved it up every single one of those who dared to say he was finished. That it was over. That he *can't*.

'What's that?' he might ask them. 'Didn't hear you.'

Here, underneath the famous wrought-iron arch of the Flemington mounting yard, the signature yellow roses flanking each side, it's just as quiet. It's the morning after the 2015 Melbourne Cup. The stillness is jolting. The calm *after* the storm.

The day before, the racecourse fizzed as more than 100,000 people shoe-horned themselves into every available space.

On the other side of the mounting yard fence, the sweaty and sozzled in the cheap seats cheered as enthusiastically as the sweaty and sozzled wearing top hats and tails watching from the committee room in the grandstand. Few expected Michelle Payne to return from the 2-mile battle aboard 100 to 1 prospect Prince Of Penzance as the winner. As she came back along the lane and then underneath the arch, it dawned on all concerned that the first female jockey in history had won the Melbourne Cup.

A year or so earlier, in the shadows of this arch, another history-making jockey, Roy Higgins, was farewelled with a befitting memorial service following his sudden death at the age of 75.

Les Carlyon, whose words over many decades have painted the picture of Flemington better than anyone, started his tribute like this: *'This racecourse, beautiful as it is, is not consecrated ground. Not in the accepted religious sense anyway, but for many of us it comes close. For 174 years it's been a place dedicated to a divine purpose, a divine purpose we all love, and it's alive with the ghosts of jockeys past and it still hums with the distant music of their heroics.'*

Jimmy Cassidy has one more day left before the music stops for good. We're alone in the mounting yard right now, but the ghosts of the past are everywhere he looks.

He goes back to 1983 and sees a familiar face.

'There's Snow over there, relaxed, standing on his own, away from Bart Cummings and Colin Hayes and Tommy Smith,' he says. 'He looked at Kiwi walking around and said, "Geez, he's parading well".'

There's the clocktower just over there.

'To be joining him at the clocktower, and being fifth, and then to win by a length and a half . . . it was incredible that Kiwi could do it. When we came back under this arch, the crowd was just jam-packed around us. People were still blowing up because of the way he had won it. They could not believe he'd done it – but I knew.'

What about Might And Power? There he is, just over there, and now we are back in 1997.

'Might And Power, he was different to Kiwi,' Jimmy continues. 'He was walking around, chest puffed out, charging around like he owned the place.'

Jimmy leads me into the jockeys' room, where there are more ghosts.

'Malcolm and I had turned up about 5 am, and parked out the back. He worked on me here, in the jockeys' room. *The rest is up to you, Pump. I gotta go.'*

We go back out to the mounting yard. Now it's 2013. Derby Day. The day he reached The Hundred.

Reached? Jimmy grabbed it and history by the throat that day. I was standing right near him when he came back to the mosh pit near the winner's stall. The sweat poured out of him like he'd just come from the sauna. He was wearing his red gloves and he pointed his index fingers to the sky in victory like they were the devil's horns, like Dennis Lillee appealing in the middle of the MCG.

'I mean, I remember Zoustar coming back through there,' he says, pointing at the arch, 'and me thinking, "Fuck, I've finally done it". I didn't do it in Sydney, or Brisbane, but here on the big stage. Standing here, looking back at those grandstands, seeing this all full on Derby Day . . .

'A hundred Group 1's was just something I didn't dream about. I dreamt about a Melbourne Cup, but being the third jockey to reach a hundred . . . That never entered my head.

'It's all about your heart and your head. You never say never. I was washed up. They said I couldn't do that. But I did.'

*

Few places purr with gossip as much as the track. I can't think of a sport with as many whispers. Usually, there is no place for spin at the racecourse. But it can be as bitchy as the Kardashians.

There had been widespread chatter about Jimmy's retirement for a year or more. After the autumn? After the spring? After the Cup? After one last ride in Sydney? After the Magic Millions?

In truth, nobody had a clue – because he didn't know himself.

And then, out of nowhere, it came. A week out from the Melbourne Cup, we met in the foyer in the Rydges Hotel adjacent to Rosehill racecourse for a story to appear in *The Sydney Morning Herald* on Derby Day.

It was an ugly morning, the dark skies rumbling overhead as Jimmy rode two barrier trials while the rest of Sydney made its way to work.

'How do you want to handle questions about your future, Pump?' I asked before the dictaphone came on.

'How about we just get it over and done with?' he replied. 'How about we just say Oaks Day will be my last day before I retire? Put all the speculation to bed. I'm sick of people asking me about it.'

Before we turned the recorder on, he phoned Vicki.

'Let's go,' he said, ending the call.

And with that, in the foyer of the Rydges Hotel at

EPILOGUE

Parramatta, with nobody around save for a handful of businessmen in the corner, he started to close the book on one of racing's most colourful and controversial careers.

'I want to go out on my terms – I don't want to be pushed out,' Jimmy said. 'I don't want people to say: "He's too old, he should've given it away six months ago". Someone said to me at Moonee Valley [on Cox Plate day] last Saturday, "Don't you retire!" It's all right for them to say that, but 30 years in a tough game is a long time. It's time to say goodbye. I feel teary thinking about it, but I'm happy. I've made the decision. It will be in writing. There will be no comebacks.'

Foremost amongst the reasons, he said, was the lack of faith invested in him from trainers and owners.

'A lack of opportunities, the lack of quality rides has made the decision for me. The younger generation is coming through, and I am honoured and privileged that I can still compete at the top level. But consistently quality rides are obviously drying up. I don't want to be punching slow horses around. I don't feel like I'm being pushed out. I'm not disillusioned. I'm happy.'

There was some pain in there, too. In his head and heart.

'I've had a lot of pain in my body the last couple of years. I've been saying I haven't, but the body's taken a lot of wear and tear. Once I stop doing the hard yards, a lot of the pain will go. You're not doing the cold and early mornings, smashing feet and legs and heads on barriers. Just all those things. It will be nice to have a bit more fun. A normal life. And there have been other things that have put racing in perspective.'

There are two Jimmys. There is The Pumper, the supremely confident Hall of Fame jockey who stands at five-foot fuck-all but walks like he's a hundred tall.

The on-course persona often betrays the turmoil off it. The past year had been tough: his father was diagnosed with cancer; his sister-in-law, Marian, suddenly passed away during the Sydney carnival; his good friend and prominent horse owner Tony Mittiga was cut down and taken by cancer.

'I want to spend as much time as possible with Dad, too,' he said. 'That's gutted me a bit. Without him, I wouldn't be here.'

At Flemington, a book of rides awaits, and they tell their own story of why Jim Cassidy is calling it a day.

He has again secured the ride on John Singleton's Dawnie Perfect in the Wakeful Stakes (2000 metres) on Derby Day as she prepares for the Victoria Oaks (2500 metres), the race he's won five times.

'Singo's a headline person so he needs a headline horse. He makes the paper as much as me, if not more. He's always been solid with me. He abuses you when you lose and when you win. I take it all with a grain of salt. He's fun to be around.'

He's also on Pornichet, who is trained by Gai Waterhouse, in the Mackinnon Stakes (2000 metres).

'It would be fitting to have a winner for Gai, too, because I haven't had a ride for her for a while. Not a decent one. I've had my ups and downs with Gai. You have to be riding work and riding winners for her. If you're not getting opportunities, you aren't getting winners. I mean, quality rides. Five of my last twenty winners are flat-out being under 4 to 1. The rest have all been out in the market. That tells me that I'm not getting quality rides.

'There's a few horses in Sydney I hoped I would get on in Melbourne, but I haven't. It doesn't make it hard, but other blokes are riding more winners consistently because of opportunities. I just feel that there's a bit of support there but it's not how it used to be.'

And then there's Grand Marshal, his Melbourne Cup horse, who has flown under the radar this preparation but a galloper Jimmy has entrusted to deliver an epic conclusion to his career.

'He's a two-miler, and you need a good one of those to win at Flemington. He's far from being the best horse in the race, but he's tough. He's had a good prep, he's fit, he's hard, he's ready, and if I give him the right ride he'll run the race of his life, I believe.'

Then we joke around about suggested headlines for this retirement story.

Ring-a-ding-ding, the spring will be Pumper's final fling . . . Clicketty-clack, Pumper's about to leave the track and never come back . . .

Then we settle on one: *Ring-a-ding-ding, that's it for The King!*

He roared with laughter.

The next day, he rode Feast For Eyes to victory in a race at Canterbury. He shook hands with chief steward Ray Murrihy.

'That will be my last ride in Sydney,' he confided.

Nobody else at the track knew it would be his last ride in Sydney.

Before he flew to Melbourne, the reality of his decision started to sink in.

'That's what I will miss the most – the rush, on the big days. The rush starts when you know you've got a good chance of winning that race. There's a difference between having a good chance and believing you're on the horse that can do it. Then going out and doing it, judging it right, knowing that you've made every right move, and no matter how many people are there, when you pull up and see the enthusiasm and the cheering and all that blood rushes through your veins, and you think, "Fuck, I've done it".

'I pride myself on believing I can do it, that I can conquer it. I enjoy seeing the rush on the faces of other jockeys now. I get a lot out of that because I know what that feeling is like. I still live those moments. I'll live them when I walk back onto Flemington. All those moments come back. It was an honour to be there to start off, and it will be magnificent to be there when I finish.'

*

Nobody cuts a lonelier figure at Flemington in the moment before the Melbourne Cup than the jockey who isn't riding in the Melbourne Cup.

In the minutes before the race in 2013, I spied Jimmy in the weighing room. He didn't have a ride that year.

'When am I writing your book?' I asked.

'I need three blokes to die first,' he laughed.

Exactly two years later, he is in the same space, on the soft, beige carpet of the weighing room, and he is down on his haunches talking to Chris Waller, who is sitting on one of the wooden benches.

Ten days earlier, Waller had claimed the Cox Plate with his superstar mare Winx. It was his first win of one of the Big Four – the Caulfield Cup, the Cox Plate, the Victoria Derby, the Melbourne Cup.

Right now, in his usual race-day attire of black suit and black-and-white tie, Waller is grey with nerves. He has three horses who can deliver him the Cup: Preferment, the Victoria Derby winner from the previous year; Who Shot Thebarman, who finished third behind Protectionist in last year's Cup; and there's Grand Marshal.

This is his best chance to win the Melbourne Cup. Listen carefully enough and you can hear the conversation between trainer and jockey.

'What was it about Kiwi?' asks Waller. 'Did you think he could win?'

'I thought he was unbeatable,' says Jimmy, who then tells the story about Eric Temperton and his advice to be wound up at the clocktower, ready to pounce.

Waller's mouth is dry, but Pumper is soaking up every single drop of his final Melbourne Cup moment.

Now the 24 jockeys are lining up, from the front of the weighing room all the way back to the jockeys' room. Jimmy is the oldest and the smallest but he's the most relaxed. He hugs Joao Moreira.

'Be safe and good luck,' he tells Joao.

He then gives a cheeky wink as he pulls on his red gloves. 'First one home buys the pizzas,' he says to Roger Elliott, Gai Waterhouse's stable foreman.

Just before the conga line of jockeys makes its way out to the enclosure, an official from the VRC issues last-minute instructions.

'When the announcer says your name, please wave enthu-siastically to the crowd,' he says.

Ryan Moore, the ice-cold European jockey who won on Protectionist the previous year, unsurprisingly does not. Jimmy waves like he's already won the race. The loudest cheer from the sweaty and sozzled is reserved for The Pumper.

Then it's time for the Australian national anthem. Jimmy is a proud New Zealander, especially when it comes to the All Blacks, but Australia has been his home for more than three decades. He belts out 'Advance Australia Fair'.

Vicki is at home in Sydney, watching the coverage, and as the camera zooms in on the two-time Melbourne Cup winner, who is about to ride in the race for the final time, it's hard to establish if he's crying.

'But I was,' he advises later. 'I deliberately got out and bellowed out the anthem.'

Whenever Bart Cummings became teary on a racetrack – most notably when Viewed won in 2008 when the master trainer was 80 years old – he dismissed it as hayfever. He often said there was no place for sentimentality in horseracing.

There is plenty at the end of the 2015 Melbourne Cup, but it doesn't belong to the retiring 52-year-old. Instead, it belongs to Michelle Payne, who had weaved her way through the field to carve out her own slice of history.

She climbs down off Prince Of Penzance, and when a microphone is waved under her nose she tells those who insist females make for inferior jockeys to 'get stuffed'. The remark echoes for days.

As Michelle makes her way back to the weighing room, Jimmy hugs her.

'I'm really proud of you,' he tells her. 'It will sink in one day, what you've achieved. I know how you feel; what's going on in your belly.'

Later, he says this: 'Good on her. She's proven herself. She's beat all the boys in the big race. She was inside of me the whole race. Her horse was hummin' and pullin' and she just sat there and didn't panic. When the split came, she got it. Purton,

Cassidy, Oliver, Boss, Moreira . . . nobody could've ridden it any better. She deserves all the accolades. She's created history. That's something they can never take away from her.'

Now, many of the best jockeys in the race are locked away in the stewards' room, answering questions from chief steward Terry Bailey for a collision at about the 400-metre mark.

The door shuts just as Michelle begins her acceptance speech. There are six jockeys at the end of the table: Frankie Dettori (Max Dynamite), Chad Schofield (Gust of Wind), Hugh Bowman (Preferment), Craig Williams (Hokko Brave), Colm O'Donoghue (Kingfisher) . . . and Jim Cassidy (Grand Marshal).

The replays, from a variety of angles including an aerial view from the helicopter above, are damning. Schofield wears the look of a man who's guilty as sin, but most fingers are pointed at Dettori, who almost took down several runners when he shifted sideways.

When Bailey asks the jockeys if they would like to say anything, Pumper can't help himself.

'Do I get a prize for staying on?' he laughs.

The jockeys file out of the room. The next time Dettori is in there he'll be copping a one-month ban and a $20,000 fine, the heaviest penalty imposed for careless riding in the race's history.

Jimmy throws an arm around Frankie's neck. It's caught on Channel 7's coverage and some speculate from the lounge room at home that it's not a hug but a headlock.

'I'm sorry, Pump!' Frankie says in his unmistakable Italian accent. 'I tried to fucking kill you in your last Melbourne Cup!'

Jimmy laughs it off. But the next morning, here under the Flemington arch, his neck is sore and stiff.

'I bet Grand Marshal's is, too,' he says. 'That's racing. We're in one piece to talk about it. Everyone came back after the race, and there weren't jockeys sprawled all over the Flemington track.'

So now there's one more day. The final meeting of a 40-year career and all that's left to do is go out under the arch, and then make it back in one piece, alive.

*

The silence of the early morning on Oaks Day breaks with the news that Dawnie Perfect has been scratched from the main race. The reason is a leg injury that's emerged over-night, but the heavy rain at Flemington would've put the race beyond her anyway.

'That's racing,' says Jimmy.

There is not one hint of hesitation about his decision.

'A lot of people keep asking me if I've made the right decision,' he says. 'Chris Waller was going on that I should do a national tour. I'll do that, but it will be a drinking tour. I respect other people's opinions, but all the people who mean a lot to me know it's the right time. I'm not going to let anyone dissuade me. There's a $10 million meeting at the Gold Coast. There's $10 million on offer at The Championships. Racing will keep going if I'm not there. They thought it would be hard when Darren Beadman stopped, but it kept going. It stops for no one.'

So no doubts?

'Not one.'

The yellow roses on the arch have been replaced by pink ones. The rain abates as the crowd makes its way into Flem-ington for the meeting better regarded as 'Ladies' Day'. But there's also a feeling that it's Pumper's Day, too. Can he ride a winner on his final day? In his final race? With the scratching of his Oaks ride, he has a book of just three rides to get it done.

Yet the notion of a dream send-off is seemingly the pre-occupation of everyone at the track except for the man of the hour. Instead, he wants to soak it all up.

So he arrives early and heads straight to the stewards' room. His home away from home. But this time he's not in trouble. He wants a photo with Terry Bailey and his panel of stewards. Cheekily, he grabs the pork pie hat off one steward and slaps it on.

'I've spent enough time in there over the years, so why not?' he laughs.

Before the fourth race, he is presented to the crowd and makes his way through a guard of honour formed by his fellow jockeys.

At the end of it, Glen Boss pops an oversized magnum of Mumm champagne and soaks Jimmy in it. Never one to let an opportunity pass, Jimmy opens his mouth and tries to catch a few drops.

By the time we get to the final race, the final minutes, of his career, he hasn't won.

He has Distant Rock, which is trained by Lee and Anthony Freedman and about $10 in the betting markets.

Jimmy comes out and spies Lee in the mounting yard. As they talk tactics, the Channel 7 cameras swoop on them.

Freedman throws an arm around his jockey.

'If this horse doesn't win,' says Jimmy, 'I'm never riding for Freedy again!'

And with that, he mounts Distant Rock and heads out under the Flemington arch.

Jimmy and the horse don't come back first. No place for sentimentality in racing. But the story of the last at Flemington on Oaks Day explains much about his enduring ability.

The Flemington track had been a source of much debate and anger for days. It had been watered the day before Derby Day, and then when rain had flogged down on that Saturday morning, the track became a labyrinth. The passage along the inside rail became the quickest way home. A strip down the middle of the straight was quicksand, and the money of punch-drunk punters was disappearing there and then.

By Oaks Day, the track was truer than what it had been at any time during the Melbourne Cup Carnival. But there were ways to get home other than the inside. Only the streetwise and the ones without fear knew where.

As they hit the top of the straight, Jimmy hooks Distant Rock very wide, finding the outside rail. Greg Miles calls it:

Now, Cassidy's pulled one out of the hat here, he's gone to the outside rail, but Zebrinz has gone past him . . .

Miles calls Craig Williams on Lord Athenaeum as the winner past the post, but the photo shows it's Zebrinz, with James McDonald on board.

When they come back to the enclosure, Jimmy says this: 'I was asked to go to the outside and I did. If he [McDonald] went to the inside, he wouldn't have won. He tried. I won the race for him.'

'There was no way in hell I was going there [to the outside rail],' says McDonald. 'He just started to go and I followed.'

What isn't revealed until later is their conversation in the jockeys' room just before the race.

McDonald is the hotshot Kiwi who in 2014 was secured as the number-one rider in Australia for Godolphin, the global racing enterprise owned by the ruler of Dubai. But so far the Group 1's over the carnival have not come his way.

He finds a place next to Jimmy in the jockeys' room, and laments his misfortune.

'They're over, mate,' Jimmy tells him. 'Be prepared to back your own ability, and your own judgement. A lot of times you might make the wrong decisions, but if you keep doing this job long enough you'll make more right ones than wrong ones. That's the difference between being a good jockey and a great one. Back yourself.'

As the crowd filters out of Flemington, Jimmy emerges from the jockeys' room.

For the past week or so, I've watched him closer than most. He's lived the moment but he's definitely been pulling back, trying to keep the emotion inside him. He's used the trademark one-liner to dodge the tears, but now the lump forms in his throat and the bottom lip quivers.

Maybe there's some place for sentimentality in racing. Just a little bit.

'I've had a great time, mate,' he says. 'I've had a great life. It's over. It's finished. It's just finally there.'

Then the emotion is replaced by relief.

'I'm in one piece. Fuck. I have finished a career in one piece. And that's what I wanted to do for my girls, to be with them. Not in a wheelchair, or a fucking broken down old crock, you know? I've stood the test of time.'

The next morning, he flies back to Sydney and watches Piper perform in the local production of the musical *Annie*.

'Daddy's getting off the big stage,' he tells her, 'and you're getting on it.'

Weeks later, Jimmy is on a stage at a private function at Rosehill racecourse. In lieu of a farewell day while he was still riding, the Australian Turf Club has thrown a celebration on one of its race days to honour him.

The room is typical of the man. There is barely an identifiable face in sight. No celebrities or big names have made it into this room. Nobody with a pinkie in the air. Instead, he is surrounded by family and friends. The battlers, as he would call them.

Longy is there. Jimmy plants a kiss on his forehead and, soon after when he's asked to say a few words, he singles out the man at the back of the room.

'People don't realise the injuries I've had over the years,' Jimmy says. 'He's kept me going for fifteen years.'

There is one man who isn't there and that's Boss. You suspect this kind of function is not his scene anyway. And if it was, there's every chance he wouldn't be wearing socks.

'He's been a father, a brother, my best mate,' says Jimmy. 'Through good times and bad times, he never changes. As a person, I've learnt so much from him. He's helped the needy, the greedy, anyone who needs it. He's been there for them. I've got goosebumps talking about him.'

After lunch, Jimmy walks downstairs and is presented to the crowd, many of them wearing 'I love Pumper' trucker hats. He poses for photos in the jockey room, and with the punters.

Then it comes to the last race of the day: the ATC Farewells Jimmy Cassidy Handicap.

He decides to have a bet – his first and only one for the day. He opts for a 'first four' for which the punter must pick the first four runners for a dividend to be returned. But he doesn't know how to fill the ticket in. For more than three decades, he's been a licensed person who cannot bet. He wouldn't know how to get on with a TAB operator.

At the start of the function, Chris Waller had addressed the room and tipped his own horse, Cauthen's Power, in the last.

'Hey everyone!' Jimmy yelled before the race. 'Go and back the nine here!'

Jimmy stands out Waller's horse, and then boxes another four. He invests $50, which is all he has on him.

Waller's horse wins, and then, before long, Jimmy realises that he's snagged the first four. The payout: $48,000.

Jimmy erupts. So does the rest of the room.

'My first bet as a free man!' he says.

*

Months later, Jimmy is back where it all started in his hometown of Lower Hutt in New Zealand for the Hutt Valley Sports Awards.

He's been inducted into the Australian and New Zealand Halls of Fame, and collected trophies for the biggest races in both countries. But he says walking along the red carpet towards the stage, before 700 cheering locals at the black-tie event, to receive a Legends award stands as one of his proudest achievements.

'Because this is where I come from,' he says.

Not far from here, his mum and dad had nervously sat in their lounge room to watch the 1983 Melbourne Cup. The last words of this book belong to Jimmy's father, Blue, who told Jimmy as he sat on the armchair, pretending to be a jockey, that nothing was impossible if he worked hard enough.

He said the same things to his son just before he lost his courageous battle with cancer as this book was going to print.

'All my life, I told him to be honest and up front with everybody – that's the way I raised him,' he says. 'On that day in 1983, we didn't have any visitors and I can still hear the racecaller saying, "And Kiwi three lengths last . . . " Francie jumped up and said, "He's no chance of winning from there!" I told her sit down, "The race isn't over yet".

'The rest is history.'

Acknowledgements

Jim Cassidy

I always knew I would tell my story in a book one day to set the record straight.

Many thanks have to go to Angus Fontaine and the Pan Macmillan team for making it come to life. And to Andrew Webster for putting the book together. Nobody could've written it any better.

There are so many people over the course of your life and career who help you along the way, and I can't mention them all here, but there are a few who stand out.

I've already written about Malcolm and Longy in this book and what they mean to me, but thank you to their families for letting them spend so much time with me over the years to keep me going. Thanks to the trainers and owners who have all supported me, too. Without them, I'd not be writing this book.

My three girls – Nicole, Sarsha and Piper – mean everything to me. So does my wife Vick, who has stood the test of time looking after me. And finally to Mum and Dad.

They gave me all the opportunities I've had, and told me I could achieve anything if I worked hard enough.

Andrew Webster

This book would not have been possible without the help and contribution of so many people.

John Jenkins, who covered the early parts of Pumper's career and ran a close eye over the manuscript. Special mention, too, to Helen Thomas, who allowed us to quote liberally from her superb book *A Horse Called Mighty*. Keiron Long from the Australian Racing Museum and the Australian Turf Club provided invaluable material from the archives.

Thanks also to Darren Pearce, Peter V'Landys, Brett Devine, Ray Thomas, Max Presnell, Ken Callander, Chris Roots, Adam Pengilly, Brent Zerafa, Paul Langmack, Billy Malouf, Les Carlyon and the dozens of people who also provided advice and insight into the racing world.

Pumper would never have made it onto the track without 'Longy' Nguyen and Malcolm 'The Boss' Ayoub and this book wouldn't have been written without their support and knowledge.

The team at Pan Macmillan, from publisher Angus Fontaine, editor Alex Lloyd and copy editor Susin Chow, have been absolute pros to deal with.

Finally, thanks to Vick and Jimmy, who welcomed me into their home like I was one of their own.

Index

A Horse Called Mighty 157, 193
AAMI Classic 218
Acumen 50
Adelaide Cup 50
The Age 213, 241, 247
Ajax 194
AJC Committee 144, 145, 151
AJC Derby 49, 50, 87, 95, 96, 102,
    153, 208, 214, 230, 257, 258,
    266, 303
AJC Oaks 236
Alice 16
Alister Clark Stakes 218
All Aged Stakes 88, 237, 309
All Blacks 1, 26, 334
All Too Hard 285
Allez Suez 259
Amarant 28, 33, 208
Americain 263
apprentice jockey's premiership
    12, 19
apprenticeship 8, 10
  leading apprentice 12
Archer 41
armed robbery 52–4
Arwon 208, 209
ASADA scandal 132
Ascot Lane 65

ATC Farewells Jimmy Cassidy
    Handicap 340
Auckland 19, 20–1
Australia 3, 13, 23
  first win in 14
Australian Crime Commission 246,
    252
Australian Cup 104
Australian Federal Police 108,
    143
Australian Guineas 141, 218,
    309
Australian Jockey Club (AJC) 55,
    69, 143
Australian Oaks 141
Australian Racing Hall of Fame 265,
    341
Australian Rule of Racing
  rule 135(a) 74
  rule 175(a) 128
Australian Turf Club 268, 340
Avdulla, Brenton 278
Avondale cup 16
Awapuni 20
Ayoub, Malcolm ('Boss') 95–105,
    135, 142, 150, 154–6, 162,
    169, 171, 179, 204, 205, 228,
    229, 260, 278, 284, 325, 340

INDEX

bad falls 11, 50, 61–2, 67, 92–3, 101, 178, 273, 278
Bailey, Terry 335, 337
Balaklava 67
Banner Headline 184, 186–9
Barker, Jim 98, 103
Barker, Noel 61
barrier trials 10, 61, 316
Bartle, Ted 67
battlers 316–17, 340
Beadman, Darren 48, 91, 336
Beau Zam 49, 64
Begg, Neville 64
Beldale Ball 45
Bell, Murray 143
Belle du Jour 225
Bensley, Andrew 257
Berry, Nathan 313–15
Berry, Tommy 313–15
Better Loosen Up 194
Bezeal Bay 163, 250, 252
Biggs, Keith 218–19
Bint Marscay 226
Black Caviar 285, 308, 312
Black Knight 41, 208
Blarney Kiss 25
Bledisloe Cup 1
Blue Diamond Stakes 91, 202
BMW Stakes 305
Boasting 64
Bonecrusher 49, 194
Bonza Crop 273
Boss, Glen 116, 227, 273, 337
Bounding Away 226
Bourke, John 41
Bowman, Hugh 311, 318
Bradley, Phillip 140
Brassel, Tommy 35–6
Brazen Beau 302
Breakfast Creek Hotel 13
Breasley, Scobie 266
Brew 211
Bridge, Les 301
Brisbane cup 13–15
Brit, Edgar 98
Brown, Cliff 216

BTC Cup 219
Bureaucracy 84
Burletta 39

Callendar, Ken 168, 216
Cameron Handicap 230, 273
Campbell, Aikey 98
Campbell, Maurice 8, 11
Campbell, Patrick ('Felix') 7, 9–12, 18, 24, 39, 52
Camperdown Children's Hospital 80
Canterbury Guineas 101, 152, 153, 230
Canterbury racecourse 50, 69, 126, 149, 151, 218, 316
Canterbury Stakes 187, 285, 285
Cappellin, John 213
Captain Sonador 273
Carbine Club Stakes 64
careless riding 60, 67, 153, 190
the Carlton Hotel 26
Carlton, Tom 115
Carlyle Court 67
Carlyon, Les 88, 326
Carnegie Express 230
Carr, Bob 131
Carry The Star 187–8
Cassidy, Arthur ('Blue') (Father) 2, 5, 6, 154, 180, 181, 309, 330, 341–2
Cassidy, Francis (Mother) 1, 2, 7, 154, 180, 181, 342
Cassidy, Helen 52–3, 206
Cassidy, Jim
    100th Group 1 race 283–4, 288, 290–2, 295–6, 327
    baby, as 2
    birth 1
    bullying 4
    dietary habits 203–4
    eighteen years old 12, 20
    fame 278
    first ride in race 8
    first win in race 12
    flexibility 177
    grandparent 321
    headaches 180–1

INDEX

height 1, 3
knees 273–4
licence to ride 8
pain 274–5, 278–80, 329
pain threshold 178
retirement 280, 282, 320, 328–9
returning to racing 155
sacrifices by 203
schooling 4
siblings 2
size 1, 59
speaking up 19
Sportsperson of the Year 183
success 67
The Hundred 283–4, 288, 290–2, 295–6, 327
trifecta, winning 138
weight 6, 9, 151, 156, 205
wins 265
Cassidy, Larry 116, 154, 166, 187, 204, 230–1, 260
Cassidy, Nicole 80, 132, 138, 169, 206, 321
Cassidy, Piper 230, 261, 280, 310, 322, 339
Cassidy, Ricky 2, 7, 154
Cassidy, Sarsha 132, 138, 169, 206, 321–2
Cassidy, Vicki 207, 228–30, 274, 280, 306, 309, 310, 312, 320, 322, 328, 334
Caulfield Classic 230
Caulfield Cup 60, 65, 89, 91, 99, 150, 156, 158–62, 190, 192, 208, 215–16, 291–2, 332
  Diatribe winning 208–11, 214
  Inaflury 215
  Might And Power winning 159–60, 316
Caulfield Guineas 79, 201, 205, 285, 290
Caulfield Stakes 88, 101, 192, 193, 195, 198
Cauthen's Power 341
Cenchire 55
Chairman's Handicap 303, 306

The Championships 299, 303–4, 309–10, 336
Channel 7 163, 165
Channel 9 213
Chapman, Doc 87
Chautauqua 309, 311
Chelmsford Stakes 192
Chiamare 34, 35
Childs, Greg 165
Chipping Norton Stakes 185, 256
Chiquita Lodge 31
Chugg, Chris 138
Colour Page 65
Comely Girl 226
Commissionaire 40
Compton, Bruce 48, 50, 79
Congressman 209
Conners, Clarry 195, 225, 235, 236
Cook, Billy 67
Cook, Peter 13, 48, 225, 317
Cooksley, Grant 102
Coolmore Stakes 283, 290, 292, 294, 302
Coolmore Stud 45
Coongy Handicap 90
Coronation Day 154
Corstens, Leon 292
Costi, Andrea 66
Costi, George 65–6, 135, 245
Courier Bay 60
The Courier-Mail 175
Cox Plate 49, 60, 64, 101, 192–5, 285, 332
  Might and Power winning 196–8, 207
Craig, Ian 227
Croome, Rod 23, 37
Cross, Merv 274
Crown Lager Handicap 64
Crowned Glory 225
Cruising 73–7, 80, 81, 84
Crying Game 165
Cummings, Bart 28, 31, 34, 49, 51, 63–4, 71, 77, 81, 83–7, 90–1, 93, 99, 194, 199, 208, 210, 257, 258, 261–2, 266–9, 281, 301, 302, 308, 326, 334

347

INDEX

Cummings, Val 64
Cups King Syndicate 71

The Daily Mirror 36
The Daily Telegraph 143, 145, 167,
    168, 207, 216, 260, 261, 268, 280,
    284, 291
Dance Hall Girl 51
Dane Ripper 194
Danehill 103, 202, 206
Darley Stud 287
David Jones 259
David Jones Cup 90
Dawnie Perfect 330, 336
de Castella, Robert 97
De Costi Seafoods 65
Dear Demi 235, 285
deaths on the track 61, 314
Denham, Allan 141, 156, 168,
    189–90, 192, 199
Denham, Jack 46, 141–2, 149, 152,
    153, 156–7, 160, 164, 168, 184–6,
    187, 189–90, 192, 194, 198, 199,
    207, 313, 319
Derby Day 40, 64, 64
Derobe 158
Diabolical Liberty 67
Diamond Jubilee Stakes 308
Diamond Shower 56, 65
Diatribe 208–12
Diddy Do It 91
Dignity Dancer 218
Dillon, Mike 78
Dimsey, Clem 33, 35
disqualification
  6-month 116
  12-month 78
  Jockey Tapes inquiry 129–30, 132,
      143–4, 147
  meaning of 137–8
Dissident 290, 309–12
Distant Rock 337–8
Dittman, Mick 13, 48, 50, 56, 84, 87,
    91, 317
Dominant 304–5
The Dominion 20, 36

Don Eduardo 230
Doncaster Handicap 43, 60, 286, 303
Doncaster Mile 256, 260
Doomben 10,000 219, 322
Doomben Cup 88, 192
Doon, Teddy 73
Doriemus 166, 219
Dr Grace 87, 102, 259
The Dragon's Journey 174
drug testing 275–7
Duffy, Gavan 13, 66
Duggan, Johnny 51
Dulcify 194
Dunn, Dwayne 257
Dye, Shane ('Billy Idol') 60, 79, 107,
    114, 117, 119, 147, 152, 191, 193–4,
    195–8, 317

Eades, Gavin 114, 119, 132
Eades, Kevin 114
Eades, Shane 114
Eagle Farm 13, 14, 88, 152, 273
Eales, Noel 40, 44
Egmont Cup 28, 34
El Donte 10
Ellerslie, Auckland 16
Elliott, Roger 333
Emancipation 43
Emirates Stakes 268, 279
Empire Rose 168
The Enforcer 86, 317
Enright, Dave 13, 14
Epsom Derby 45, 259
Epsom Handicap 153, 156, 230, 273,
    302
Europa Point 147
Excellerator 217, 221, 225, 227, 230

Fannie Bay racecourse 61
Feat For Eyes 331
Ferguson, Rob 224
Filante 153, 184–5, 187, 194
The Filbert 79
Fine Cotton scandal 86, 130
Fiorente 148
Fiveandahalfstar 286

INDEX

Fix The Date 49

Flemington 5, 28, 29, 50, 63, 64, 83–4, 93, 218

Flight Stakes 230

Flindell, Darren 305, 311

Flying Spur 107, 116, 226, 228

foot injuries 178, 318

football 2, 3

Foreteller 285, 286, 288

Four Corners 244, 254

Fox, Millie 46, 48

Fox, Stan 46, 48, 141

Foxton 2, 40

Four Crowns 12–15, 47

Frank Packer Plate 153

Freedman, Lee 89, 107, 158, 160, 166, 226, 245, 257, 337

Freedom Rings 75

Freeman, George 70–3, 241

Fulton, Bob 172

Gadsden Stakes 64

Galange, Ellio 218

the Galaxy 87

Gale, Megan 259

Galilee 99

gambling 61, 130

Gauci, Darren 92, 208

Geelong Cup 41, 250

George Main Stakes 43, 192, 273, 291

George Ryder Stakes 43, 60, 256, 259, 260, 286

Giles Gym 96, 98

Gleeson, Des 212–13, 242–4

Glen Vista 49

Godolphin 287, 305, 316, 338

Gold and Black 51

Golden Rose 289, 290, 292

Golden Slipper 59–60, 115–16, 141, 179, 187, 189, 209, 221, 225–6, 228, 234, 285, 315
  1986 60
  1995 107
  1996 139
  2014 313

Grand Marshal 299, 303–4, 308, 331, 333, 336

Granite King 14–15, 47

Grant, Brett 156–7, 193, 316

Grant, Trevor 244, 245

Grimley, Duncan 236

Gunsynd 85, 194

Gurner's Lane 28

Ha Ha 222, 224–7, 230, 234

Hall, Greg 166–7

Hall of Fame 329
  Australia 265, 341
  New Zealand 266, 341

hand healing 176

Handy Proverb 50

Hanlon, George 28, 34, 208, 213

Harris, Noel 11, 37

Harris, Wayne 47, 48, 67, 84, 317

Hartnell 305

Harvey, Gerry 224

Hastings 7, 25, 40

Hastings Boys High 4

Havana Wind 231

Have A Guess 139

Hawke, Bob 49, 225

Hawke's Bay 39

Hawke's Bay Cup 12

Hawkes, John 226, 276, 292, 309

Hawkspur 218, 288, 291–2

Hayes, Colin 28, 34, 45, 67, 99, 210, 326

Hayes, David 203

Hayson, Eddie 246

Heart Ruler 153, 154

The Herald 78, 80

Herald-Sun 242, 244, 245

Herald-Tribune 10, 27

Hewitt, Marie 138

Hibberd, Michael 91, 212

Higgins, Roy 31–2, 35, 36, 266, 267, 284, 295, 296–7, 326

Hill, Terry 172

Hilton, Tony 20

Hobartville Stakes 309

Hollindale Stakes 191

INDEX

Hong Kong Vase 305
Hore-Lacy, Rick 91, 202–3
horses 71
  affinity with 7
  passion about 139
  riding 6
  special 88
Hot Zephyr 67
The Hundred 283–4, 288, 290–2,
  295–6, 327
Hunter 72
Hutt Old Boys 3, 89
  Australia tour 3, 89
Hyperno 28, 63

Iglesia 187
Imperial Baron 60, 225
Inaflury 208, 215–16
Ingham, Bob 287
injuries 59, 67, 92–3, 99, 173, 178–80,
  271, 278–9, 318, 340
Innocent King 95, 101, 102, 259
Interfere 246
Intergaze 152
Irish Moss 9
Iskander, Sherrif 292, 294, 296

Japan Cup 42, 199, 267
J.B. Cummings Ming Dynasty Quality
  268
Jenkins, John (Johnny) 10, 16, 27
Jeune 88
jigger 152–3, 185–6
Jillings, Colin 18
jockey(s) 62
  aiming to be 1, 4, 5
  first steps as 10
  leading 8
  methylated spirits, rubbing with 163
  mistakes 62
  New Zealand, bias against 70, 79
  number of 317
  payment 214–15, 263–4, 296
  preparing 155, 203
  prizemoney 214–15
  punting 38, 340
  respect for 301
  riding instructions to 214
  sacrifices by 203
  success as 11
  superstitious 30
  tipping, 117–18, 125–6
'Jockey Tapes' 107–33, 138, 143, 145,
  150, 183, 190, 191, 222, 224, 243,
  253, 264
  transcripts from inquiry 119–20,
  122, 123, 124–5, 126–7, 128,
  129
'Jockey Tapes Mark II' 242
Jockeys' Association 151
jockey's premiership 56
  apprentice 12, 19
Johns, Gary and Gayle 246
Johnson, Dave 23, 26, 37
Johnston, Malcolm 'Miracle' 14, 15,
  47, 86
Jordan, Kerry 72, 95, 101, 121
Just A Dancer 91
Just A Dash 85
Justice Prevails 226

Kaapstad Way 211
Kaaptive Edition 102
Karaka yearling sales 25
Kay, Alan 5
Kenny, Brett 80
Kent, Paul 136
Killian, Brian 77
Kingston Bay 101
Kingston Rule 90–1, 267
Kingston Town 28, 40, 85, 194
Kiwi 23–42, 46, 79, 90, 333
  bet on 38–9
  Melbourne Cup 24, 28–35, 48, 69,
  167, 295, 297, 326
  scratching 41
Koch, Phillip 136
Kolivos, Greg 286

Lady Purpose 92
Lai, C. C. 304
Langby, Kevin 48

INDEX

Langmack, Paul 201–2
Lapointe, Bob 43, 46–7, 50–1, 56, 70, 75, 79, 178
Lee, Greg 135
Lee, Jim 135
Lees, Maxie 54, 55, 72, 135, 152, 300
Lees, Vicki 54
Letts, Johnny 45, 163, 166
Levin Bayer Classic 49
Lexus Stakes 263, 276
Light Fingers 31
Lightning Bend 84
Lightning Stakes 1991 83, 91, 259, 293
Lilley, Susan 45
Lillye, Bert 46
Linesman 154, 166
Linton 276
Lord Athenaeum 338
Lord Axel 139, 140
Lord Raywood 21
Lotteria 230
Love Conquers All 263
Lower Hutt 2, 13, 44, 287, 341
Lowy, Frank 171, 174, 176, 181
Lupton, Anne 24–6, 29, 37, 42
Lupton, Even 'Snowy' 24–6, 28–9, 37, 41–2
Lynch, Mark 77

McClymont, Kate 108, 113, 117
McDonald, James 318, 338
McEvoy, Kerrin 257–8
McGinty 18
McKenzie, Nick 244, 247, 250
Mackinnon Stakes 40, 330
McLean, Peter 6, 7
McMahon, Otto 98
McNab, Chris 11, 12
McNulty, Rob 218
McSweeny, Tony 194
Magic Flute 60, 260
Magic Millions 221, 224, 290, 313
Magnier, John 45
Mailbox 103
Makybe Diva 41

Maluckyday 263, 276
Manikato 43
Manikato Stakes 203, 205, 219
Mannerism 88
Marauding 60, 226
Marble Halls 158
Marooned 50–2
Marscay 141
Marsh, Bruce 18, 28
Marshall, John 64
Martin, Brian 195
Martin, Tim 246
massage/masseurs 171, 176, 178
Masters, Roy 80
Mayfield-Smith, Brian 46, 48–51, 56, 60, 66, 73, 75, 77–80, 223
Melbourne Cup 5, 40, 60, 63, 69, 85, 88, 148, 153, 154, 161, 190, 192, 193, 208, 211, 214, 239, 263, 292, 305, 315, 332, 333
1966 99
1971 34
1977 51
1980 45
1983 23, 174, 297, 326, 341
1988 168
1990 90
1995 219
1997 327
2000 208
2011 281
2013 332
2015 325, 334
aim to win 5
clocktower 33, 34–5, 166, 295, 333
dinner 37, 38
Kingston Rule winning 91
Kiwi winning 24, 28–35, 48, 69, 167, 295, 297, 326
Might And Power winning 165–70, 327
regret about 90
winning 24
Mercedes Classic 191
Merchandise 180
Meridians 176

351

INDEX

Metallic Crown 268
Metropolitan Handicap 72, 153–4
Might And Power 24, 40, 150, 152–4,
    156–62, 164, 183, 187, 189,
    190–4, 196–200, 219, 256, 264,
    286, 316, 318
  Caulfield Cup, winning 193
  Cox Plate, winning 196–9, 207
  Melbourne Cup, winning
      165–70–4, 316, 327
  record of 197
Miles, Greg 165, 206, 210, 295, 338
Miller, Johnny ('J.J.') 99, 104
Miller, Kay 104
Miss Octopussy 147
Mitchell, Billy 308
Mithen, Anthony 213
Mittiga, Frank 217, 221, 245
Mittiga, Tony 217, 221, 245, 330
Mokbel, Tony 239–54, 255
money, rolling in 23, 39
Montgomerie, Simone 61
Montjeu 259
Moody, Peter 288, 308, 310–12
Moonee Valley 64, 84, 195, 203,
    218
Moonee Valley Cup 90
Moonee Valley Vase 195
Moore, Gary 194
Moore, George 67, 194–5, 209–10,
    212, 214, 266, 267, 284, 295, 296,
    305
Moore, John 305
Moore, Ryan 333
Moraitis, Nick 149, 161, 167, 168, 170,
    189, 197, 256, 261, 263–4, 276
Moraitis, Stephen 264
More Joyous 118, 237, 273, 285
More Strawberries 233
Moreira, Joao 302–8, 333
Moseley, Dianne 24
Moses, Kevin 113, 116, 119, 129, 132,
    187–9
Mossman 195
Mr C 108, 114, 129
Mr Jazz 34, 35

Mr Rogers 150, 151
Munce, Chris 59, 221, 322
Munro, Darby 266
Muollos, Tony senior and junior 218
Murdoch, Rupert 117, 171, 174
Murphy, Chris 107, 114, 115, 117,
    119
Murrihy, Ray 141, 180, 183–6, 187–8,
    192, 230, 232, 234, 246, 247–50,
    275, 276, 299–300, 331
My Tally 231

Natski 168
Naturalism 88
Nebo Lodge 46–9, 50–1, 64, 69, 75,
    79, 80, 84, 113, 141, 178, 222
'necking it' 74
New Plymouth 25
New Zealand 1, 3, 5, 12, 14, 23, 39,
    43, 53, 62, 70
  bias against jockeys 70, 79
  Racing Hall of Fame 266, 341
  Racing Personality 39–40
Newmarket 72, 93
Newmarket Handicap 83, 91, 302
Newquay 225
Nguyen, Duy Long ('Longy') 171–82,
    229, 278, 325, 340
Nguyen, Teresa 175
Nicholson, Bob 116
Nikolic, Danny 244, 254
Noble Comment 34, 35, 36
Northern Meteor 294
NSW Crime Commission 131, 140
NSW Industrial Court 79
NSW Thoroughbred Racing Board
    184
Nurmi 126, 129

Octagonal 194
Oliver, Damien 147–8, 194, 205–6,
    215, 219, 284, 295, 311, 318
Omnicorp 63, 64
Once We Were Wild 276
O'Shea, John 194–5, 305, 316
Our Jug 65–6

INDEX

Our Magic 273
Our New Horse 85
Our Sophia 209
Our Waverley Star 49
owners 118, 190, 214–15, 217–19, 264, 286, 296, 315, 329

Packer, Kerry 117, 164, 167
Pahiatua Cup 26
Palmerston 2, 44
Palmerston North 26
Paris Lane 88
Parramatta Eels 80
Party Mood 85
Paterson, Ian 119, 121, 126
Patinack Farm 272–3, 282
Payne, Michelle 326, 334, 335
Peace Pipe 20
Peacock, Andrew 45
Peake, David 20–1
the Phantom 40
Phar Lap 29, 74, 160, 194
Phillips, Troy 77, 186
Pierro 285–6, 288
Piggott, Lester 8, 59
Piping Lane 208
P.J. O'Shea Stakes 13, 14
Platinum Scissors 230
Poetic Prince 79
Porchinet 330
Potrero 87
Potter McQueen 67
Preferment 333
Presnell, Max 78, 143, 163
Price, Mick 245
Price, Ray 80
Pride, Joe 256, 261–3, 309
Prince of Penzance 315, 326, 334
Pringle, Alan 9
Privato, Matt 257
Prix de l'Arc de Triomphe 45
Protectionist 305, 333
publicity 58, 202
The Pumper 57–68, 87, 329, 333
punters 61, 123, 135, 319
Purton, Zac 321, 334

Queen Elizabeth Stakes 49, 88, 191, 199, 261
Queensland Cup 65, 66
Quinton, Ronnie 43, 48, 50, 51, 60, 67, 87, 317

racehorses 7
  Europe, from 315
  number bred per annum 31
races 2, 6
  race fixing 108–13
racing 59
  changing nature of 316
  danger in 314
  hypocrisy in 241
  improper actions in connection with 128
  industry, as 313
  innuendo 216–17
  life and death 314
  love of 320
  returning to 155
  sentimentality in 334, 338, 339
Racing Appeals Tribunal 78, 136
Racing Conference 5
Racing NSW 247
Racing Victoria 148, 242
Raging Planet 121, 129
Rain Affair 285
Rain Lover 41
Randwick racecourse 43, 48, 50, 61, 67, 86, 88, 101, 150, 153, 316
Ranvet Stakes 187, 190, 256, 285, 286
Rauhine Lass 9
Rawiller, Nash 235, 236, 285
Rayner, Evan 21
Real Jester 203
Red Anchor 101
Red Dazzler 256
Red Handed 31G
Redoute's Choice 202–3, 205–6
Renouf, Lady Susan 45, 52
reprimands 61, 85
riding gear 136–7

INDEX

riding racehorses 58, 198–9
  'lifting a horse' 59
  pulling up 215–16
Rising Fast 194, 197
Robbins, Glenn 57
Rogerson, Graeme ('Rogey') 18–20,
  91, 135, 218, 231, 279
Roman Consul Stakes 290
Roman Emperor 257–9, 261–2
Ropiha, Eric 17–18
Rose, Danny 215, 217
Rose of Kingston 90
Rosehill Gardens (racecourse) 43, 46,
  47, 52, 55, 57, 60, 66, 67, 74, 101,
  144, 180, 187, 199, 232, 316, 339
Rosehill Guineas 153, 208
Rough Habit 87–9
Royal Ascot 290, 308
Royal Courtship 225
Royal Descent 236
Rubiton 64
Rudolph, Greg 299–300
Russell, John 158
Russell, Rod 218–19

Sacred Falls 286
safety 11, 63
Saintly 24, 194, 197, 257
Salinger Stakes 275
San Domenico Stakes 64
Sandown cup 65
Sandown Guineas 65, 101
Sandy's Pleasure 64, 65
Sangster, Robert 44–7, 50–6, 65, 70,
  224, 226
sauna, in 155, 163, 204–5, 323
Savabeel 218
Schillaci 89
Schreck, John 55, 60, 67–8, 69–70,
  73, 74–7, 85, 115–26, 128, 141,
  147, 184, 226, 228
Sea Siren 219, 322
Secret Flash 74
Secret Savings 260
Secretariat 90
Sellwood, Don 10

Selwood, Neville 67
Shaftesbury Avenue 83, 84, 91, 93,
  259, 293
Shean, Mark 258, 261, 289
Sheikh Mohammed bin Rashid Al
  Maktoum 287
showjumping 138–40, 168–9
Silver Knight 28, 34
Silver Slipper 221
Silvester, John 241
Singleton, John ('Singo') 224–5, 228,
  232–7, 245, 264, 276, 285, 310,
  325, 330
Sir Zephyr 49, 50, 101, 178
Sires Stakes 303
Skelton, Bill 11, 20, 30
Skelton, Bob 28, 31
Sky Filou 64
Smith, Dave 89
Smith, T.J. (Tommy) 14, 15, 18, 28,
  34, 46, 49, 56, 58, 66, 67, 80,
  85–7, 95, 101, 103–4, 141, 194,
  202, 210, 222, 226, 302, 326
Snowden, Peter 257, 288, 316
So You Think 257
Somers, Daryl 37–8
Sousa 257
South Australian Derby 50
Spectatorial 225
Spink, Victor 114, 117–22, 131, 147,
  241
Spring Carnival 239
  1987 64
Spring Champion Stakes 230
St Kilda baths 92
Stanley, Brent 158, 165
Star of The Seas 288
Star Watch 226
Starstruck 104
Sterling, Peter 80
stewards inquiries 19, 67, 74–8,
  183–6, 187–8, 213–14, 215, 230,
  232, 247
Stewart, Brad 273
Stradbroke Handicaps 88, 89
strappers 6, 139, 316

INDEX

Stratton, Bruce, QC 132
Sullivan, Anthony 79
The Sun 57
The Sun-Herald 48, 136, 306
Sunday News 78
Sunday Star 79
The Sunday Telegraph 85, 136, 145, 227
Sunny Lane 165
Super Impose 88, 194
Supreme Court 115
suspension 59, 60, 67, 72, 80, 84–5, 100, 132, 144–6, 150, 153, 187, 189, 190, 260, 276, 280
Sutherland, Paul 96
Sydney Cup 50, 51, 304, 306, 310
  1986 52
  2015 299–300
The Sydney Morning Herald 46, 47, 54, 108, 113, 262, 292, 328
  Kate McClymont's race-fixing article in 108–13
Sydney Olympics 2000 140

Taksan 209
Tan Chin Nam, Dato 257
Tapp, Johnny 102, 116
Tarlton 12
Tauherenikau 2
Tea Rose Stakes 232
Temby, Ian, QC 131
Temperton, Eric 34, 333
Tempest Morn 230
Terravista 309, 311
Testa Rossa 205–6
Think Big 41, 257
Thomas, Helen 157
Thomas, Ray 145, 268, 280, 291
Thompson, Antony 294
Thompson, Jack 98
Thompson, John 211–15, 217, 273
Thompson, Robert 280, 281
Thompson Handicap 150
Thomson, Brent 20, 67
Thousand Guineas 39, 87
Tinkler, Nathan 272–3, 282, 285

TJ Smith Stakes 303
Toorak Handicap 256
Top Innings 64
Toparoa 85
Toyota Welter 74
track maintenance 319
trainers 5–6, 17, 190, 300–1, 303, 312, 315, 329
  premiership 56
  road maps 301
transcripts from inquiry 119–20, 122, 123, 124–5, 126–7, 128, 129
Trentham 27
Triple Crown 218, 219
Triscay 141
Tristanagh 87, 281
Trusting 273
Tulloch 85, 160, 194
Tulloch Lodge 103, 222
Turf Monthly 53, 59, 66, 84
Turnbull Stakes 208
Tycoon Lil 191, 193–4, 195–6

Unencumbered 313

Van der Hum 28, 31
Victoria (VRC) Derby 63–4, 101, 332
  1985 50
Victoria (VRC) Oaks 56, 64, 65, 87, 235, 281, 330
Victoria Racing Club (VRC) 37
Viewed 257, 334
Villiers Summer Cup 67
Vision And Power 256, 259, 260–2

Waikikamukau 187–8
Wairoa 8, 12, 18, 19
Wairoa Cup 9
Wakefield Stakes 65
Wakeful Stakes 235, 330
Walker, Michael 278
Waller, Chris 180, 268, 283, 286–9, 291–3, 296, 299–302, 304, 306, 316, 332, 336, 341
Waller, Stephanie 287
Walsh, David 60

INDEX

Wandjina 309, 311
Wanted 246
Warwick Farm 43, 64, 121–2, 192, 291
Warwick Stakes 192
wasting 204, 304
Waterhouse, Gai 86, 104, 148, 154, 157, 166, 217, 221–25, 228, 230–4, 237, 260, 276, 285, 288, 309, 316–17, 330, 333
Waterhouse, Robbie 86, 222–3, 230–1, 302
Waverley Cup 27
Weekend Delight 87
Wellington, New Zealand 1, 2
Wellington Cup 1, 27, 37
Whanganui 11, 17, 20
Wheeler, Johnny 88
whipping 77, 185–6, 228, 290, 318
Whitby, Max 218
White, Beryl 141, 152
White, Geoff 141, 152

White, Harry 28, 63, 152
Whitefriars 275
Who Shot Thebarman 299, 333
Widden Stud 283, 294
Willesee, Mike 60
Williams, Craig 338
Wilson, Julian 45
Wilson, Neville 280
Wilson, Wayne 15, 89
Winx 197, 332
Woodlands Stud 287
Woodville 40
Worthington, Rick 275

Yalumba Stakes 192
Yippyio 150, 152, 153
York, Brian 153, 156, 191, 192, 225
Young, Les 48

Zebrinz 338
Zerafa, Brent 261
Zoustar 283, 286, 288–97, 302, 327